Don Harvel
BRIGADIER GENERAL (RETIRED), UNITED STATES AIR FORCE

ROTORS

IN THE

SAND

Follow on: https://www.facebook.com/rotorsinthesand
https://www.instagram.com/rotorsinthesand
https://twitter.com/rotorsinthesand
rotorsinthesand@gmail.com

AUTHOR'S NOTE

June 28, 1972, the day I reported to the United Stated Military Academy at West Point, one of our class's first military acts was to subscribe to the Cadet Code of Conduct, swearing not to lie, cheat or steal ... nor tolerate among us anyone who does. I also pledged, as a cadet, and later as an officer, to preserve, protect, and defend the constitution of the United States. Any future allegiance I incurred fell subordinate to these two.

Perhaps that's why I developed an affinity to the flying safety field which resides in a sacred niche within the sphere of flying. At the pinnacle of this citadel of truth resides the accident investigation process ... where there is no room or tolerance for politics or innuendo.

I accepted the job to investigate the April 9th, 2010 CV-22 Osprey accident with reservations concerning the magnitude of the task and the inherent barriers preventing the collection of evidence a half-a-world away. But I failed to account for the obstacles of full disclosure, politics, and the reluctance of the same entities that assigned me the task, to accept the controversial findings of the investigation.

If, at this point, you have read the first few pages of this book looking for an indictment of the government, Air Force, or the contractors who supply weapons of war, put the book back on the shelf ... or click "remove" from the digital cart. This is no vendetta, tell-all, hatchet job.

This book is about facts and truth. Over a period of five months, the Air Force CV-22 accident investigation board traveled thousands of miles, interviewed over one hundred witnesses, and collected mounds of evidence in an inhospitable environment searching for the reason an Osprey aircraft impacted the ground in the remote desert of eastern Afghanistan. The accident took the lives of four personnel aboard the accident airplane.

The following pages chronicle the unpublished and exhaustive investigation process, ending with my opinion of the cause of the Osprey accident on the morning of April 9th, 2010. My opinion included "two-engine power loss" as a contributing factor of the accident. Power loss as a factor was very controversial ... but to this day ... I am sure it is correct. Nearly ten years later, the Osprey continues to have power loss issues as outlined in a November 2019 Inspector General report stating dirt and debris continues to take a toll on Air Force and Marine Osprey aircraft. Pentagon inspectors found the vacuum filtration system known as the Engine Air Particle Separators (EAPS), which were redesigned twice in the last nine years, are inadequately protecting the engines … resulting in numerous power loss incidents.

The crews who strap tons of metal onto their backs … hold thousands of pounds of horsepower in their hands … employ state-of-the-art technology and fly into the face of our nation's enemies … deserve the truth. The soldiers, sailors, airmen and marines who ride these machines into battle deserve the truth. Family members, who every day bid their loved one's farewell for a day … a week … a month … six months … a year or more, deserve the truth about their heroes, some of whom never return.

Telling the truth can be challenging at times, but that does not give leaders the right to alter the truth. Leaders must tell the truth no matter how difficult it is. Altering the truth risks destroying your credibility and trustworthiness: two traits essential for all leaders. Leaders must emulate the behaviors they expect from their subordinates. This book is the truth.

CV-22 Osprey Crew in Afghanistan – Two Days Prior to Accident: L-R – Captain Luce, Major Voas, Senior Master Sergeant Lackey and Staff Sergeant Curtis

CV-22 in "helicopter mode" on ground and in-flight.

This book is dedicated to the families of the four people that did not survive the accident on the morning of April 9, 2010 in Afghanistan. The accident report turned into a controversial lightning-rod, causing the families to suffer and struggle beyond imagination. My heart goes out to the families affected by the accident.

A special thank you to Lt Col (Retired) Michael Leikam and Nan Harvel for their talented editing and content contributions. They made great sacrifices of time and energy to make this book a reality. I am forever grateful.

I have great respect and admiration for the accident investigation board members who worked with me to investigate the CV-22 Osprey accident. They stayed true to their moral compass and respected the Air Force Core values of integrity, service, and quality. All have my utmost gratitude for working 12–16 hours a day for months without a day off. I was blessed to work with all of you.

All profits from book sales will be donated to select veteran organizations to help gold star families.

TO THE LIVING WE OWE RESPECT,
BUT TO THE DEAD
WE OWE ONLY THE TRUTH

Voltaire

CONTENTS

PROLOGUE

April 9, 2010

Approximate Local Time – Midnight in Afghanistan

Twenty-five hundred feet over Taliban-held territory in southern Afghanistan, three U.S. Air Force CV-22 Osprey tilt-rotor aircraft droned through the inky black sky. The mission of the forty-eight U.S. Army Special Forces, Third Battalion, Seventy-Fifth Rangers aboard the airplanes was to engage in direct action with the enemy. The Air Force crews' mission – insert the Army troops close to their objective, a landing zone (LZ) near the town of Qalat in eastern Afghanistan.

Major Randell Voas, a Minnesota native and twenty-year veteran commanding military helicopters, led the three-ship formation on the planned fourteen-minute trip. With a layer of high clouds obscuring the night sky, screens on his instrument panel burned green with aircraft performance and navigation information, the only visible illumination.

In the cockpit, the navigation page revealed their progress – late. Anticipating the descent for landing, Voas adjusted his night vision goggles and keyed the microphone switch on his control column advising his formation of an updated time over target (TOT). The new TOT would have the three CV-22s landing on the LZ at forty minutes after midnight. Approximately twenty miles from the LZ, Voas reduced power, allowing the nose of the aircraft to fall toward the obscured horizon. He trimmed pressure on the control stick to neutral for the gradual letdown to a lower altitude.

At six minutes from touchdown, he passed a required advisory to his crew and passengers. The two aircraft behind him followed his lead and reset the alert height in their radar altimeters to five hundred feet. The Army troops acknowledged, ensured their weapons were safe, checked that their hand-held GPS tracked normal, and lowered their night vision goggles over their eyes.

Level at six hundred feet above the ground and two minutes out, an A-10 Thunderbolt II orbiting above illuminated (sparkled) the LZ. The crew, expecting a single shaft of light to identify their objective, instead watched multiple rays of infrared energy streak toward the planned touchdown point.

The copilot leaned forward in his seat questioning what he saw.

With no apparent concern, Voas acknowledged and modified his crosscheck, focusing on the TOT and the approach to landing.

At three miles and one minute from landing, the trio of aircraft descended to three hundred feet above the ground. The troops in the rear of the airplane acknowledged the "one-minute" advisory from the CV-22 tail scanner and took a knee facing the open ramp and door, preparing for a rapid egress once on the ground.

Descending into a valley and drifting away from their desired track, the crew noted an unexpected wind shift and corrected their heading to remain on course.

At two and a half miles to landing, Voas slowed to approach speed, and tilted the nacelles on the ends of the CV-22's stubby wings toward the vertical, altering their configuration from airplane to helicopter mode. The flight engineer lowered the landing gear. Hydraulic fluid compressed to 5000 psi (pounds per square inch) hissed through stainless steel lines to release the up locks fixing the landing gear assemblies into the wheel wells. Giant pistons ported fluid that extended the landing gear into position with an audible clunk.

Suddenly, at one hundred feet above ground, the airplane's nose unexpectedly pitched earthward in a rapid rate of descent. Unable to arrest the aircraft's vertical velocity or his speed over the ground, and with the plane headed for the center of a deep gully, Voas elected to abandon a vertical helicopter landing in favor of a seldom-practiced emergency maneuver. With his speed slightly exceeding ninety knots, he opted to land like any fixed-wing airplane, rolling the wheels onto the desert floor. Nearing touchdown, and amid a cacophony of aural electronic altitude warnings, the tempo of cockpit conversation intensified.

The tail scanner annunciated heights above touchdown beginning at ten feet, but before he could make the six-foot call, the main gear touched down firmly.

The nose wheel rolled a short distance then bounced, causing the open ramp to plow a furrow in the desert sand centered between tracks made by the main gear. Contacting the ground a second time, the nose gear collapsed. The now damaged airplane plowed across the desert, the nose of the CV-22 striking a shallow three-foot-deep ditch. The aircraft pivoted, tail-over-nose, crushing the cockpit, flipping onto its back. As the upside-down airplane skidded to a stop, its proprotors dug into the sand tearing the wings from the fuselage. The engines exploded, igniting fuel pouring from ruptured tanks into the hull and over the ground. The burgeoning inferno trailed the aircraft's deadly path.

The hard points securing the copilot's seat to the floor failed when the cockpit was crushed, sending him tumbling through a hole ripped in the aircraft's skin and across the sand for over thirty yards. He came to rest facing the rear of the fuselage, still strapped in his seat.

The larger section of hull, aft of the cockpit, came to rest inverted facing the direction from which they had landed. With the tail section missing and the fuselage separated at the bulkhead between the flight deck and what remained of the aircraft, the cargo compartment became a hollow tube grotesquely gaping open at each end with severed wires, tubing, and structural supports protruding into the void in a random, disordered tangle.

Shocked and injured passengers disencumbered themselves from their restraints; the less impaired assisting others away from the wreckage as quickly and safely as possible.

At first thought to be dead, the tail scanner remained one of the last brought to safety. His wounds appeared so severe he was left dangling by his safety line from the floor of the cargo compartment. Only when one of the Rangers heard him moaning, was he cut from his restraints and carried away from the aircraft. Thirty yards behind the airplane, another soldier cut the dazed copilot's restraints freeing him from his seat.

Light from the orange flames of burning jet fuel illuminated the dark night. Anticipating a rescue they were sure would soon arrive, the survivors administered first aid and triaged the wounded beneath a cloud of black smoke towering over the wreckage.

The fated Osprey flew only fourteen minutes, from takeoff to impacting the ground - less than a quarter mile short of their point of intended landing. Once on the ground, it skidded over the desert floor for seven seconds, traveling nearly three hundred feet.

Of the sixteen passengers aboard, fourteen, with varying degrees of injuries, survived. The most severe were treated at hospitals in Afghanistan and Germany, the rest at military trauma centers in the United States. Five sustained no or minor injuries, allowing their return to duty once evacuated from the crash site.

Two passengers riding in the back of the airplane died at the scene; one a U.S. Army Ranger, the other, a female civilian embedded with the unit as an Afghan interpreter.

Two U.S. Air Force members of the crew perished when the Osprey flipped onto its back, crushing the cockpit; the flight deck engineer, Senior Master Sergeant James Lackey, and the pilot, Major Randell Voas.

10 Hours Earlier

After less than a week of deployment at their main operating air base in Kandahar, Afghanistan, Major Randell Voas and his crew rose at 2:00 p.m. - dawn for special operator's duty. Expecting to be on alert or fly that night, they ate at the chow hall closest to their quarters then drove their crew vehicle, a Polaris 4-wheeled ATV, a quarter mile over unmarked dirt and gravel roads to their squadron operations. The crew shielded their faces against the mushrooming clouds of choking dust thrown into the air by rough terrain tires on most of the bases' vehicles, and the pungent odor of raw sewage saturating the Kandahar atmosphere.

They entered from the main base side of the semi-permanent building into a large room crews used for flight planning. Once inside, they made straight for a whiteboard where the squadron dispatcher posted general notices and the day's schedule.

Before they could digest the hand-written information, their commander greeted them. "Good, you're here. The Joint Operations Center (JOC) called. They require three aircraft from the Eighth Special Operations Squadron (SOS) to transport members of the Seventy-Fifth Rangers to a landing zone near Qalat ... TOT around midnight. Voas, you're senior in rank and experience. You have mission command and lead. The Planning Operations Center (POC) is drafting the mission plan. They're ready to brief you and the other two pilots when you get there."

Needing no further instructions, Voas's copilot and two enlisted crewmembers departed operations for the flight line and their assigned aircraft. While his crew configured and finished pre-flighting the airplane, Voas headed to the POC.

Before huddling with the two other aircraft commanders in his flight and the mission planners, he checked the weather forecast by calling the base weather shop. With no meteorological stations or observers in the target area, he relied on a general area forecast for the period – starlit night, light winds, high to mid-level ceilings, typical temperatures for the area and time of year. He had been studying the skies since childhood and could rely on his experienced, albeit primitive, predictions. In spite of the bleak environment, Voas always appreciated an opportunity to fly. He emailed the data to the POC.

Voas and the other two pilots consulted with the imagery analysts to determine a precise landing zone location and coordinated support units providing security and infrared for the landing zone. When they had completed their planning and mission briefing, the pilots loaded into a vehicle and were driven to their respective aircraft.

By the time Voas arrived, maintenance personnel and his crew had removed all non-essential equipment including the cargo compartment seats. The airplane weight had to be minimized to allow for maximum army personnel and fuel required for the mission.

The crew completed operational checks of the aircraft and systems, then proceeded to start both engines. The aircraft first assigned to Voas and his crew earlier in the day had developed mechanical problems that could not be fixed in time to fly. Maintenance substituted another airplane - tail number 06-0031 – to fly the mission. During the preflight, the right engine failed to start normally. The crew discontinued the start, letting the engine cool for a minute. On the second attempt, the engine accelerated to the required speed without any issues. Because this scenario happened periodically, the crew noted the malfunction mentally, and continued to prepare for takeoff.

The mission included a stop at a classified forward operating base (FOB) to on-load forty-eight Rangers. With sixteen Army personnel per aircraft, the three-ship Osprey formation would then fly a fourteen-minute low level route to insert the special operations team at an infiltration point near their objective along the southeastern border of Afghanistan.

With mission planning and aircraft preflight complete, Voas briefed his crew and prepared for departure. At a prearranged time, the three aircraft started engines, departed Kandahar, and flew a thirty-minute, eighty-mile route to the forward operating base.

After making a vertical approach and landing, the airplanes were shut down to allow the flight engineers to start loading the army personnel. The three aircraft commanders huddled with the ground forces commander, Major Carter, to go over the route of flight and the selected landing zones for each airplane at the infiltration site. A few Rangers complained about having to ride in an airplane to get to a landing zone only fifteen miles from their base. Had they double-timed the fifteen miles, they reasoned, they would have already completed their mission and be hoofing it back. Despite personal preferences or considerations, no one had a choice but to comply with tasking orders.

The soldiers had been loaded into the Ospreys in reverse order they would have to exit after landing. With the seats removed, the soldiers sat on the floor and leaned on their packs to rest against the sidewalls of the cargo compartment. For restraint, they cinched a rope around their waist, securing the opposite end to a line strung along the axis of the fuselage. With the last soldier in place, the three aircraft started their engines and quickly prepared for takeoff.

Due to the altitude of the forward operating base (over 4,000 feet elevation) the weight of each aircraft, and the absence of a prepared runway to provide a clear area to accelerate and climb, the three aircraft performed an *80 Jump[1]* departure with the rotors tilted to near vertical and the engines at maximum power. Because the copilot had no combat experience and little practice performing the maximum weight take off, Voas allowed him the honors.

The copilot advanced the thrust control lever (TCL) to maximum. The powerful Rolls Royce engines gorged on the additional fuel while accelerating to maximum power. The mammoth, thirty-eight-foot-long blades clawed at the near mile-high air sending vibrations shuddering throughout the airframe. The airplane jumped into the air, climbing out at a steep angle, without the landing gear rolling over the ground.

The copilot nervously shook his head and made a quick glance at Voas.

"She feels very heavy."

"Yeah," Voas nodded in agreement.

---

1 "80 Jump" Takeoff – A technique used by V-22 pilots to get off the ground in a short distance.

CHAPTER ONE

ACCIDENT INVESTIGATION PROCESS

Wall, Robert. "CV-22 Crashes in Afghanistan" *Aviation Week*, April 9, 2010.

> *Three U.S. military personnel and a civilian have died in the first crash of a U.S. Air Force Special Operations CV-22 Tiltrotor.*
>
> *The cause of the accident has not been determined yet according to a statement issued by NATO's International Security Assistance Force, which runs much of the military campaign in Afghanistan.*[1]

Newnan, Georgia
Friday – April 9, 2010
7:40 a.m.

On the morning of April 9th, I sat down in front of my computer and scanned my new email messages. I had been out of town for four days working my civilian job as a commercial airline captain flying the Boeing 777. I skipped over the few personal emails, focusing instead on the twenty-five or more dealing with my other job – Air National Guard (ANG) advisor to the commander of the U.S. Air Force Special Operations Command (AFSOC). Before tackling official military communications, news pop-ups with the words *Crash, CV-22*, and *Afghanistan* in the *Aviation Week* online newsletter seized my attention.

The post provided few details, so I turned to a cable news network in the middle of their report. My mouth went dry and chills radiated down my arms as I listened to the words every U.S. Air Force commander fears – the loss of a U.S. military airplane with the probable loss of the crew.

When the reports began to repeat the scarce details, I returned to the internet for information. Over the next few hours, I learned survivors had been taken to medical facilities in theater. The aircraft and crew were assigned to the Eighth Special Operations Squadron (SOS) based at Hurlburt Field, Florida, about thirty-five miles east of Pensacola. Since my position as the Air National Guard advisor to the commander of Air Force Special Operations Command kept me at the Florida Panhandle's base often, I was very familiar with the command and the base. Though I most wanted to know the names of the crewmembers involved in the accident, the information would not be available until the next of kin had been notified. I tried to call Major General (two stars) Clay McCutcheon, United States Air Force Reserve Advisor to the AFSOC commander. With no answer on his or any other line at headquarters, I left a message with my executive officer, Captain April Pierce.

Because of the fatalities involved and the loss of an eighty-six-million-dollar airplane, the accident fell into the category of a "Class A" mishap. The commander at Kandahar Air Base (KAB) would have already assembled an Interim Safety Board (ISB) to preserve evidence and conduct preliminary interviews of witnesses. He would pass their findings to a Safety Investigation Board (SIB) that would arrive at Kandahar Air Base within days.

Assigned by the Air Force Special Operations Commander, the Safety Investigation Board would conduct the next level of investigation. That board would grant *privileged* and *confidential* status to persons providing testimony and hold those findings solely for the benefit of the commander with the object of discovering and recommending any immediate action that might prevent another accident. The findings of the safety investigation board are not releasable to anyone except the commander and selected personnel.

The top tier of the accident investigation process, the formal Accident Investigation Board (AIB), would then convene with a general officer as president. Upon completion, their findings and complete detailed report would be released to the public. The AIB's independent investigation would collect and assess their own evidence, as well as non-privileged evidence shared by the SIB. The AIB would interview witnesses and study evidence in order to find the probable cause of the accident, or the contributing factors contributing to cause the accident. The board would also make recommendations about remedial actions to the commander.

Over the weekend, news anchors and organizations (CNN, FOX and MSNBC) polled military and aviation experts about the accident. One-by-one, they offered opinions that ran the spectrum of possibilities. Some offered that the airplane was shot down. Others insisted the CV-22 had a mechanical malfunction causing it to impact the ground unexpectedly. A few pundits even offered that the crew inadvertently hit the ground while flying too low.

Monday morning the identity of the soldiers and airmen killed in the crash were released. I did not recognize any of the names, but I shared every Air Force airmen's anguish for those associated with the accident – the families, survivors, and those at every level in the chain of command. Given the scrutiny and history of horrific accidents spanning nearly three decades during its development, the media attention for this accident would persist long after the completion of the investigation.

Tuesday morning, three hours before I planned to depart my home and drive to the Atlanta airport, my cell phone rang. I recognized the name and number on the screen. It was the vice commander of Air Force Special Operations Command, Major General Kent Dobrinski.

"Don. It's probably no secret why I'm calling. Have you been watching the news?"

"Yes, sir," I answered. "I can't believe this has happened. I'm heartbroken. Can I help in any way?"

"I'm glad you asked. How soon can you get down here to Hurlburt Field?"

CHAPTER TWO

SEALING THE DEAL

My brief conversation with General Dobrinski included a reference to news concerning the accident and ended with a summons to Hurlburt Field in Ft. Walton Beach, Florida. Since further discussion would have no doubt included classified information, we agreed to continue the discussion once I arrived on the base.

As I sorted through the flood of events now requiring my immediate attention, I informed my commercial airline crew scheduling office to remove me from my scheduled trip. I changed into my Air Force utility attire, battle dress uniform (BDUs) and repacked my suitcase for military duty in Florida. I considered my travel options. The six-and-a-half-hour drive from Atlanta to Hurlburt Field would consume most of what remained of the day. If I went to the airport and caught a flight, I could cut that time closer to two hours. I called my executive officer at Air Force Special Operations Command, Captain April Pierce.

She had anticipated my call and after a brief greeting, cut straight to business.

"I have you scheduled on a Delta Airlines flight departing Atlanta at 4 p.m. I'll pick you up at the Ft. Walton Beach airport with your staff car. I've also reserved a room for you at the Visiting Officer's Quarters (VOQ)."

"That's great. I'll make it, if I leave my house within the next half hour," I said.

I placed several calls postponing or cancelling events scheduled for the following weeks. I threw my bags in the car, then made a personal call to my wife as I drove to the airport. I endured the ensuing silence while she digested what she'd been told about the change in plans. Six months from my scheduled military retirement, she had to have believed this part of our lives had come to an end. I waited for her first question for which I would have no answer.

"How long will you be gone?" she asked.

"Days at least … maybe weeks … I don't think months. I have no idea what they expect, but I promise to call you later tonight."

I could feel her disappointment through the phone. Balancing a military and commercial airline career had many challenges – most of them carried as weight on the shoulders of my wife and daughter. I knew they would handle it, as they always did, but that didn't make it any easier.

I parked at the airport and scurried through the security checkpoint. Arriving at my departure gate, I boarded the flight. As soon as I was seated, I started working on calls, texts, and emails. Before long, the commuter airplane touched down on schedule at the Valparaiso Airport, a facility shared with Eglin Air Force Base. The civilian and military traffic made the airfield one of the busiest airports in the Southeast.

Eglin Air Force Base, a sprawling United States military reservation located roughly fifty miles from Panama City to the east and forty miles to Pensacola to the west, consumed a vast portion of the Panhandle coast of Florida. Numerous special operations units were based in the area, including the headquarters of Air Force Special Operations Command at Hurlburt Field.

Captain Pierce met me on the street side of the terminal and handed me a chilled bottle of water.

"Welcome back, sir."

I loaded my bags into the trunk and slid into the passenger seat.

"Thanks, I guess. So, what's happening at headquarters?" I asked.

"I'm not aware of everything, but it's been crazy-busy since the accident. Word in the command area is that you'll be here a while. I reserved your room for a month."

A month? I had not envisioned being away from home for a month, nor could I guess what I would be asked to do. There had to be senior officers detailed from their duties to manage events triggered by the accident. Perhaps I would backfill a position for someone engaged in one of the investigations. Having been to military and commercial aviation safety courses, I could also serve as liaison with the accident victim's families, or coordinate headquarters' staff with investigation teams deployed to the accident site.

Despite traveling in a blue United States Air Force staff car, sentries guarding the main gate checked both of our identification cards and made a cursory inspection of the car's interior. Since the attack on 9-11, security at every military installation remained on heightened alert. Hurlburt Field, home of the Air Force Special Operations Command, and numerous special operations units, had always been very serious about who had access to the base.

After driving through the main gate, we passed by the Hurlburt Air Park, where static displays of aircraft employed by special operations crews from as far back as the Korean and Vietnam wars, were restored to perfection and gleaming in the Florida sun. Unlike most airplanes on exhibit in parks and museums, these airplanes were not the worn-out old hangar queens relegated to glorified bone yards. Each specimen in the collection had proudly flown in the days prior to being moved, or flown to Hurlburt, for the purpose of being on display. The aircraft stood as silent sentinels reminding passersby of historic milestones of Hurlburt's contribution to the special operations, air commando mission. With special operations occupying an expanding role in modern warfare, on May 22, 1990, the Air Force designated Air Force Special Operations Command as one of the ten major air commands. Hurlburt Field boasts state of the art training and operational facilities for conducting worldwide combat operations.

After we passed the airpark, Pierce turned right then made a quick left onto the street leading to the AFSOC headquarters parking lot, stopping at the three-story building's front door.

"I'll park the car in your designated spot, and see you upstairs in a few minutes, sir."

"OK, thank you," I said as I jumped out of the car.

I scanned my ID cards at the headquarters entry door and double-timed up the stairs to the third floor. My heart pounded as I took a deep breath and entered the command suite.

The AFSOC command suite of offices occupied most of the building's third floor. The commander and senior staff occupied space around the perimeter of a large, open outer office separated from the corridor by a glass wall and doors. The workspaces for secretaries and senior administrative personnel sat near the officer they supported. My office stood between the vice commander and my counterpart from the USAF Reserve.

Before the glass doors closed, the commander's secretary greeted me.

"Hello, General Harvel … it's good to see you again … and so soon. The vice commander is expecting you. I'll let him know you're here."

Within seconds General Dobrinski, a barrel-chested six-foot figure, appeared in the door and shook my hand. He carried weight which some might seem unusual for his training and previous assignments as an F-16 and F-117 fighter pilot, but I credited his size to a chronic ankle injury which prevented him from a routine of rigorous exercise rather than a senior officer's sedentary existence.

His office included pictures and knickknacks from his numerous Air Force assignments. In the center of the room, between two stuffed chairs, a glass-topped coffee table displayed fifty or more challenge coins exchanged in military tradition with other senior commanders or gifted as an expression of gratitude or acknowledgement to those exhibiting outstanding performance.

"We've assembled the Safety Investigation Board for the CV-22 accident," he said. "They'll depart for Kandahar in a few days."

His manner had always been forthright; direct without being curt. He seldom engaged in small talk or pleasantries to ease into a subject, going right to the reason for my being summoned.

"Have you attended the Accident Investigation Board (AIB) President training?"

"Yes, sir. I completed the course in 2006."

"Great, that makes my next question a little easier. Would you be willing to serve as the AIB president for the Osprey accident?"

I had assumed the position would be filled by an officer currently serving on active duty. I expected to be involved in some capacity for sure, but being six months from my planned retirement, I had not considered the commander would choose me to sit as president of the official accident investigation.

"Me, sir? You want me to preside over the accident investigation?"

"You were the boss's choice. You're familiar with the Osprey and seem close to the 8th Special Operations Squadron. So, will you do it?"

From the first day as a cadet at the United States Military Academy at West Point, I had been taught to accept orders without question. I considered myself a good officer who acknowledged orders in the affirmative and charged toward the objective, whatever it happened to be. With my mouth dry, unable to swallow, I choked down a gulp of air.

"Yes sir."

"Excellent," he said. "You have a lot of work to do and not a lot of time to get it done. Clear your schedule for the next six weeks. Will that work for you?"

"I'll make it work, sir."

"If you need to bone up on duties of the Accident Investigation Board President, check with the safety office at the First Special Operations Wing (SOW). They'll get you up to speed. We'll have the remainder of your board assigned in the next few days. You have any questions?"

"Where will the board conduct its work?"

He confided that two options were being considered, revealing the location of neither. He would decide within a few days.

We sealed the deal with a handshake and a salute. I walked two doors away to my office.

While the regulations regarding aircraft accident investigations printed, I composed a "to do" list. The print job had completed, but I continued to write. When I pushed away from the desk, I had three pages of notes.

I scanned the regulation outlining the duties of the AIB President. In the four years since I had completed the course, I had forgotten about one block of training during the class. I was reminded about it, and how much it bothered me, as I reviewed the Air Force Instructions (AFIs) concerning accident investigations and the duties of the board president.

I suddenly had second thoughts about what I had agreed to do minutes prior and considered walking back to the vice commander's office.

CHAPTER THREE

NO CHOICE

The one-week Safety and Accident Investigation Board President Course at the Air Force Safety Center, Kirtland Air Force Base, New Mexico, had faded into my distant memory. It had been the last course I attended in the Air Force flight safety field. With retirement on the horizon, I had no reason to expect I would have to draw on the experience.

I searched my memory for a loophole in the Air Force Instructions that required the president of the accident board to personally visit the families of the accident victims in their homes once the investigation was completed and the commander of the Air Force Special Operations Command (AFSOC) had been briefed. Air Force regulations required the accident board president to deliver a copy of the report to each family of the critically injured and deceased personnel involved in the accident and brief them about the accident findings. The fact that one of the casualties had been a foreign national troubled me. I couldn't recall the course dealing with surviving families of foreign contractors who lived half a world away.

The knot tightening in my stomach eased knowing that AFSOC had assigned representatives from public affairs, the chaplain's office, and 8th Special Operations Squadron personnel dedicated to the support of individual family members in the aftermath of the accident. I would treat them with the same honesty with which I intended to conduct the investigation, whatever the outcome. The command, the mission, the crews, and their loved ones deserved no less.

In the meantime, I had a lot of work to do in preparation for conducting the investigation. I needed a piece of information that Captain Pierce had at her fingertips. There were seven desks in the main area outside my office, and when I opened my office door, they were empty. I had lost track of time. Everyone had shut off their computers, straightened their desks, and departed. The call to retreat at the flagpole outside the building had passed hours before, as had the sunset. At 8:15 p.m., I remained the only one in the command section. I began cleaning up my desk, making a note to call home as soon as I got settled in my room. I knew if my wife and daughter didn't hear from me soon, they would become worried.

Though the command, and my job, provided an office in the command suite of AFSOC headquarters, my temporary duties in Florida did not justify a permanent residence. During my brief tours of duty, the base provided temporary quarters. On the short drive to the visiting officer quarters (VOQ), I mentally scripted what I thought I could divulge about my part in the accident investigation and still keep my family involved.

Quarters for visiting senior officers mirrored a second tier commercial Residence Inn or a small condominium; not luxurious, but clean and very comfortable. The two-story unit had a sitting area, bath, and kitchen downstairs, with a bedroom and bathroom upstairs.

Before making the call, I raided the familiar honor bar and pantry. After heating up a can of soup and mixing a rum and coke, I called to update my wife and daughter on all the surprising events of the day.

The following morning my alarm awakened me at 6:00 a.m. I slid into my usual day while performing duties at AFSOC, arriving at the office by 7:00 a.m. where I would prepare for the commander's daily "stand-up" briefing at 8:00 a.m.

The meeting followed a standard format prompted by PowerPoint™ slides projected on a screen opposite the commander's end of the long conference table. Members of the Commander's Action Group (CAG), select civilians, junior officers, and a few senior officers, who often included Captain Pierce, presented the status of assets and missions – a command-wide "how-goes-it" and a projection of activities over the ensuing twenty-four hours. Fourteen members of the senior staff representing the major elements of the command sat in descending order of rank along the two sides of the table. Other officers, non-commissioned officers (NCOs), and ranking civilians with interests in, or presentations to make, sat in chairs placed along the two long walls of the conference room.

With Lieutenant General (three stars) Charles Becker away from the base on a temporary assignment, General Dobrinski conducted the meeting, starting by introducing me as the president of the accident investigation board for the Osprey accident. If I had harbored any illusion of absolving myself of this assignment without prejudice, he smashed it in one simple, declarative sentence during the morning meeting.

At the conclusion of the briefing, most returned to their work, while a few remained to conduct informal business or engage in small talk. Neither the commander when present, nor the vice in his stead, ever remained beyond the conclusion of the meeting.

When I returned to my office, post-it notes on my desk indicated I had missed six calls in my absence, one from the pilot member assigned to my investigation board. He wanted to meet me as soon as possible. As I reached for the phone, Captain Pierce knocked on my door.

"We're compiling a checklist of requirements for your deployment to Afghanistan, sir. You need to update your weapons qualification, which is scheduled in thirty minutes. The pilot member of your board requires the refresher course, too. He has called a couple of times and is anxious to meet you," she said. "Then you have a working lunch with the hospital commander. He will check your records for theater medical requirements, which, I have to tell you, includes an impressive array of immunizations. If you get a minute somewhere in between, stop at the supply squadron. They'll issue you a mobility bag, and equipment required for deployment to Kandahar Air Base in Afghanistan. Sir, you have a busy day ahead of you. As always, let me know if I can help with anything."

Though I had no need to remind her, I did anyway.

"Call me if anything important changes," I said.

I had not qualified with the 9mm pistol for a couple of years, but anticipated no problem with updating my qualification. When I arrived, there were only two people - a Master Sergeant, the instructor - and the pilot member of what would soon be my accident investigation board, Lieutenant Colonel Jeff O'Leary.

O'Leary stood an inch or two shorter than me with a marathon runners build; a definite asset in the cramped cockpit of a helicopter. Like most aviators, he wore the sleeves of his flight suit pushed half way over his forearms with a crew neck t-shirt showing at his neck. Moving with little wasted motion, he smiled and looked me straight in the eyes when we exchanged greetings.

"General Harvel ... Jeff O'Leary ... I'm the pilot member assigned to your board."

"I'm glad you're here before everyone else. We're going to spend a lot of time together during the next couple of months," I said. "Have you served on an accident investigation board before?"

"Yes, sir, the CH-53 accident six years ago."

"You have no idea how happy that makes me. This is my first," I replied.

I turned my attention to the range master.

"Sergeant, we're ready to start when you are, unless we're waiting for the others to join the class?"

"No, sir, just two of you," he said, as he laid boxes of ammunition and two freshly oiled 9mm pistols in front of us.

We quickly completed the short course. I invited O'Leary to join me for my working lunch meeting with the First Special Operations Wing Medical Group commander. We drove to The Reef, a fast food restaurant a few blocks from AFSOC Headquarters.

While we waited for the flight surgeon, O'Leary and I exchanged pleasantries and talked about our careers. O'Leary had instructed and evaluated pilots in most of the rotorcraft in the United States military arsenal, which included training Afghan pilots how to fly the Russian built MI-17. He also was one of the first active duty U.S. Air Force pilots to have flown the CV-22. When the aircraft underwent flight-testing prior to its acceptance for production and deployment to active units, O'Leary served as an Air Force test pilot for the program.

He appeared shy at first, perhaps intimidated by my rank and the task to which we had been assigned. Being fellow Air Force aviators gave us a lot in common and during our conversation, I discovered he had also graduated from the U.S. Military Academy. I immediately knew we would become very good friends. Besides being a seasoned aviator, he had been schooled in technical aspects of flight. I hadn't considered it beforehand, but the team might require a numbers guy, a trained engineer and expert in aerodynamics. Dobrinski had chosen well by selecting O'Leary to be on the accident board.

Midway through lunch, the Medical Group commander, Colonel Stuart Lund, arrived with a briefcase packed with papers. Command requirements for individuals deploying to a forward combat area and the near east exceeded general U.S. Air Force or Department of Defense minimums. He provided a detailed record of inoculations, briefings, training, and computer based tests to be accomplished by all members of the AIB prior to departure. He pledged to make the process as smooth and easy as possible.

Toward the end of our working lunch, I felt my cell phone vibrating continuously in my pocket. Captain Pierce's familiar number showed on the screen.

"General Harvel, she said, "can you come back to headquarters immediately? General Dobrinski wants to speak with you right away."

CHAPTER FOUR

INVESTIGATION SNAG

I drove to headquarters expecting to deal with bad, if not dire, news. I entered the command suite, and a secretary directed me to the vice commander's office, miming, "He said for you to go in immediately."

I stood at the door for a moment while he finished a phone call. I tried to step away, but he motioned for me to come in and have a seat.

"I talked to the boss," he said after hanging up. "He wants you to conduct your investigation from here."

"Here? Here in Florida, sir … at Hurlburt? What? I don't understand. How do we conduct an investigation without traveling to the accident area?" I asked.

"We've located workspace for your team. Make a list of supplies and equipment you'll need."

He leaned toward me, eyebrows pushed up onto his forehead, expecting a response. I had met only one member who would serve on my board and knew nothing about the remaining board members. To this point, I harbored no expectation of conducting an investigation from behind a desk; then he asks me for a list of supplies for space in a facility I would need but had not yet seen.

"Questions?" he said. His steely eyes bored into mine.

Stunned for what seemed to be a full minute, I couldn't form a logical response.

"Has the cause of the accident already been determined?" I asked. "News reports say pilot error."

"We haven't been briefed by the Safety Investigation Board. When that happens, we'll have their answer, and a good idea of what happened."

Except for media reports, I had no indication whether pilot error was or was not the cause. When the Safety Investigation Board completed their investigation, I would have their data, with possible exceptions, but I still wouldn't know what they concluded. It made little sense to me; however, if the commander insisted, I would have no choice but to conduct my inquiry without deploying to Afghanistan.

"Sir, can I get back with you about supplies? I would like to see the office first, then let you know what is needed."

He leaned back in his chair and said, "Sure. Have it on my desk first thing in the morning. I sent you an email with my attached letter convening the Accident Investigation Board and assigning six members including two legal representatives. You'll find a side letter outlining what I expect regarding their part in the investigation along with other instructions. Coordinate your team's arrival, here at Hurlburt Field, with the Safety Investigation Board president, Brigadier General Michael Kingsley, in order to make sure your board members are here prior to his investigation being completed."

Considering the Osprey's troubled history, the loss of four lives, destruction of an expensive weapon system, scrutiny by the media, Congress, the public, and the aircraft's manufacturer, the results of the investigation promised to be intensely scrutinized. With their days being packaged in fractions of a minute, neither the commander nor his vice needed to be handcuffed to a legal, or public relations nightmare.

"Will do, sir," I said.

"In the event we've not anticipated all your board member requirements, send a request for what you need through the command's legal office. They'll forward it to me, after it has been reviewed, along with their recommendation."

"Yes, sir," I said as I stood up and departed his office.

I trudged to my office hauling the truckload of wet sand Dobrinski had just heaped on my shoulders. I pushed everything aside and placed a clean yellow legal pad in the center of my desk. I drew a line, top to bottom, down the middle of the page. On the left side, I wrote "*Reasons to Deploy to the Accident Site*" or a base near the site for whatever time would be necessary to conduct what I envisioned to be a proper investigation. On the right side of the page, I noted reasons, valid reasons, for "*Conducting an Accident Investigation from Hurlburt Field.*" Assuming that sort of scrutiny would be possible, or even legal, I would study options that supported both alternatives.

I scrolled through my inbox until I located Dobrinski's email. I read it thoroughly, then printed the attached letter.

> *Item One: An AIB is hereby convened under the provisions of Air Force Instruction 51-503,* **Aerospace Accident Investigations**, *to investigate the subject mishap. This appointment letter is your authority to interview witnesses, take sworn testimony, and review all documents, files, and wreckage relevant to your investigation. Upon receipt of the evidence and Part 1 of the Safety Investigation Board (SIB) report, you and the other detailed members of your team are relieved of all other duties until the AIB report is completed.*
>
> *Item Two: If, during the course of your investigation, you determine additional expertise is required please advise AFSOC legal office of your requirements.*
>
> *Item Three: A legal advisor is required to be present during all interviews, and must review all evidence, documents, transcripts, and statements prior to inclusion in your report. All witnesses, documents, records, and other evidence within the control of the Air Force will be made available to you, other than privileged safety information. All witnesses who testify must do so under oath or affirmation. Your report shall be releasable to the public and may not contain any privileged safety or Privacy Act-protected information.*
>
> *Item Four: Your Statement of Opinion must be supported by clear and convincing evidence contained in your report. Your legal advisors will assist you in evaluating evidence. Do*

not include recommendations for corrective or disciplinary action in your report. You and the other AIB members are not authorized to disclose board findings or opinions, except to members of my staff, prior to approval of the AIB report.

Items Five, Six: Outlined specifications for travel and logistical support.

Item Seven: Your investigation should be completed within thirty days from the receipt of the SIB's [report] Part 1. [2]

Though the note included no contact information other than email addresses in the BC/CC section, I jotted the names of the other board members.

Scanning emails again, I noticed a message from one of the legal advisors assigned to the investigation board, Lieutenant Colonel Gordon Winsett. He had taken it upon himself to communicate with the other board members soliciting their cell phone numbers. He closed by asking me to call him as soon as possible. I was appreciative of his aggressive assistance.

Every successful group has at least one person without whom the organization could not function; the glue that holds it together. Winsett appeared to be such a person. A graduate of Boston College Law School he came to the board from the special operations wing at Cannon AFB in Clovis, New Mexico. I made the call.

He answered after two rings.

"Hi Colonel, this is Brigadier General Don Harvel. I see you've been assigned to my Accident Investigation Board."

"Yes, sir, thanks for the quick response. How are you settling into the job?"

"Behind, but working hard to get caught up."

"I can help. I'm sending you contact information, emails and phone numbers, for the remaining board members as we speak. With your permission, I'll coordinate travel, billeting, and rental cars as well. Do you have a date for us to report to Hurlburt?"

"Go ahead, send me what contact info you have and pencil in travel arrangements. I haven't set a date. I need to coordinate with the Safety Investigation Board president to see how fast their investigation is proceeding. I'll send you a date tomorrow."

"I suggest we report to Hurlburt about ten days from when the Safety Board thinks their report will be complete," said Winsett. "That'll be plenty of time for us to organize, set up an office, and prepare to deploy to the accident site."

His last comment reminded me of the meeting I'd had with Dobrinski minutes before. Winsett also assumed we would have to see the crash site. In either case, ten days would be ample time to organize and lay out a timeline to conduct the investigation. When, or if, we traveled to Afghanistan remained the question.

I hung up the phone and printed the roster of team members. Next to O'Leary's name, (the pilot member of the board with whom I'd shared the firing range) I penciled, *Top notch helo-pilot … smart … numbers guy, experienced special operations pilot.* Beside Winsett's name I wrote, *Glue … organized … high energy … very smart … detail oriented.*

As I studied the members assigned to the board, it was apparent to me that I would need a communications specialist. Whoever it would be should be a non-commissioned officer - someone affable, smart, and accomplished. Technical Sergeant Bryan Scott came to mind. He would be perfect, but I would have to convince Lieutenant Colonel Rique Gwin, chief of the Commander's Action Group, to loan him to me for a couple months.

Few in AFSOC knew Scott had survived the 1996 terrorist attack on the Khobar Tower barracks in Saudi Arabia. The explosion blew him through two walls. He had sustained back injuries making the act of standing up or sitting down painful, but no one outside his workspace noticed.

Offered an opportunity, he would want to be a part of the investigation. Despite the CAG's hectic schedule, I would have to convince his boss to detail him to me for a few weeks. If you asked Gwin about it today, he would swear I begged, but I didn't care as long as I had him. With the numerous deployments, communications personnel were in high demand.

I would have to release him back to his job the minute I no longer needed him.

With the normal duty day coming to a close, I walked across the hall and asked TSgt Scott if he could help me for a few minutes. We walked to my office where I showed him the partial list of equipment and supplies I had compiled. He scanned the single hand-written page and made a few suggestions.

"The CAG is about to roll up for the day," he said. "Let's go take a look at the office they've allocated to your team."

I grabbed my hat and we drove three blocks to a building across the street from the Air Force Special Operations Training Center. A photo lab and the Military Personnel Flight occupied one end of the single-story structure and a spacious office sat vacant at the other end.

"This is it," I said.

Scott walked the room with a contractor's sense of space, paying special attention to electrical and communications capacity.

"How many people will work here?" he asked.

"If I negotiate the details with your boss and you want to join the AIB, there will be eight."

"I'd love to see how the accident investigation process works. Working for you will be a bonus. I have a friend in the communications squadron. He can back-fill my spot in the CAG for a few weeks."

I admired his enthusiasm and expertise, plus he knew and had a great rapport with every unit and person on the base, regardless of their rank.

"Then consider yourself part of the AIB team."

"Thank you, sir, and don't worry about this office. There'll be eight desks, each with a telephone and a computer. I'll get a high-speed copier for the room. I should have it set up in three days."

"Perfect," I said.

As we walked back to my car, I was confident I had a home for the investigation team and a first-rate communications specialist. Though I had checked two large items off my "to do" list, I still had no plan for the issue that bothered me most … how to do justice to an accident investigation conducted half a world away from where the accident occurred.

By the time I returned to headquarters, the building had been vacated by all except those whose duties involved twenty-four-hour attention. Working alone in the command section, I moved bullets from my legal pad to a PowerPoint™ slide. I planned to consider it overnight and finish the following morning.

Neither the commander nor his deputy tolerated push back on orders once issued from their respective desks. They hadn't been promoted through the officer ranks to preside over one of the top tier United States military commands by making ill-conceived, or ill-advised decisions. Though I enjoyed their confidence and respect, no comment from me on a personal or professional level would reverse their decision. If, however, they became convinced that the command's best interests and their own were better served if I deployed the team to Afghanistan, I would lead the investigation there and wherever the facts led.

Before leaving the building for the night, I sent an email asking Winsett to send a formal request for TSgt Bryan Scott to be added as a member of the Accident Investigation Board.

I also checked for posts on the Secret Internet Protocol Router Network (SIPRNet) concerning the Osprey accident. The SIPRNet is a system of interconnected communications networks used by the Department of Defense (DOD) and the Department of State to transmit information up to and including *TOP SECRET*, a classified version of the internet. In my search I found no new posts on the accident but did see an email from the CV-22 Safety Investigation Board president requesting I call him later in the evening (Florida time). I immediately picked up my office phone and dialed his number. While waiting for the call to connect, I reread the last line in his email.

"Don, it's critical we speak before you attend the commander's stand up briefing tomorrow morning. Please call me immediately."

CHAPTER FIVE

ACCIDENT INVESTIGATION BOARD CONVENES

To my good fortune and contrary to my habit of checking email in the morning prior to the commander's stand up briefing, I went through my inbox before heading back to the visiting officer quarters. Even though I remained the only person in the command suite, I closed my office door for privacy.

I was acquainted with the safety board president, Brigadier General Michael Kingsley. Our paths had crossed, although we had never worked on the same or related projects. With his extensive special operations helicopter experience, the commander requested he be detailed from his Pentagon post to be the safety investigation board president.

I had two landlines in my office. One was for local and unclassified long distance calls, and the other, a Secure Telephone Unit (STU III), enabled telephone conversations of classified (Secret) information with other people who had the same type of phone at their work location. The device scrambled voice inputs on one end of the line and descrambled the transmission on the other. Once the connection was established, callers turned a key at the same time to enable the encryption software that secured the conversation. The clarity suffered from the process, but speaking in a deliberate manner and tone rendered the quality adequate and, most importantly, secure.

I waited through the characteristic STU III ring tone.

"Hi Mike, Don Harvel, you ready to go secure?"

We both turned a key on our phones linking the devices in SECURE mode.

"Mike, how goes the investigation?"

"Well enough, I guess," he said. "We've completed a dozen or more interviews in country and plan to meet with the surviving crew members being treated stateside as we travel back to Hurlburt. You may or may not be aware that two A-10s bombed the crash site a few hours after the accident."

"No, no one's mentioned that," I said. "Why would they bomb the accident site?"

"We haven't had access to the accident site; it's pretty deep into Taliban held territory. What wreckage we recovered fits in a medium-sized box we'll be carrying on the airplane when we fly home. It's not much. We're about finished with our work at Kandahar. Once we complete our report, I should be able to give you Part One sometime during the first week in May. Have you set a date to convene your board?"

"The last of the board members should arrive on April 28th," I answered.

We discussed the transfer of evidence and his redeployment plans, but avoided discussion of his findings, which might taint our own investigation – not that he would have divulged any such information anyway. Before we signed off, I had one final question.

"Mike, is any of your safety board information privileged?"

"No, nothing yet, but we've yet to interview the co-pilot and tail scanner.

The safety investigation board report included two parts. Part One – non-privileged and non-confidential information which would be given to the accident investigation board, but not released to the public unless included in the accident investigation board's final report. Distribution of Part Two … confidential witness and contractor statements, board findings, deliberations and recommendations confined to safety channels and the senior command structure only. The information would be very "close-hold" and not released to anyone in order to protect the people sharing their testimony with the safety board members.

With the safety investigation board's report in hand, my board would have a head start unless interviews with the two recovering crewmembers became labeled as privileged or confidential. If the interviews had protected information – it would not be shared between the safety board and the accident investigation board. This would not prevent me from interviewing the two crewmembers, and asking any question I desired. The crewmember might answer the questions differently to my board – and perhaps request an attorney to be present while being questioned by the accident board. The two crewmembers' testimony to the accident board could result in punitive action against the crewmember. Their testimony to the safety board could not be used against them in any way.

Kingsley ended the phone call with a request for me to tell the AFSOC commander that he and his seven-member team would depart Kandahar as soon as they could secure seats on a military flight returning to the United States. I assured him I would pass the message.

After speaking with Kingsley, I prioritized elements of my investigation, with the accident site and the reason the aircraft had been destroyed being at the top of the list. Next, I needed to work on the logistics and updating the medical condition of the survivors, which might dictate whether those interviews would be done before or after we traveled to Afghanistan.

Kingsley's team had interviewed a dozen or more individuals, yet if they had talked to just the survivors of the mishap aircraft, the number would have been sixteen. I tallied the numbers as I ran the catalogue of possible people to interview:

- The crews of A-10 aircraft flying cover and support for the mission

- Crews and passengers in the other two Ospreys flying that night

- Personnel on duty in the task force command center who watched the event unfold in real time and their contemporaneous video and recordings of radio transmissions

- Air traffic controllers at the main operating base and the forward operating base

- Special operators and support staff at the forward operating base

- Air crews and resources involved in the rescue and recovery of the deceased and injured

Those face-to-face interviews could only be accomplished while the subjects remained in theater. When personnel in the Area of Responsibility (AOR) rotated to the U.S. or received other assignments, tracking them down would be a nightmare, and I had a timeline to complete the investigation. Our probable success waned with every passing hour.

The mishap aircraft had been mostly destroyed during the accident. The accident site, cleared of personnel and classified equipment, was bombed by two A-10 Thunderbolts. I wondered how there could only be enough remaining wreckage that could be contained in a box carried by one person. If not recovered soon, pieces of the aircraft would be converted to souvenirs and trophies in the local souk (market) or junked. Kingsley had not mentioned what other evidence he had collected, if any. We couldn't search for or discover missing aircraft wreckage or other evidence from behind a desk at Hurlburt Field. With my meager staff, we couldn't even track down and interview most of the witnesses over the phone. Trying to conduct our accident investigation without leaving the base sounded like a bad idea – and it got worse by the minute.

Perhaps Kingsley had discovered unequivocal evidence indicating the cause of the accident. If someone at the upper echelons in AFSOC's chain of command, or on the safety board had not leaked the information to the media, why were the reports of pilot error credited to an *official source close to the investigation*?

Most of the following week, O'Leary and I completed our personal requirements to deploy to Afghanistan and laid the groundwork for the arrival of the other team members. He saved me countless hours of preparation. Without his help and that of TSgt Scott furnishing the office, we might not have been ready to receive the board members as they arrived on base.

By April 26th, Scott had equipped, supplied, and organized the accident investigation board office space. Winsett arrived on April 27th and came straight to my office. His six-foot frame was slight of build, and he appeared young for his rank. We exchanged greetings and engaged in a few minutes of casual conversation about his trip and how we each arrived at being selected for this assignment.

Winsett offered to share a PowerPoint™ presentation he had prepared for the board members. It was obvious he had spent a lot of time working on it. His narrative flowed smoothly with every slide.

The third slide piqued my interest:

AIB Responsibilities

- *Brief next of kin of crewmembers, military personnel and civilians killed in the accident or seriously injured*

- *Inform the public and media*

- *Inform Congress upon request*

- *Inform other interested government agencies*

- *Provide the Air Force with adjudication of wrongful death, personal injury, and property damage claims resulting from the accident*

- *Help the Air Force determine if any punitive or administrative action should be taken against those whose negligence or misconduct contributed to the accident*

The first three bullets reasoned that a credible investigation required deployment to the AOR. When I contrasted Dobrinski's written and verbal instructions with Winsett's slide, it became evident how the command had tied our hands with contradictory mandates. Without gathering the information first hand, we would have no credibility with the accident victims' families. Congress, should they have questions about the accident, and the media, if they dug into the accident board's findings, would be appalled once they heard the investigation board was not permitted to travel to the accident site. If I had entertained thoughts about not pressing the commander to allow my team to travel to Afghanistan, Winsett had dashed them with a few words and his PowerPoint™ slide.

His presentation complete, Winsett stepped away from the computer, anticipating a reaction.

I allowed him to reflect for a moment.

"What do you think about conducting the investigation without leaving Hurlburt Field?" I asked. "Do you see any legal problems by failing to access the accident site or interview witnesses in person?"

His reaction appeared to be just as mine had been the previous week. He looked away in obvious thought then broke the silence.

"Sir, we can't conduct interviews unless we're at Kandahar. The safety board traveled to Afghanistan, so the accident board should as well. Conducting your investigation without traveling to the accident site, and interviewing witnesses in person, casts a dark cloud over the entire process. Sir, pardon my asking, but, why do you want to conduct the investigation from here?"

"Not my choice, believe me," I said as I leaned back in my chair. "General Dobrinski relayed the request straight from the commander – 'the boss would like for you to conduct your investigation from here at Hurlburt' were his exact words."

General Becker had not assigned two attorneys to the team without good reason - concern for huge legal consequences and possible overwhelming negative publicity. Together with Winsett, I would have to convince him to deploy the accident investigation team to Kandahar.

"I've put together a PowerPoint™," I said. "I plan to make that exact point to the commander with one or two slides maximum, and a simple talking paper entitled 'AIB Travel to the Area of Responsibility.' I need your help to make this presentation convincing."

"Great, the second legal member of our board arrives this evening. Let's get together and come up with some ideas."

"If the three of us can knock it out tonight, I'll pitch it to the commander tomorrow afternoon. Get settled into your room and call me when our other lawyer arrives. I'll be here."

He agreed and departed for billeting.

An hour or more after sunset, Winsett knocked on my door with a female officer at his side.

"Sir, I would like for you to meet Captain Christine Kelly, our second accident board legal member."

She extended her hand, "Nice to meet you, sir. I look forward to working with you on this investigation."

She was very professional, blond and medium height - maybe five-six. She and her husband, also a U.S. Air Force attorney, had three elementary school children and served at the same military base near Washington, D.C. She had recently returned from a deployment to Iraq and had accident investigation experience. Having been to the desert she seemed undeterred about the prospect of deploying to Afghanistan and relished the opportunity to sit on the investigation board. I had seldom seen an officer with her universal good cheer and positive energy. No obstacle seemed to deter her ... or Winsett. Once again, Dobrinski had chosen well.

We labored over the briefing for about an hour and a half, and finished a little after 10:00 p.m. Since neither the commander nor his vice would endure a lengthy harangue about deploying or not deploying to Afghanistan, we kept the presentation to one slide and a four page talking paper. After several practice runs, I could get through the presentation in less than two minutes.

General Becker's secretary had blocked time for me the following afternoon, after which the commander would be away from the base and unavailable for ... I couldn't guess how long. I had one shot at this, but I had a sound case and the General loved concise PowerPoint™ presentations.

On the 'Pro' side of the slide:

- *In-person interviews*

  - *Evaluate body language of witnesses*

- *Recover additional data*
- *Expand on safety board testimonies and evidence*
- *Credibility*
  - *Families/Congress/courts/media*
  - *Preserve privileged information that is protected by law for Safety Investigation Boards*
  - *Air Force Legal Operations Agency (AFLOA) advises deployment*
- *Access to operations personnel in the area at the time of the mishap*
- *Access to Operations Experts*
  - *Inspect facilities and crew routine*
  - *Access to Ranger and Marine special operators at or near Kandahar – Camp Leatherneck (MV-22)*
  - *Access exhibits left at Kandahar by safety board*

On the "Con" side:

- *Security for a general officer traveling to/from Afghanistan and while in theater*
- *Imposition [time, assets] on host unit (site overfly and bed-down of accident investigation team)*
- *Potential delay of operational equipment or personnel to accommodate accident board travel*

The AIB met, as a board, for the first time on April 28th. I worked through the morning, excited to get on with the investigation, yet dreading the looming presentation and possible confrontation with the commander. At 2:00 p.m., I walked down the hallway and entered the second floor conference room. When I entered, everyone immediately stood at attention. Winsett had seated members according to rank. I stood at the head of the table with Winsett on my right and O'Leary to my left.

"Please be seated, everyone," I said as I sat in the one oversized chair.

I introduced myself, then worked my way around the table with each person introducing themselves:

Lieutenant Colonel Chance (Doc) Harper, Flight Surgeon based at Cannon Air Force Base, New Mexico. Standing just under six feet, his casual demeanor exuded the confidence of a military professional who served aviators by keeping them flying rather than wielding the power of a doctor who could ground a pilot, or any crewmember for the slightest medical issue.

Captain Christine (Christie) Kelly, Assistant Legal representative, with whom I had worked the previous evening. Positive, smart and bubbling with enthusiasm.

Master Sergeant William Dolan, CV-22 Maintenance representative, assigned to the AFSOC flight crew training wing at Kirtland Air Force Base, New Mexico. A little over six feet with hair clipped flat-top close, his biceps strained the material of his shirt sleeves. If his off-duty hours were not spent lifting weights, flight line maintenance must have kept him in top physical condition.

Technical Sergeant Bryan Scott, Hurlburt Communications specialist borrowed from the AFSOC commander's action group office. Always one of my favorite non-commissioned officers at AFSOC. A "can do" guy that gets any job done without question.

Technical Sergeant Nicole Adams, assigned as the accident investigation board recorder. A slender brunette, she was the only board member, who by reason of rank or the task at hand, appeared to be intimidated by the number of officers and rank in the room. I had to make sure she shed her reticence. For me it was important to set the tone for acceptance of participation and sharing of ideas as the investigation proceeded.

I shook her hand. "Thank you for volunteering."

Everyone laughed. No one had volunteered for this assignment. Dobrinski had selected each by name due to their great reputations, expertise and work ethic.

"We'll spend a great deal of time together over the next couple months, so from here on, don't call the room to attention when I enter. I refuse to interrupt our work every time I move in and out of our office. I hope each of you has been offered the same option proffered to me … can you spare the days in the next two months to do this? If this is a problem, speak up before we get started. I realize all of you have lives and jobs elsewhere. Commitments to your family, your regular job, and yourself don't cease because you are on this board. I expect you to devote your complete attention to this work, but if you need assistance with handling other issues, we'll do our best to help you get things resolved. To get us started, our senior legal member will provide an overview of what we can expect."

Winsett detailed the role and responsibilities of the board. When he finished, he updated the deployment readiness of each board member by referring to a deployment readiness checklist.

"Sir, two of us require multiple inoculations, one weapon qualification, and one needs an updated passport. We will all be ready to deploy by the end of the week."

"Very good," I said. "I appreciate the effort. You should know, as of this moment, we have not received permission to travel to Afghanistan. This afternoon Lt Col Winsett and I intend to convince the commander otherwise. In the meantime, TSgt Scott will escort you to our office. Check out your new digs and I'll meet you there later. By then we'll know where we'll be conducting our investigation."

Convinced that our credibility depended on our ability to deploy to Afghanistan, I had a precious few seconds, a single slide PowerPoint™ presentation, and a four page talking paper to persuade the strong-willed AFSOC commander to change his mind. Failure would doom the credibility, and perhaps nullify the entire accident investigation.

CHAPTER SIX

DO WE STAY, OR DO WE GO?

I stood at the door while members of the team filed past me into the corridor behind TSgt Scott. Winsett hung back and I stopped him before he stepped into the hall.

"Can you stay a few minutes? I need you in the room when I pitch this to General Becker."

TSgt Scott stopped across from the command suite and looked back at me. I waved for him to continue without me. Winsett and I sat down at the table.

"Have you read the media reports about the accident being caused by pilot error?" I asked.

"Yes, sir."

"What do you make of it?" I said as I studied his reaction to my question.

"Nothing," he replied very nonchalantly.

"So, you don't think the safety board found the cause of the accident and somehow their findings have been leaked to the media?"

"Maybe they have … and … maybe they haven't," Winsett said. "It's immaterial. At some point they'll complete their investigation, give us all the evidence as allowed by regulations, then we'll conduct our accident investigation. Aside from sharing information, one has nothing to do with the other. We'll consider their material while we discover our own evidence and make our own logical conclusions. You know that, and so does General Becker."

"What if General Kingsley has told the command, under the table, that the crew screwed up? What if he's vested in 'pilot error' being the cause of the accident and doesn't want to commit resources for a full-up investigation? Or … he has another agenda?"

"Or he has a death wish for his career," Winsett said. "You've been to the schools, sir. Even if you've never served on a board you know the investigation process is not linear. One level of inquiry doesn't pick up where the previous leaves off. It's more like a pyramid of three mixing bowls, each larger than the previous, placed up-side-down over each other. The second investigation, Kingsley's, has an inviolate marble in his bowl. That's the privileged and confidential information he collects plus what his board determines to be the cause of the accident – Part Two of his report. We'll definitely get the Part One of his final report information to consider while we build a case of our own – the largest of the three mixing bowls. The only part of Kingsley's report that will ever be shared with the public is what he hands over to us – the Part One of their final report. Ours will be posted on the internet and made available to anyone who has a desire to read the interviews and all the other data we find. It will get ultra-microscopic scrutiny. You can bet your last dollar on that," he said confidently.

"Okay, you're right," I said. "That's what I'll present to him … without the cookware analogy."

"Good," said Winsett. "I know you wouldn't be comfortable filing a report having never seen the accident site, setting foot in country, or looking into the faces of personnel we'll be interviewing. I strongly advise you request permission for the board to do its job. The accident board must be allowed to deploy."

"I don't want us huddled over a computer screen, so I printed copies of the PowerPoint™ slide and the talking paper. We have a few minutes and my office is in the command suite, so why don't we wait there so we are ready when the commander calls for us."

Becker's secretary greeted us entering the commander's outer office.

"He's on schedule, sir," she said as I waved to let her know I was ready to brief at the commander's convenience. "He'll call you in a few minutes."

Before she finished her last word – the commander appeared at his office door.

"Come in and have a seat," he said as he turned and walked to the small conference table in his office.

I took a deep breath and walked inside with Winsett right behind me.

"Sir, this is Lt Col Winsett, our senior legal representative for the accident board."

Becker shook his hand and gestured toward his conference table.

"What have you got for me?" he said.

His schedule did not allow for, nor did he have the slightest interest in, socializing during his hectic workday. I would only have two or three minutes to make my case. His final decision would be the end of the discussion concerning the accident board traveling to Afghanistan.

I handed him the printout of the PowerPoint™ slide and the talking paper.

"Sir, General Dobrinski asked me to study the feasibility of conducting the accident investigation without deploying to Afghanistan."

He set the slide on the table in front of him and leaned back in his chair while he leafed through the four-page paper.

"Okay, go on," he said.

"Sir, we're aware a general officer into a war zone places a unique burden on combat assets in the region. I assure you we'll make as small a footprint as possible while we minimize our stay in country."

I made the case for a broader scope for the investigation than the safety investigation might have conducted. I emphasized the public release of the accident report, personal briefings for the families of crew members and the Army personnel killed and critically injured as a result of the accident. I also spoke of the high possibility of pushback that might result from acquiring information using a remote location, and the inability to search for physical evidence not yet collected or to conduct face-to-face interviews of personnel whose testimony had not yet been taken. I looked over at Winsett. He gave me an approving nod. I had made all the points to outline the case – we waited for the commander to ask questions – or to give us his answer.

Becker flipped the talking paper onto the table and scanned the PowerPoint™ slide. After a few seconds, he added the single page to the stack in front of him and peered at Winsett.

"Do you concur with General Harvel's assessment?"

"Without equivocation sir, if for no other reason it might put safety investigation privileged information at risk of being compromised. Consider the real possibility of a suit being filed if the accident board conducts an investigation from a remote location, while the safety investigation board deployed to Afghanistan. The command risks the possibility of a federal judge ruling that privileged information must be publicly released. That would set a dangerous precedent for any investigation of future aircraft mishaps in this or any other military organization."

We sat in silence for interminable seconds. Becker stroked his chin then pushed the PowerPoint™ slide and the talking paper into the center of the table.

"Okay, the accident board travels to Afghanistan with two restrictions. One, minimize your time in the country. Two, you must be out of the Middle East by May 31st. I'll underwrite your team's combat pay for May, but I won't answer accusations from the wannabes and the media that we're running a combat pay scam here at AFSOC."

"Agreed, sir," I said as I quickly stood up. "Thank you for your time."

Becker nodded and returned to his desk on the other side of his office. Winsett and I departed before he had a chance to change his mind or levy additional restrictions.

We walked into my office and closed the door.

"Thank you," I said. "We just averted a disaster. You did a great job of making a key point. I am very pleased to be working with you on this investigation."

Winsett smiled and said, "That's the first of what will probably be many more obstacles. I'll get the team ready to travel once the safety board completes their report. In the meantime, I recommend we use what time we have to interview CV-22 crew members who are here at home station.

With your permission, sir, I'll share the news with the team and start preparing for the upcoming interviews."

I enjoyed a few seconds of euphoria, then started thinking about all the work I needed to get done. Waiting to deploy until the safety board filed their report ate up the precious days we had to get into Afghanistan and get out again by the end of May. Working seven days a week for the next two months might get us ahead enough to complete our accident report before mid-summer.

Since I probably wouldn't return to my AFSOC office for a few weeks, I cleared my desk and boxed a few personal items I would need over the following months. Then I stopped by Capt Pierce's cubicle to pick up gear she had assembled for my deployment. I told her the AIB team had arrived and we would deploy as soon as possible after getting the safety board's final report.

"The uniforms and gear you ordered from supply are in the bag, sir," she said. "If you need anything else, let me know."

"I'll inventory this later tonight. Meanwhile, please transfer my calls to the accident board office. I won't be back for a few weeks. As always, I appreciate your work, thank you."

I grabbed my gear and headed to the car. As I drove to the accident board office, I thought about all the things we needed to do to get ready. I felt overwhelmed.

I parked my car and walked into the building. As I entered the accident board office, someone shouted, "room attention." Everyone rose and stood at attention as I closed the door behind me.

"Wait a minute," I said. "I thought we agreed not to do this. Everyone, please be seated."

Someone in the room replied, "Sorry, sir. It'll take time."

Full and half-empty boxes sat on the floor and on all the desks. As team members set up their personal workspaces, TSgt Scott flattened the empty cartons and stored them behind a bookcase for use when we would be done with the investigation and vacate the office. I gathered everyone around the conference table.

"Let's brief every morning at 8:00 a.m. I'm not big on meetings, so we will pass assignments, collect completed work, plan future activities, and exchange essential information during the morning meeting. TSgt Scott, do you think you can get us three or four white boards to cover this wall?"

"Yes, sir, the boards will be here by the close of business tomorrow."

Captain Kelly approached me with a clipboard and several pages of hand-written notes. "Sir, we're locating the personnel who were on board the mishap aircraft the night of the accident. They're spread from Afghanistan to Walter Reed Army Medical Center, to Fort Benning, Georgia, and some are traveling at this time – with plans to arrive here at Hurlburt Field next week. The copilot has been cleared by doctors and is home recovering from his injuries."

"Has he been interviewed by the safety board yet?" I asked Kelly.

"If he has sir, it would have been a telephone interview, so I bet he hasn't."

"As long as we're not breaking protocol, schedule a time for us to interview him. Check the implications regarding privileged and confidential information, if the safety board hasn't talked to him. What else?"

"Sir, with your permission, I'll schedule a trip to Fort Benning," said Kelly. "We'll interview members of the Third Battalion, Seventy-Fifth Ranger Regiment recuperating there."

"Great, please do it."

"There are 8th Special Operations Squadron key personnel on station, the squadron director of operations, the chief of standardization, and crewmembers who've rotated from Afghanistan to their homes here. TSgt Scott and I will secure a location and schedule interview times. Please give me or L. Col Winsett a list of your proposed questions. We will review and approve the questions prior to each interview. Just a couple more issues."

"Okay so far, Kelly," I said. You're not saving the bad news for last, are you?"

"No sir, two procedural matters. Prior to each interview you'll have to read a legal narrative that Lt Col Winsett and I will draft."

"Which encompasses what?" I queried.

"It's the legal, necessary mumbo-jumbo that sets the ground rules for the interview. Lt Col O'Leary calls it the Rules of Engagement (ROE). He said you would know what that meant."

"Okay, and the second?"

"The safety board investigating officer will send us all the interviews they've completed. Once we receive and document the transfer, they'll be available for the team to consider."

"Well done, Kelly. Our work is going to increase substantially, so we'll need to work every weekend. I apologize in advance for having to ask all of you to give up your weekends. Any questions?" Everyone remained silent.

"All right then … no questions. Let's get to work."

I walked to the back of the L-shaped room where TSgt Scott had set up my work station. I sat down and adjusted the tilt on the flat-screen monitor on my desk.

Scott hovered over my shoulder and said, "You have access to your AFSOC email account, as well as your classified secret email account. I've set up a discrete, secure network for the team with eight computers logged in. I'll work with individual team members to get mobile devices online too."

"Nice work, Scott. Thanks for setting up the room; it's perfect. I am very fortunate to have you on this team. I only have one question for you. Where'd you find a refrigerator?"

He smiled. "Better you didn't ask, sir."

"And it's stocked as well, I see."

"The 'honor jar' on the table beside the fridge will repay my initial investment and fund what anyone wants to have available after that," said Scott.

From across the room, Winsett raised his voice over the low-level din. "General Harvel, the safety board president wants to send us a video they recovered."

"Recovered where ... of what?" I asked.

"It's a video of the accident. Filmed by a support airplane orbiting overhead the landing zone. It's the final twenty seconds of flight and shows what happened after the Osprey hit the ground."

CHAPTER SEVEN

ACCIDENT VIDEO

The team hovered expectantly over Winsett's shoulders, staring at his monitor, while he opened the safety board's email and downloaded the attached video.

"I don't know about the resolution, so if you're ready, sir, let's see what we've got."

"Lt Col O'Leary, tell us what we're seeing once the video starts." Winsett clicked on the link and a bright green screen appeared.

UNCLASSIFIED
09 April 2010
CV-22 Mishap (Afghanistan)

After a few seconds, video of the CV-22 Osprey appeared. It traveled from the upper left to the lower right of the screen, descending toward the ground. An oval marker with a thin line cross in the center overlaid the video. The overlay marked the intended point of landing.

On the left side of the screen, a digital clock displayed Greenwich Mean Time (GMT/ZULU time) in hours, minutes, and seconds. The video captured the airplane flying over a few ditches (wadis) eroded into the desert floor. The wadis appeared as squiggly bold dark lines. After passing over the last wadi in the video, the airplane touched down. Dust went flying into the air as the airplane rolled on the sand.

Adams gasped when a second later a black indistinct blob mushroomed over the light background indicating an explosion.

"Geez … all right, once more," Winsett said as he started the video again.

During the second screening, O'Leary narrated while we watched.

"In the first frames of the video you can see the Osprey is in a steep descent. It is traveling way too fast for a hovering approach. The Osprey crossed over three wadis. At this point, the speed over the ground should be slower. There, look at the dust cloud kicked up when he touched down. The dark blob that follows is the aircraft catching fire and exploding."

O'Leary fielded random questions from the team for the next couple of minutes.

"Why is the fire black instead of bright red or orange?" asked Adams.

"This is a low-light infrared video. Hot objects appear black. Cool or cold objects appear white."

"How and why was this video taken?" asked Kelly.

"This was a High Value Target (HVT) mission," O'Leary said. "Almost all those type of missions are filmed. One of the airplanes flying overhead that night had the intelligence, surveillance, and reconnaissance (ISR) capability to provide the video."

"One of the airplanes … there were others?"

"It's not uncommon for infiltration missions to have a stack of airplanes operating at or near the target area, some providing fire support, others capable of illuminating a target with infrared electronic beams (sparkle) invisible to the naked eye. Then, there are the ISR aircraft providing live video feeds to command centers or any number of intelligence or other U.S. agencies."

"Why didn't they land like a helicopter?" asked Adams.

O'Leary shook his head. "Great question. They configured the aircraft by tilting the rotors to near vertical to do just that. We can see that in the video. I don't know why they didn't and fly a normal low visibility approach."

He put his hand on Winsett's shoulder. "Go back to the point where they cross the wadis."

"You got it."

"Watch as they cross the ditches, said O'Leary. The aircraft pitches up in what appears to be an attempt to clear the last ditch. They succeeded in that, but the rate of descent and forward speed is still too fast. What were they doing?"

"So you're saying they couldn't, or for some reason elected not to, land like a helicopter?" asked Winsett.

"When we know why that didn't happen, we'll know what caused this accident. The questions at this point are: Why did the airplane descend so fast? Why did the crew attempt, and succeed, for a few seconds to make a roll on landing? Or, did they inadvertently fly the aircraft into the ground?"

I looked at TSgt Scott.

"Make sure we have this video available when we question the crew members at the 8th Special Operations Squadron."

"Yes, sir."

"Play it once more," I said. "I have a question for Lt Col O'Leary."

When the video showed the Osprey at seventeen seconds prior to hitting the ground, I tapped him on the shoulder.

"Stop … there … look … look at the white smoke coming off the airplane. Is that something from the engines?"

CHAPTER EIGHT

COPILOT INTERVIEW

In the days following our first meeting, we prepared to accept the SIB team's report. If we received it during the first week of May, we would have most of the month in Afghanistan. In either case, the thirty to sixty day clock to complete our investigation would start ticking.

I was very disappointed as the first week of May rolled by and we did not hear from the safety board. We called again on May 6th, and were told they had delays transcribing interviews and compiling information. General Kingsley informed me he planned to brief the AFSOC Commander and release Part One of his report on May 12th. I was disheartened by the bad news. Half of our potential time in Afghanistan evaporated in one phone call.

My accident team members organized their personal and our collective workspace, and Winsett prepared the briefing I would deliver prior to starting each interview. The narrative advised the person being questioned about the nature of our inquiry, followed by an oath swearing their truthful testimony.

TSgt Scott would not deploy to Afghanistan due to his nagging medical issues, but the remaining team members trekked to base supply numerous times gathering supplies, equipment, and uniforms. Capt Kelly and TSgt Scott secured an on base site to interview key personnel who were at Hurlburt Field. Everyone on our list was in Afghanistan at the time of the accident.

We conducted our first interview at the home of one of the two surviving crewmembers, the copilot, Major (Maj) Brian Luce. After being evacuated from the accident site, Maj Luce underwent treatment at the Kandahar Air Base hospital. After a few days, he was transferred to Bagram Air Base, in northern Afghanistan. Then he was flown to Landstuhl Regional Medical Center (LRMC), Kaiserslautern, Germany. From LRMC, he traveled to Walter Reed Army Medical Center in Bethesda, Maryland. After a week, doctors released him for air evacuation to Hurlburt and his home in Fort Walton Beach, Florida.

A hero's welcome and a promotion to major greeted Luce when he arrived. Headquarters staff and AFSOC personnel not otherwise engaged turned out for the reception. Festivities surrounding Luce's homecoming made no mention of the two crewmembers who lost their lives in the crash. Their services had occurred a few weeks prior.

Capt Kelly coordinated our interview with Maj Luce for May 4th at 11:00 a.m. On that morning, the team met two hours prior in the AIB office. I outlined the process we would follow, from our arrival, to our departure from Luce's home. Afterward, we would return to the office, debrief, and organize the information to be included in our final report.

We traveled in two vehicles for the trip - a rental car, and van. If any conversation transpired during the drive, I don't remember it; my mind was otherwise occupied.

Despite the delay of the safety investigation board report, their investigation appeared abbreviated for the magnitude of the event, unless … they had come to a definitive resolution of the cause of the accident. And if, as new accounts indicated, they had concluded pilot error to be the cause, they had done so without interviewing either of the surviving crew members. It just seemed wrong to me.

We parked at the curb in front of the Luce home. As we gathered our briefcases and recording equipment, we noticed someone inside peering at us through the curtains.

When I stepped onto the porch, Mrs. Luce appeared at the door, a baby cradled in her left arm, and an older child clinging to her leg. Slender, with short hair, and wearing Florida casual attire – t-shirt, shorts, and flip-flops, she invited us inside. I introduced the team members and myself as we filed through the front door.

Mrs. Luce ushered us into their family room where toys littered the floor and Maj Luce rested, fully reclined, in an easy chair. The air carried a hospital-like smell of topical medications used for treating his wounds. The aura, perhaps, mingled with preparations used in the care of their infant.

Dark-circled, swollen eyes, and deliberate movements testified to Mrs. Luce's stress and fatigue. Consumed with the care of two children and her injured husband, neither she nor the house showed signs of expected guests. I suspected she spent her energy just getting the family through each day.

"Feel free to rearrange the furniture or bring chairs from the kitchen if you like," she said with a tired smile.

Luce was bandaged around his head and over portions of his arms and legs. His face showed cuts and abrasions with bruised swelling over one eye that appeared to slightly limit his vision. He attempted to stand when we entered, but I quickly insisted he remain seated. He seemed lethargic and had difficulty making eye contact or focusing for any length of time when team members introduced themselves.

I moved close to Lt Col Harper. "Hey Doc, find out what meds he's taking. Make sure he's not still in shock, drugged, or in a condition that would prevent an effective interview. Let me know if you think we should come back at a later date."

Together with the two legal reps, Doctor Harper conferred with Luce and his wife. After a minute, Mrs. Luce disappeared into the interior of the house, soon returning with three prescription bottles. Harper studied the labels and consulted with the legal reps and the couple.

When he finished, he spoke to me in a hushed tone.

"Sir, he's tired. He's still taking pain medication, but in small doses. The three of us agree he is mentally and physically fit to conduct the interview. He, and his wife, want to get it over with."

While Winsett moved dining chairs from an adjoining room, I offered Mrs. Luce the opportunity to be present while we interviewed her husband. She pressed her lips together, looked at the floor, then her children, and shook her head.

"We'll be in the next room, if you need anything," she said. "I apologize for not having any refreshments, but ..."

"Please ma'am, that's OK. We have everything we need," I said.

Winsett arranged seating with Luce at the top of a semi-circle, and indicated who should sit where. He moved a coffee table into the center and placed TSgt Adam's equipment on top. When everyone had taken their place, she completed a sound check.

"I'm ready, sir," she said, as she waited to start the recorder.

Winsett nodded. "Everything is set, sir. You may begin."

I introduced myself for the record. I made sure Luce understood the difference between the proceedings conducted by the Safety Investigation Board (SIB) (even though they had not interviewed him) and the interview we (the Accident Investigation Board) were conducting. I made sure he understood the accident board's report would be released to the media and public via the internet and hard copies when the report was completed.

"Do you understand what I have just explained to you?" I asked.

Luce nodded his understanding.

"I apologize, Major. For the recording, I need a verbal answer."

"Oh, yes sir, I understand," he said.

I then administered the oath. Once he answered in the affirmative, I reminded him that his recorded testimony would be released as part of the final report.

"Yes, sir, I know," he said.

"Very well then, before we start, any time you feel you need to take a break, tell me and we'll stop for as long as necessary."

He indicated he could continue and I asked the first in a series of simple questions to put him at ease.

"How long have you been in the United States Air Force?"

"Almost ten years," he said.

"What is your current unit of assignment and location?"

"The 8th Special Operations Squadron (SOS), Hurlburt Field, Florida."

"What aircraft have you flown prior to the CV-22?"

"The UH-1N and the UH-1H, Hueys."

"How many flying hours do you have?"

"Total hours in Hueys, I had about 2,400 hours. In the Osprey, I have 130 or 150 hours."

"How many times have you deployed to a combat zone?"

"Sir, this was my first deployment."

"Very well. Now we'll skip to the night of the accident. Are you okay?"

"Sure."

To this point his answers to simple questions from his distant memory seemed to help him become more comfortable as we progressed. At first he limited his eye contact to me, but as we proceeded he addressed his answers and made eye contact with the other board members.

"What were your duties and responsibilities for the mission on the evening of April 8th?"

"I was the copilot on the lead Osprey for the mission. The way we ran it that night is the aircraft commanders went and got the brief of what was going to happen and the copilots and flight engineers went right to the aircraft and got it ready to go. So, when the aircraft commanders got to the airplane, it was already running and we were ready for takeoff. So, we got a brief from the aircraft commander, hey [sic] this is our first stop, we are going to go up to the forward operating base; have a face to face meeting with the team [Army Rangers] and press from there. My duty there was just to back-up the pilot. I was able to fly most of the first part of the mission up to the forward operating base, and back-up radio calls; you know the four radios we've got … radio calls … back up checklists."

At the mid-point in his answer he slowed his reply, halting at intervals before continuing. When searching for the correct words he looked away, but not in any consistent direction.

"What happened after landing at the FOB?" I asked.

"The aircraft commanders and lead engineers got off the airplane and went to brief with the Army personnel. When they returned to the aircraft, the pilot had imagery of the landing zone. The pilot briefed the crew about the landing zone and the landing zone elevation. He also had a paper copy of the route we would fly. He brought a data card that allowed us to load the flight computer on the airplane so we could display the route on the screens in front of the pilot and the copilot."

"Was the takeoff from the FOB normal?"

Luce nodded. I reminded him that we needed a verbal answer for the record.

"I was able to get the takeoff. We did an '80 Jump' out of there. That means we rotated the nacelles to 80 degrees. I pushed the power in and we were off the ground. At the first turn point, the pilot took control of the airplane and I started performing my copilot duties. The pilot briefed that we would fly a standard Low Visibility Approach (LVA) with a three-mile deceleration. We always briefed a LVA profile. It would keep us in a safe regime. We talked about landing 'at the zeros' - which means landing at the selected waypoint at zero feet above the ground and zero forward speed."

Halfway through his reply, he began reciting procedure rather than answering the specific question. I pressed for his recollection of events on the night of the accident.

"Do you remember crossing the initial point?" I asked.

"Yes, sir, the initial point was ten miles from the landing zone. We descended to eight thousand and five hundred feet. Initially, we had the terrain following radar on. After the initial point, we descended to five hundred feet above the ground."

"Are there radio calls you were making to the other aircraft or to the team sitting in the back of your airplane?"

"For the team in back of the airplane, they get a ten, six, and one minute to landing call. All those calls were made. The one I remember the most is the one-minute call. Normally, one of the pilots, or the flight engineer up front would call the engineer in back of the airplane [tail scanner] and tell him to pass the ten minute, six minute, or one minute warning to the team."

Again, his answer ran tangent to the question - reverting instead to published procedure. I simplified the question, hoping to elicit something more specific.

"You definitely remember the one minute warning being passed to the team?"

"Yes, the pilot told the tail scanner to pass the one minute warning."

"Do you recall the tail scanner starting an altitude countdown starting at ten feet above the ground?"

"I don't remember. The approach was going as—it was on the LVA profile. I don't know if it is my mind playing tricks on me, or if this is something I actually remember …"

Team members leaned forward and stopped taking notes. Their eyes fixed on Maj Luce.

From this point his recollection drifted from events of that night to what seemed to be procedures memorized from the flight manual. His memory of events beyond the "one minute warning" appeared to be disjointed at best, and at worst, missing altogether. He failed to maintain eye contact and his gaze darted about the room focusing on nothing in particular.

I leaned over to whisper to Doctor Harper.

"Hey Doc, what the hell is he talking about?"

"Sir, I think he has a false memory of the last half minute of the flight. I've seen this happen to people involved in traumatic events."

Luce continued but was now visibly shaking. Even though he was looking at me, he didn't seem to register that I was there. I had interviewed innumerable trauma victims before but this was different. It was clear he didn't understand what happened. He wasn't simply blocking it out.

"Like I said, the one minute callout was given," he said as he struggled for memory of the event. "Unfortunately, that was the last thing I remember or can understand. It all happened so fast. I remember watching the radar altimeter, the tape … ummmm … not the tape, but you know 100, 90, 80 and 70. I remember watching it rapidly go from 100 and some feet to zero. It shouldn't have been happening that way. I don't remember if this actually happened or if it's my brain playing tricks again [sic]. When I remember seeing this, I felt as if not that I was outside the aircraft, but I was just not in my copilot position. I was watching this from outside the aircraft. I didn't feel like I was – it was kind of like I was a spectator. I wasn't part of the crew."

When he confessed to experiencing an out-of-body event, each member of the team cast curious looks at one another. He stated the radar altimeter readings but could not relate them to the approach that night nor could he recount any event in the approach thereafter, or any malfunction that might have occurred.

I looked at Winsett, O'Leary and Harper and whispered "Any ideas on how to jog Maj Luce's memory? We needed something more concrete."

When facing imminent injury or death the brain can dissociate in what can feel like an out-of-body experience. If I were in that position I would wish I could escape any way possible. But this was not helping us figure out what happened.

O'Leary looked at Luce and asked, "Can you describe what type of low visibility approach profile the pilot used that night?"

"If you had the 11-222, [AFSOCH 11-222 a procedures manual for Combat Aircraft Fundamentals CV-22] it has the diagram in there," Luce said. "So, at the three mile deceleration point, you are at 210 knots, roughly 200 feet above the ground. We start slowing down. At 170 knots, you will 'beep', which is to get the rotor revolutions per minute (RPM) from 84% to 100%. By 1.5 miles from the landing zone, you should be roughly 150 knots airspeed and slowing …"

From that point, he recounted procedures used for the low visibility approach not as an event of that night, but as we might have expected, procedure substituted and inserted from his recollection of the CV-22 flight manual.

O'Leary glanced at me, then the other team members. He asked a question that changed the subject. This was a good interrogation technique to take the interviewee out of the trauma memory. It was like a reset. Sometimes it worked to take us deeper into the answers.

"Can you describe flying with Maj Voas?"

"I think you can pretty much ask anybody in the squadron. He's a laid back aircraft commander. He doesn't get spun up real easy. His demeanor is very calm. I don't think I have ever flown with him where he has raised his voice or gotten excited in the cockpit. He's a guy that's able to maintain a very level head in flying."

O'Leary asked a few more questions about training and procedures then yielded the questioning to Lt Col Harper.

"You told us about the last thing you remembered during the approach to the landing zone. What is the next thing you remember after that?"

"The next thing I remember, I was in my seat and I was sitting upright but I was not in the airplane. I remember tipping over in the seat. I remember lying there on the ground trying to push myself."

Luce began to tremble again. I had seen pilots after an accident who could still relate incidents with a level head. This man was clearly shaken beyond anything I had witnessed before. He continued slowly.

"I was thinking what a horrible dream this was. It didn't really seem real. It took me a few moments on the ground to figure out what had actually happened. My left leg was in pain and my lower back was in pain. I looked over to my right and saw the airplane. It was on fire. I couldn't tell if the airplane was upside down or right side up. I saw some guys that were in the back part of the airplane. I could hear someone yelling about his leg but that might have been me. I could see some of the Army personnel setting up a casualty collection point (CCP). I saw them dragging the female Afghan interpreter out of the airplane and placing her at the CCP. It was all chaotic, guys yelling in severe pain, people running. I don't remember how I wound up getting out of my seat. I know I asked if everybody made it out of the Osprey. One of the Army guys told me that they got everyone out of the airplane. At first that is all he would say."

Luce asked for some water. I noticed him tearing up which I didn't expect. It was rare for officers to show emotion. Perhaps I was just seeing how I would have felt at the senselessness of this tragedy.

"I kept asking if everyone was okay and no one would tell me," Luce continued. "An army guy finally told me the news. He said, 'I don't think your crew chief made it.' This didn't make sense to me. It was all supposed to be routine. I could hear the other two Ospreys flying above us. Then I remember being strapped to a backboard. When an H-60 rescue helicopter landed, I was carried to the helicopter and evacuated from the crash site."

At this point his wife returned and asked if we wanted something to drink. We were finished with the official interview, so I took the time to ask if the family was doing alright. Luce looked up at his wife and managed a slight smile.

"I'm just glad I get to come home to my family," said Luce. "Wounds heal but at least our family is still together. And the command, unit, and Air Force are giving us excellent care." [3]

We returned the furniture to the dining room and thanked Mrs. Luce for allowing us to use her home. As we filed out the front door, I gathered the team on the front lawn.

"What do you think," I asked.

"Aside from discovering he's still shook up, I don't think we learned much. I've never experienced anything like it," said Winsett.

"Yeah, me neither," I answered. "Doc Harper, I know you've seen patients with loss of memory. Will he ever regain the memory of what happened during the last thirty seconds of the flight?"

"I am not sure he has lost his memory," Doc replied. "He's obviously traumatized, but it appears that it happened so fast and unexpectedly there may not have been information for him to retain. Obviously, something went wrong. It's possible the crew had no warning .. there may be nothing for him to recall."

CHAPTER NINE

OSPREY HISTORY AND MYSTERY OF THE FLIGHT INFORMATION RECORDER

Our discussion continued as we ordered food and drinks at a nearby restaurant.

"Maj Luce is the first of many interviews we will conduct over the next few weeks," I said. "I'm curious to hear your opinion about the interview now that you've had a few minutes to think about it."

"Sir, I am still stunned," said Kelly. "The memory loss, lack of usable information and then … the out-of-body experience. I just don't get it."

TSgt Adams looked around the table and saw no one was speaking.

"Sir, can I offer my opinion?" she asked.

"Sure," I answered.

"I take depositions all the time," she said. "From where I sat, I noticed he made eye contact with us during the first thirty minutes of the interview. I think he was telling the truth. Then, when he told us about the approach they flew to the landing zone, he seemed to struggle. He stared straight ahead, or at distant objects on the ceiling. Maybe he couldn't remember, or maybe he was trying to hide the facts he didn't want to talk about? Do you think he may have been concerned about resuming his flying career? Will the Air Force let a pilot fly again after admitting to an out-of-body experience?"

"His injuries will keep him grounded for a while," said Doc Harper. "I don't think his mental state will affect his ability to return to flight status. It's possible he can recover the lost memory of the accident. Then, we can interview him again."

"Any chance of that happening?" I asked.

"He could," answered Harper. "But, the chances are slim at best."

"If he had any type of mental health counseling as a part of his treatment, will we have access to it?" I asked.

Doc Harper shook his head and said, "No, that falls in the area of confidential medical information. We'll only see the complete medical records of the accident casualties."

"Okay, then we all agree that Maj Luce talked us through a low visibility approach," I said. "It was not the approach the crew flew in Afghanistan prior to the accident. He described the text-book approach in the crew flight manuals."

"Yes, sir, I agree," said O'Leary.

"He substituted what he already knew to be the ideal approach for the memory of the approach prior to the accident ... transference ... it really happens."

I looked over at the two lawyers and asked, "What does our legal community think?"

Winsett answered, "Sir, we consider his interview as sworn testimony. Let's wait to see what the safety board finds, and passes on to us. We know they have not interviewed Maj Luce yet. But, they could interview him prior to wrapping up their report. We have conducted one interview. By the time we are finished, I think we will have plugged most of the holes of the investigation. I'm not concerned ... not yet."

"Thank you for the open and honest discussion," I said. "This afternoon, I want to take everyone out to the flight line. For those of you who have never seen an Osprey up close, today is your lucky day. We will have a chance to walk around, and sit inside the flight deck. Everybody ready to go?

Seeing inside an Osprey would be a first for several of our team. We would also have a familiarization mission including a flight so the team could understand the machine. When we got to the AFSOC aircraft maintenance building, a couple of CV-22s were parked on the flight line in front of the building.

"I know you are all anxious to examine these beautiful specimens. But, before we walk out to the Osprey, I think you should know the history of this machine," I said.

Before I could begin Capt Kelly caught my attention.

"Sir, I have a comment and a question. I've been stationed at Air Force bases where they had fighter jets, bombers, and cargo aircraft, and even helicopters, but this thing looks like it spawned from a mutant Ninja aircraft factory. Is it true it flies as fast as most propeller airplanes?"

"Yes, the Osprey can fly as fast as most propeller airplanes," I answered. "The mystique of this aircraft is that it is a brilliant combination of helicopter and airplane technology. The Osprey was born from tragedy. The idea of designing an airplane that could take off and land like a helicopter, but fly as fast as an airplane from point to point, gained momentum due to a very unfortunate military event." With everyone looking expectantly at me, I told the story.

"On November 4, 1979, militant Iranian students in opposition to the deposed Shah (Reza Pahlavi), being admitted to the United States for supposed cancer treatment, stormed the U.S. embassy in Tehran. They captured the Americans working in the building. When the Ayatollah Khomeini gave his blessing to their actions, they abandoned their original aim of a temporary demonstration, and held the embassy staff hostage while demanding the U.S. extradite the Shah back to Iran. When President Jimmy Carter refused their demands, and declined to negotiate with the terrorists, an impasse ensued. President Carter came under pressure from all quadrants to do something. While back-channel talks proved fruitless, President Carter authorized the military, using special operations teams with the burgeoning U.S. army 'Delta Force' at its core, to plan and execute a mission to rescue the hostages.

"Combined U.S. forces from the navy, air force, marine corps, and the army planned and trained for the mission. The mission was named Operation EAGLE CLAW. It would require a rendezvous in a remote part of the Iranian desert three hundred miles southeast of Tehran. The rendezvous point was named DESERT ONE.

"Six C-130 Hercules cargo aircraft transported personnel into Iran and airlifted fuel for the eight RH-53D Sea Stallion helicopters. Painted in Iranian air force markings, the helicopters planned to refuel and then wait, in plain sight, close to Tehran until the next night. Under cover of darkness the special operators intended to breach the embassy compound, free the hostages, and airlift them to a third site where they would be flown out of Iran.

"Dust storms and mechanical problems plagued the helicopter force before they arrived at DESERT ONE. One of the Sea Stallions returned, with maintenance problems, to its launch point, the carrier Nimitz, positioned in the Persian Gulf. Another Sea Stallion had to be abandoned in the Iranian desert while enroute to DESERT ONE.

"Operation EAGLE CLAW then had the bare minimum number of vertical lift machines (6) required to execute the mission. As the helicopters arrived at the rendezvous point, one of the remaining six helicopters reported a failed hydraulic pump. With only five flyable helicopters, the on-scene mission commander had to report to the National Command Authority (NCA) that they did not have the assets to complete the mission. The NCA ordered the commander to abort the mission.

"Mission architects, fearing a disabled aircraft at the rendezvous site, had planned for all airplanes to leave their engines running, even while refueling the helicopters. The visibility, due to the engines stirring up dust, was reduced to where the people and airplanes could hardly see each other."

"With the order given to abandon the site, the aircraft prepared to leave. But, before the first C-130 could depart, one of the helicopters had to reposition clear of the area selected for takeoff. The pilot hovered the helicopter while trying to follow the marshalling signals being given by an air force combat controller. The pilot had great difficulty seeing the person trying to give him signals. With the thickening cloud and sand fiercely pelting his body, the ground marshaller sought refuge under the wing of a nearby C-130. The Sea Stallion, with a full tank of fuel, crashed into the cockpit of the cargo plane and exploded. The blistering inferno destroyed the two aircraft and killed eight of the ten crew members aboard them.

"The two survivors staggered out of the burning helicopter wreckage and were spotted by the loadmaster on a C-130 as it taxied toward the take-off area. The loadmaster notified the on-scene commander about the two personnel. The on-scene commander ordered the C-130 to stop and pick up the two men who were quickly boarded through an aft paratroop door. As soon as the door closed, the airplane immediately started its take off roll and departed. As the C-130 climbed into the dark night sky, the pilot looked back at the ground where he could see the airplane wreckage and the five Sea Stallion helicopters that were being abandoned.

"After-action analysis of the debacle fixed on the limited range and payload of the vertical lift aircraft. Military commanders petitioned Congress for the authorization and funds to research and develop an aircraft that bridged the gap between the C-130 and helicopters in the current U.S. arsenal. Their vision was a conceptual aircraft that could fly into a forward area with the speed of a fixed-wing aircraft, then alter its configuration to land vertically like a helicopter. Drawing boards at several aircraft companies, Bell, Boeing, and Sikorsky developed prototypes for the Department of Defense to review. Eventually, Bell and Boeing teamed up to build early versions of what would morph into the V-22 Osprey.

"The CV-22 Osprey is the U.S. Air Force version of the U.S. Marine Corps MV-22 Osprey. Its mission is to conduct long-range infiltration, exfiltration, and resupply missions for special operations forces. The aircraft combines the vertical takeoff, hover, and vertical landing capabilities of a helicopter with the long-range, fuel efficiency and speed characteristics of a turboprop aircraft. With its engine nacelles and rotors in a vertical position (helicopter mode), it can takeoff, land, and hover like a helicopter. Once airborne, its engine nacelles can be rotated ninety degrees forward to convert the aircraft to a turboprop airplane capable of high-speed (351 miles per hour) and high-altitude flight (up to 25,000 feet).

"The Osprey can carry up to twenty-four combat troops (with seats installed in the cargo compartment), or a maximum payload of 10,000 lbs. at twice the speed of a helicopter.

"The cross-coupled drive system ensures aircraft viability in the event of a single engine failure – with either engine capable of driving the proprotor on the opposite wing. The Osprey is powered by two Rolls-Royce Liberty AE1107C engines that develop 6,200 shaft horsepower. Advanced electronics allow the CV-22 to conduct combat operations at low altitude in adverse weather and in medium to high threat environments.

"AFSOC and the 8th Special Operations Squadron accepted delivery of the first USAF airplane in March 2005, and achieved combat ready status in 2008. They flew the first operational mission in support of Operation Flintlock in Africa, December 2008. Making trans-Atlantic flights to and from the African continent using two entirely different routes, the CV-22 demonstrated the aircraft's worldwide self-deployment capability.

"The aircraft is built by Boeing Rotorcraft Systems and Bell Helicopter Textron. Boeing builds the fuselage, empennage, and all subsystems – digital avionics and fly-by-wire flight control systems. Bell is responsible for the wing, transmissions, rotor systems, engine installation, and final assembly at its facility in Amarillo, Texas."

"This sounds like a miracle machine," Adams interjected. "So what's the problem?"

"From design … to roll out … to deployment, the aircraft and its innovative technologies found the road often troubled, sometimes deadly, and always expensive," I explained. "During development, four prototype aircraft crashed with the loss of thirty personnel. After two of the prototypes crashed in 1992, President Bush's Defense Department abandoned what they considered a beleaguered program as too costly in funds and lives. The Osprey program was reinvigorated and resurrected by the newly elected Clinton administration in 1993.

"Over the life of the program, the per-unit cost soared from initial projections of $15 million per unit to over $87 million per airplane in 2010. The U.S. air force ordered fifty of the aircraft, while the Marine Corps committed to over four hundred MV-22s." [4]

We finished the discussion of the Osprey history and everyone walked out to the airplane. O'Leary put two team members in the pilot seats and conducted a cockpit orientation, while Dolan explained the equipment and its use to other team members in the cargo compartment.

The most asked question related to the huge proprotors (38 foot arc) and what would happen if the crew could not increase the pitch of the nacelles (pylons, engines) to an angle that cleared the ground when the aircraft landed, i.e. landing the Osprey like an airplane with the nacelles in "airplane mode."

"The propellers would broomstick (splinter) into enough pieces to provide toothpicks for every hayseed and meat eater in the country," O'Leary said with his wry smile. "The engine might survive without major damage, but MSgt Dolan's counterparts in maintenance would definitely be tasked to replace the proprotors."

At the end of the tour we huddled in the cargo compartment for one last chance to ask questions. Dolan noticed that Adams kept looking up at the back of the airplane.

"Are you looking for something?" Dolan asked.

"Yes. Isn't the black box in the back of most airplanes?"

O'Leary stepped to her side and said, "For our investigation, it would have been helpful to have a flight information recorder. The 'black box,' as you call it, does not exist on this airplane. The Osprey doesn't even have a cockpit voice recorder."

"He's correct," I said. "No good reason. It's just not installed on the airplane."

MSgt Dolan stood at the crew entrance and looked at us surprisingly.

"That's true to a point, sir," he said. "There isn't a voice recorder in the cockpit. But there is a flight information recorder (FIR) that electronically logs essential flight and engine parameters."

He pointed to the top of the airplane to an area above the crew entry door.

"It's only accessible through a panel right there … on top of the airplane."

O'Leary and I looked at each other in shock. Neither of us knew this very important fact. This information was a game-changer. The FIR would give us everything we needed to solve the mystery of the accident.

CHAPTER TEN

OPERATIONS OFFICER INTERVIEW

"How could the very important fact about the Flight Information Recorder (FIR) being installed on the Osprey be left out of the flight manuals?" I asked O'Leary.

He shrugged and said, "I don't know, sir. But I promise I'll find out."

We drove back to our office. As soon as we walked in the door, O'Leary and I picked up the airplane "Dash-One" flight manual and looked for any reference to the FIR. The other team members sat at the office conference table and analyzed Maj Luce's interview answers. At her desk in the center of the office, Adams began transcribing the recording of the Luce interview.

"This is bizarre, sir," said O'Leary. "The reference to the FIR in the Miscellaneous Equipment section of the Dash-One says 'N/A,' but there are pictures of it in the Avionics and Electrical section. I also see the FIR referenced in two other chapters. It'd be easy for crewmembers to conclude the FIR is not installed on the Osprey."

"Unbelievable," I said. "I have never seen this kind of confusion in a Dash-One; especially when dealing with such a critical piece of equipment. Run this by Winsett and put out the word to headquarters about this error. We can't change what's happened, but we can make sure we plug this hole right away."

"Yes, sir, I'll shoot emails to the command safety office and the flight standards section at the 8th SOS. I expect they'll publish emergency guidance to inform the crews there is indeed a FIR installed. It will take a few weeks, but they will also make sure the Dash-One is changed to reflect the FIR's existence."

"That'll be a start." I said. "I'll check with General Kingsley and the SIB. Maybe the FIR is one of the pieces of wreckage they collected or might still recover. If the FIR survived the accident, we can't let it slip away."

Air Force Special Operations Command, the command that takes extraordinary pride in attention to detail, appeared to have overlooked the handling of this piece of essential equipment. O'Leary confided that the Air Force flight manual had been copied, in its entirety, from the Marine Corps MV-22 flight manuals. The MV-22 flight manuals included references to the FIR, which had been purchased and deployed on the MV-22 version of the Osprey. The Air Force version of the manual was changed by the initial CV-22 cadre, who were mistakenly told the Special Operations version of the Osprey would not include the FIR.

If the safety investigation board recovered the FIR, its existence might explain the media's contention that pilot error caused the crash. It would be out of character for Kingsley to breach protocol of his team's investigation and release any information outside the command. Besides, extracting data from the FIR required special equipment probably not available at Kandahar. With the time difference between Florida and Afghanistan, it would be a few hours before Kingsley would be available for a phone call. I was anxious to find out if the FIR was recovered.

We spent the remainder of the day preparing questions for our next interviews. Our schedule included the 8th SOS Operations Officer the following afternoon and the Army Rangers at their base in Columbus, Georgia, the next morning. A few Rangers had deployed home to Georgia for medical care after the accident in Afghanistan.

Late that evening, after most of the AIB members had left the office, O'Leary and I had an interesting discussion about a number of possible scenarios the crew of the mishap aircraft might have encountered during the final minute of flight, with pilot error being the least likely in our combined judgment, but still a possibility. It did not seem probable that an experienced crew would have endured, without intervention, an abnormal precipitous rate of descent in the seconds prior to landing. Data from the FIR would tell us the speed of the aircraft, and the revolutions per minute of the proprotors. We would know for certain if the engines were operating normally. Without the FIR, we would count on empirical evidence to reach a logical conclusion.

The following morning, we gathered in the office for our daily 8:00 a.m. meeting. I opened the meeting with a discussion of what I hoped to learn from our interview with the 8th SOS Operations Officer, who, while the unit commander was deployed, served as the acting commander for unit members at Hurlburt Field waiting their turn to deploy to Afghanistan.

Winsett scanned questions the team planned to ask and passed each to Kelly before returning them to individual members.

"Sir, it's time to head out," said Winsett.

We loaded up our vehicle and drove to the Hurlburt Field control tower/base operations building where the ground floor served as a flight planning area for local and transient aircrews. The base weather flight occupied a small office with a counter on one side of the room where local observers and military meteorologists provided crews with local weather conditions and forecasts for any destination they might require. Three dispatchers worked from an office behind the adjoining counter. They filed crew flight plans with the Federal Aviation Administration and posted notices of conditions regarding navigation aids and airfields worldwide.

We set up to conduct our interview in a well-appointed conference room next to a crew lounge and the flight planning area. While Winsett assigned members to their seats, Adams fine-tuned her recording equipment.

Lt Col Daugherty, the 8th SOS Operations Officer, entered the room while we were busy getting organized. He recognized O'Leary and immediately walked to him to exchange greetings.

Tall and lean, he stooped a bit when he walked. I attributed his gait and dark, sunken eyes to the stress of recent weeks. I introduced myself and expressed my condolences for the loss of his friends.

"Sir, equipment checks … we're ready when you are." Winsett said.

Winsett's eyes on the clock measured our time against a tight schedule. A five-hour drive to Fort Benning, Georgia, would consume our afternoon and early evening after the interview.

"Good. Everyone have a seat," I said.

I read the required legalese and ensured Daugherty understood how we would proceed before I administered the oath.

"How long have you been in the Air Force?" I asked.

"Sir, sixteen years," replied Daugherty.

"How long have you been assigned to the 8th SOS?"

"Sir, ten months."

"What aircraft have you flown?"

"Sir, MH-60, MH-53, UH-1 and CV-22."

"Did you participate in Operation Iraqi Freedom flying the CV-22?"

"Yes, sir. I was the Assistant Operations Officer. I flew six missions as a copilot. Most importantly, I got to see how to run operations and learned how to manage the risk of each mission. I also worked as the deployed mission commander in charge of getting the six airplanes back home from the Middle East. It took us seven days to get back to Hurlburt Field."

"I haven't thought of it until you mentioned returning from Iraq, but how did the unit get the CV-22s to Afghanistan a few weeks ago?"

"Sea lift, sir, and that was a new thing for us. We were originally going to fly them over, but considering the [flight] hours it takes, it's hard on the airplanes to get there and requires a bunch of maintenance and risk while flying over the ocean. We felt if you could put them on the ship and not use any flight time and let the crews stay home a little longer and do simulator and ground training events, then they could meet the planes over there. I feel that was a success. We launched them on March 3rd out of Corpus Christi, Texas – five planes. The crews were flown over in a charter airplane and landed in Kuwait on March 28th. By the time the crews arrived, the Ospreys had been off-loaded from the ship and were prepared to fly to Afghanistan. We are going through the lessons learned at the group and wing levels, but I think it's something we will definitely try again in the future."

"How does the unit mitigate risk of landing zone selection?" I asked.

"Sir, we would have an imagery analyst assigned to the JSOAC (Joint Special Operations Air Component) who pulls the most current imagery of possible landing sites. We ask for a two hundred by two-hundred-foot zone for each airplane to land. He finds an area with as flat terrain as possible, no trees, wires, or obstacles. The crew spends most of their pre-mission time working on the landing zone selection. The flight lead sits down with the imagery analyst and fine tunes the zone. Can we move it here? What are these ruts? Is that a farm field? What is that line? Is that something that could be a wire? Those are the types of questions asked while selecting landing zones. Then the flight lead determines if the aircraft would go in together or if they would stagger the approaches. In some cases we used a leapfrog technique where the lead airplane would land and the second or third aircraft would go past the lead, and land in front of each other, so that they would have better visibility of the landing area, without 'dusting out' from the previous landing Osprey. There are pros and cons to both formation landing techniques."

"Is there an acceptable tailwind speed allowed during landing, or is it determined by each individual pilot?" asked Winsett.

"We don't take [accept] a tailwind culturally. I have never heard anyone say they will take a little tailwind. You go in there generally knowing what your winds are and if anyone took a tailwind to me, it would be a surprise. Flying a H-53 or a H-60, you could get away with it, but you can't with the Osprey. It's ingrained during our training that you must check your winds constantly. It differs dramatically in mountainous areas from one place to another. Pilots have been surprised by winds in this thing. They thought they were calm, or they thought they were just a right or left quartering headwind and it ended up being too far to the side (crosswind), or behind them (tailwind), and ended up having a tough time with the power margin toward the end of the approach.

"The crew had to accept what they got and ride it down," Daugherty continued. "Culturally though, we teach guys to land into the wind. I have never heard of a crew intentionally taking a tailwind."

"Has the 8th SOS changed any tactics since this mishap occurred?"

"Yes, sir, some of the overall guidance. We went from saying that the crew needed OGE[2] for an infiltration, to requiring OGE + 5%. This gives the crew a little more power buffer just in case someone did not calculate the takeoff and landing data (TOLD) right, or if the outside temperature is warmer than the weather briefing projected, or maybe the wind is different."

"Earlier, you talked about unit culture," said O'Leary. "What is the unit culture toward go-arounds, especially in combat scenarios?"

"They come at a cost with the team (referencing the passengers being delivered – during an infiltration), but the most important priority is to get the team, crew and airplane home safely. I have been in units where it was said that go-arounds are 'free.' I have also been in units where it is said that go-arounds are 'not free' and you will not go-around. I think we had a moderate approach to that in the 8th SOS. If you fly a good set-up, you are going to be fine. But, if you are uncomfortable with the approach to landing in any way, perform a go-around and we will debrief what happened later. I was not aware, even in a joking manner, of anyone thinking they would lose face by doing a go-around. In fact, we routinely brief 80 and 80 as our profile for a go-around: 80 knots speed and nacelles set to 80 degrees (almost full 'up' in helicopter mode) so you would not have to fly all the way out and spend an inordinate amount of time getting the ground forces back to the landing area. Make two 180 degree turns and return to the target and land. We were fine with crews briefing that, because sometimes they needed it."

"Would you tell us your personal assessment of each of the crewmembers?" I asked.

"Sir, we really liked that crew. We like all our crews, but that crew was number one. Maj Voas was a high time pilot who we trusted to do anything with the CV-22. We trusted him implicitly and I can't say enough

---

2 Out of Ground Effect (OGE) - Minimum indicated airspeed for single engine performance - ground effect being the height above the ground equal to the wing span of the aircraft where aircraft performance is increased by a slight margin due to the cushion of air resulting from lift generated by the aircraft wing.

about him. I've flown with him since 2002 and I think he had over 3,700 flight hours. He was a skilled, experienced pilot … even-keeled, mild-mannered, and hard to rattle. He was competent and we needed that. He also had a paternalistic approach to the young guys. He wanted to train them. He wanted to get them into the fight and give them confidence and build our future capability. I have known (the copilot) Maj Luce since 2008. He had experience as a UH-1 instructor pilot. He had a great work ethic. We made him the mobility officer, which we normally do not do to someone coming to Hurlburt for the first time. He has very promising leadership potential. Senior Master Sergeant Lackey was the senior enlisted advisor of the squadron. He had 'been there and done that' with every airplane he'd flown. I can't really quantify what his loss means to the unit. We would put anybody on an airplane with Maj Voas or SMSgt Lackey. The tail scanner, SSgt Chris Curtis is a phenomenal young non-commissioned officer, and flight engineer. He has experience flying H-53s. He works very hard and is very humble. That is my assessment, in a nutshell, of the crew."

We went around the table with the remaining members asking questions. His answers provided the board with insight into the training, mission preparation, and culture of the unit. He also detailed how the unit trained the crews for operations in Afghanistan.

He further testified that he and the commander, along with his senior staff, held the utmost professional regard for everyone on the mishap crew. In the month since the accident, unit personnel had not had time to absorb their loss. They considered these men their friends. Daugherty hoped a thorough accident investigation would allow his unit to learn what went wrong so unit members could finally put the tragedy behind them.

Before closing the proceedings, I thanked Daugherty for his time. He shook my hand and offered any assistance he might provide while we conducted our investigation.

"We appreciate your offer," I said. "I may have something for you … information we've just discovered."

He laid his hat back on the table and furrowed his brow.

"What?" he asked.

"You'll receive notification regarding confusion on whether or not the CV-22 has a flight information recorder installed. You should be getting notification of an immediate change to the Dash-One flight manual. As of now, the Dash-One states the airplane does not have a flight information recorder. The Dash-One is wrong … there is a flight information recorder on all CV-22s."

"Yes, sir. I'll take care of the change as soon as I get it. I wonder how that happened? The airplanes have been here for a few years. Kind of shocked it has not been discovered before now."

Daugherty thanked all of us and departed the room shaking his head.

We packed our equipment and drove back to the office. While everyone checked email and phone messages, Winsett watched the clock and gave the team a countdown to departure in thirty-minute intervals.

"General, with your concurrence," Winsett said, "I'll drive one van and MSgt Dolan will drive the other. Travel time, traffic permitting, should be about four hours and forty-five minutes. To arrive at Fort Benning as early as possible, I suggest we make one quick stop at the half-way point to buy gas, switch drivers, and get some food to go. We can eat while we continue to drive."

O'Leary caught my attention.

"General Harvel, do you mind if I ride with you? I have an answer to the email I sent to the flight standards chief. He'll be in his office the day after we return from Fort Benning."

I looked at Capt Kelly and asked, "Is he on our interview list?"

"If he's not on the list, he should be," O'Leary said. "He identified the two crew casualties at the site of the accident. He also recovered the classified equipment and comm-sec (Communications Security) documents from the accident aircraft. He may have removed the flight information recorder from the accident site."

CHAPTER ELEVEN

THE CREWMEMBERS

In the fall of 2009, I had personally flown the Osprey with the training squadron at Kirtland AFB, New Mexico. Despite having contact with the leadership of the 8ᵗʰ SOS on occasion, I didn't know the crewmembers involved in the accident. The interview with the operations officer provided insight about the crew's personalities and collective abilities. It also left an impression about the esteem the crewmembers had earned from him and their peers.

Whenever a commander deploys to an unfriendly and demanding area of operation with aircraft and personnel, he/she builds one or more select crews from the most experienced and capable personnel. The hand-picked crew is tasked to plan and lead the most complex and dangerous missions. Testimony revealed Maj Voas was an elite pilot. His work ethic and devotion to duty was exemplary by all measures.

What follows are short biographies of these four hand-picked crewmembers.

Crew Member Biographies

Major Randell Voas – aircraft commander, lead pilot, squadron instructor pilot, flight examiner and a mission commander. He was the pilot flying the Osprey on the night of the accident. After graduating from the University of Minnesota with a Bachelor of Science degree in biology, Maj Voas entered Army helicopter training at Fort Rucker, Alabama. With pilot's wings pinned on his chest and warrant officer bars on his collar, he reported to Fulda, Germany[3] where he flew the AH-64 Apache attack helicopter. In Germany, he upgraded to aircraft commander and supported NATO missions throughout the European theater. Following his

---

3 Fulda – The expansive plain in Germany through which Pentagon planners believed the Soviet Union/Russia would attack Western Europe.

Germany tour, he was transferred to Fort Campbell, Kentucky, and the 101st Airborne (Air Assault) Division where he flew training exercises and operational missions that included duty at Camp Eagle, Korea. In 2000, Voas and a select group of Army pilots transferred to the Air Force. He completed Officer Candidate School (OCS) at Maxwell Air Force Base, Alabama, and joined the 21st SOS based at Royal Air Force Base (RAF) Mildenhall, England, for a three-year assignment flying the MH-53 Pave Low helicopter[4].

During Operation Iraqi Freedom, Maj Voas and Capt Craig Prather received the Cheney Award[5] for aerial achievement during a March 26, 2003 airdrop mission over Basur, Iraq. During the largest combat airdrop since Vietnam, the two pilots provided 1,000 soldiers of the U.S Army 173rd Airborne Brigade with fire support and casualty evacuation. While presenting the award, then Air Force Chief of Staff, General John P. Jumper said:

"These two took their (MH-53M Pave Low) helicopter from Greece and flew almost 700 miles to the drop area. As part of a 1,000-Soldier airdrop mission, the crew provided on-call fire support, immediate casualty evacuation, triage, and recovery for thirty-seven paratroopers. The flight was conducted at maximum wartime weight in deteriorating weather and included three aerial refuelings. Guys like this think these things are routine, but to those of us who don't live that life, it is very special indeed. It is a mark of our Air Force that we have officers of this caliber." [5]

After his European assignment, Major Voas upgraded to instructor pilot and for over two years taught undergraduate helicopter pilot candidates in the 23rd Flight Training Squadron at Fort Rucker, Alabama.

4 Pave Low – A Special Operations variant of the Sikorsky MH-53 search and rescue helicopter.
5 Aviation award presented annually by the USAF in memory of 1st Lt William H. Cheney, killed in an air collision over Foggia, Italy, January 20, 1918. Established in 1927, the Cheney Award is presented to an airman for an act of valor, extreme fortitude or self-sacrifice in a humanitarian interest, performed in connection with aircraft, but not necessarily of a military nature.

When the CV-22 became operational in 2006, Major Voas reported to the 8th SOS at Hurlburt Field, Florida, as an initial cadre Osprey instructor pilot. His responsibilities included being a flight commander, instructor pilot, and evaluator pilot. Senior officers and civilian dignitaries often visited the squadron to acquaint themselves with the CV-22. By regulation, the dignitaries required an instructor pilot to occupy one of the pilot seats while the guest was in the other pilot seat. Maj Voas most often found himself the instructor trusted with such duty.

Major Brian Luce (his rank was Captain on the night of the accident) was performing duties as the copilot on the night of the accident. After Maj Luce graduated from Syracuse University in 2000 with a Bachelor of Science degree in computer science, he attended helicopter flight school at Fort Rucker, Alabama. His first assignment was flying UH/TH-1H helicopters at Minot AFB, North Dakota. Over time, his experience and skill warranted advancement to the Chief of Squadron Flight Standards. In November of 2005, he returned to Fort Rucker and served as the Chief of the Operations Group Standardization and Evaluation.

Toward the end of 2009, he completed CV-22 training and reported to the 8th SOS, Hurlburt Field, Florida. As an additional duty, Luce served as the unit's mobility officer. He was responsible for ensuring the unit, and its assigned personnel, were prepared and equipped for deployments anywhere in the world. Luce's supervisors, and fellow squadron members, respected his diligence in his flying and devotion to his additional duties. His commander assigned him to crew with Maj Voas in order to hone combat experience and mentor him for a future upgrade to aircraft commander.

Senior Master Sergeant James B. Lackey - known to his friends as "JB," was qualified as a flight engineer/tail scanner, instructor and flight examiner. He was sitting in the flight engineer seat in the cockpit on the night of the accident. SMSgt Lackey enlisted in the Air Force in 1986 and worked on the flight line as an A-10 and F-15 crew chief. He re-trained as a MH-53 flight engineer in 2002. That same year, he earned the Distinguished Flying Cross for his actions during Operation Enduring Freedom. In 2006, the 8th SOS transitioned from the retiring MH-53 Pave Low helicopter to the new CV-22 Osprey. He was selected as a part of the initial cadre to train new flight engineers and tail scanners. His rank and experience warranted SMSgt Lackey's assignment as chief of the CV-22 flight engineer/tail scanner section of the squadron. He was the unit's senior enlisted advisor. Like Voas, when special, dangerous or difficult missions were tasked, the squadron scheduled Lackey as a crewmember. Not designated for the deployment to Afghanistan, he volunteered to replace another crewmember unable to deploy due to personal issues.

Staff Sergeant Christopher Curtis - flight engineer/tail scanner, was flying in the tail scanner crew position on the night of the accident. A native of Northern California, SSgt Curtis joined the Air Force in 1998, at the age of twenty-one. He worked in maintenance as a MH-53 Pave Low avionics systems specialist stationed at Royal Air Force (RAF) Mildenhall, United Kingdom. In 2003, SSgt Curtis was transferred to the MH-53 Maintenance Squadron at Kirtland AFB, New Mexico. In 2006, he cross-trained into the flight engineer career field and crewed the MH-53 Pave Low at the 20th SOS based at Hurlburt Field, Florida. After completing his second deployment to Iraq, the Air Force retired the MH-53 from the active inventory. Curtis, along with many of the Pave Low experienced crews, returned to Kirtland Air Force Base to train as CV-22 flight engineers.

After completing training, he was assigned to the 8th SOS. On the unit's first deployment to Afghanistan flying the Osprey, SSgt Curtis, the most junior crewmember, split duties as flight engineer/tail scanner with SMSgt Lackey.

Every commander can spout two quips, most often attributed to Benjamin Franklin:

One – "One bad apple spoils the barrel."

Two – "A chain is only as strong as its weakest link."

Whether inscribed on an office wall, or atop a desk, the commander knows and lives by the truth of this quip. A bad apple or weak link cannot be tolerated in military units. It would threaten successful accomplishment of the mission, and the safety of unit personnel and aircraft. Universal testimony by supervisors, commanders and peers in our accident investigation yielded only the highest accolades for the integrity, character, and ability of Voas and the other members of his crew.

CHAPTER TWELVE

THE YOUNG ARMY RANGER

We caravanned from Hurlburt Field, Florida, to Fort Benning, Georgia, the afternoon of May 6th. The command had honored my request for two vehicles in the event we needed to split the team for any reason or make an extended drive. It would have been a tight fit with eight of us crammed into a single van. The vans, as "plain vanilla" as they could be, were painted a dull white color and equipped with basic options. The only installed equipment that could have been considered a concession to comfort or convenience was air conditioning. Amazingly, the van did not even have a radio installed.

Winsett led Dolan on the first leg to our only pit stop. The break allowed us to switch drivers and stop at a fast-food restaurant. Those not driving nested in corner spaces of the van to catch up on paperwork, emails, and phone calls.

On the initial leg, O'Leary ensured he had a place beside me in the second seat of the lead van. We hadn't traveled far before he shared an email he had received on his Blackberry.

"Sir, this is from the Chief of Wing Standardization. He attended a CV-22 conference at the end of 2006. One agenda item covered the equipment to be installed on the different models of the Osprey. Opinions differed regarding the inclusion of the FIR on the Air Force CV-22. The lead service for the Osprey procurement – the Naval Air Systems Command (NAVAIR), confirmed that the Marine version would be delivered with the FIR installed. The USAF version would not. In fact, every production Osprey had been delivered to the user (Marine Corps and the USAF) with the recorder installed. Our inquiry addressing the oversight resulted in an emergency change to CV-22 flight manuals."

"Did they say if the FIR had been recovered from the mishap aircraft?" I asked.

"Sir, he has a list of equipment he removed, but refuses to get in front of the safety board's investigation by releasing information before they've completed Part One of their final accident report."

"Log our investigation's first success." I said proudly. "Discovering the Air Force Ospreys have a flight information recorder is a big deal."

I polled the occupants of our van to see who had been to Fort Benning. O'Leary had, but Winsett and Harper had not. I had no idea about the team members in the other vehicle.

After Army flight school at Fort Rucker, O'Leary had spent short periods flying support for most units on the base, including the U.S. Army Ranger School and operational units of the 75th Ranger Regiment.

Members of the 75th Ranger Regiment wear a distinguishable tan beret and the "Ranger" tab on their uniform sleeve. This distinction accords the wearer unquestioned respect, as do badges of the Special Operations forces of other services. For those outside their elite circle who might not possess a Ranger's demonstrated accomplishment and devotion to duty, most special operators tempered their regard for those less skilled and dedicated.

Traffic driving through Montgomery, Alabama, and a couple of unplanned navigation issues delayed our arrival until 10:20 p.m. We checked into our hotel and agreed to regroup at 6:00 a.m. for breakfast before departing for the short drive to the base. Kelly had coordinated our arrival and interviews with the unit First Sergeant from the 3rd Battalion, 75th Rangers. Our first interview was scheduled for 7:00 a.m.

By the time we arrived, the unit had completed their morning physical training, showered, ate breakfast, and were cleaning and refitting field equipment from recent deployments. Despite having three lieutenant colonels and a brigadier general passing through their area, the Rangers paid little attention to us. They were not intimidated by rank. If one of us had worn a "Ranger" tab on our sleeve and a tan beret on our head, we might have created a sensation. To them, we were merely nuisance spectators, an inconsequential group of Air Force personnel on a tour of the facility.

We made our way down a short hallway to an open office. The unit first sergeant immediately stood and called the area to attention. I told everyone to be at ease and shook his hand while introducing myself and the team. He ushered us across the hall to a conference room. Except for two six-foot folding tables and twenty or more metal folding chairs resting against the wall, the room made no claim to comfort or character. It smelled of damp canvass I attributed to duffels and backpacks lying in piles throughout the area.

"I didn't know how many chairs to set up, sir," said the First Sergeant. "If you want the room in a particular order, I'll detail a couple of my men to set the room to your specifications."

"That won't be necessary," I said. "We'll take care of it. Give us five minutes to get the chairs set and our equipment ready. We'll start our first interview in fifteen minutes."

"Yes, sir. Private First Class (PFC) Timothy Davis is standing by … he'll be your first interview this morning. Sergeant (SGT) Charles Claybaker will be ready when you finish speaking with Davis."

When announced, we were ready to start the interviews. Within seconds, PFC Davis marched into the conference room with all the military bearing he could Becker. His stride lacked the aura of a determined soldier, favoring one side of his body. He wore the unit's utility uniform of the day and carried a half-empty bottle of water. He was a crash survivor, although we didn't yet know the nature or extent of his injuries. He locked eyes on me and reported per military custom by rendering a crisp salute.

"Sir, Private First Class Davis, reporting as ordered."

I returned his salute and asked him to take a seat. Stunned at how young he and his comrades appeared, I marveled at the skills they had mastered at such a young age. Few aspire to the Ranger career field and fewer yet qualify for, much less complete, the rigorous training.

I likened his youth to that of my daughter's, a couple years younger, and grappled with the contrast of their lives. While my daughter struggled with the travails of high school – term papers, tests, sports, and proms – Davis chose to be a U.S. Army soldier, and a Ranger.

His life experience included an extended period of intense combat training followed by deployment to inhospitable, hostile environs half a globe away from the safety and comfort my family enjoyed. I thanked God for him and the silent minority, those precious few, who underwrite the world's freedom by frequently completing highly risky missions.

I shuffled papers listing the questions I intended to ask and, in a concession to the father in me, considered altering the order or eliminating inquiries referencing his lost comrades.

Winsett roused me out of the thought. "Sir …"

I introduced myself and members of the board. For the first time since entering the room, he broke eye contact with me and cast an assessing look at each of the board members as I introduced them. He sat in a chair facing me on the opposite side of the table. In an effort to avoid the appearance of our proceeding resembling an inquisition, Dolan and Doc Harper took chairs beside him.

He winced as he stooped to place his water bottle on the floor beside his chair, appearing uncomfortable with his posture, but sat as erect as he could. He stared into my eyes without emotion or fear. Unintimidated by a general officer's rank, the proceedings or the questions he might be asked, his demeanor was pure cool, calm and collected.

I read the legal statement used prior to every interview. Once PFC Davis understood the nature of our mission and swore his testimony would be truthful, I trudged through the qualifying questions.

Davis had begun his service a year and a half prior and had been an Army Ranger close to a year. He seemed proud of his assignment as his squad's automatic rifleman. He recounted his activity the day of the mishap from rising, through fitting out for his mission, and boarding the Osprey at the forward operating base where the unit lived in-between missions.

"PFC Davis," I said, "do you remember anything unusual about the takeoff after you boarded the Osprey at your base April 8th?"

"No sir, I don't remember any difficulties. The first thing I thought was unusual was the speed we were going when we received the one-minute call. But, being as I am not fully experienced with all the aircraft we use, I didn't think anything of it, sir."

"What were your actions at the one-minute call?" I asked.

"We, I proceeded to get up on one knee and grab my safety line. I prepared to exit the airplane when we touched down. After that, I felt a bump, which sat me back down and we proceeded to crash, sir."

"Did you remain conscious?"

"Yes, sir, as far as I know, I was conscious. I remember being knocked down, and I remember a strong jerk on my safety line which broke, and then I tumbled. When the airplane stopped, I was lying on my back, sir."

"Were you able to exit the airplane on your own?"

"Yes, sir. Out of the tail of the airplane."

"What did you do once outside the aircraft?"

"Sir, I saw an Air Force crewmember (SSgt Curtis, the flight engineer/tail scanner) lying in the dirt. He was on his back. He looked up at me and he said, 'I need help; I'm hurt.'

"I said, 'Okay, I am here. I got you sir.' I saw that his arm was pretty messed up, so I reached for my medical kit, then realized I did not have it anymore. It must have been ripped away during the crash. I grabbed the tourniquet I had rubber banded to the front of my belt. I put the tourniquet on his arm, then grabbed the collar of his uniform behind his neck and dragged him about ten meters away from the airplane.

"I told him everything would be okay. Someone else came over and asked me if I was all right. I told him I thought I was fine, but the crewmember needed more help. I can't recall who I was talking to, but he handed me his M-4 carbine and told me he would help. I took the weapon and started walking away from the airplane to conduct a security sweep. I thought we had been shot down. I was waiting for enemy forces to close in on us. I looked to my right and saw my squad leader and asked him if he was okay. He looked confused.

"The squad leader asked me, 'Where are we?' I told him that we were in Afghanistan. Our plane went down. He said, 'Okay, stay here and pull security.' I continued to watch for enemy forces for a few minutes. I was then asked to come back to the airplane to assist in dragging more people out. We were putting the people into groups. One group was personnel who were 'expectant' – they were dead or going to die soon. Another group was personnel who were severely injured and needed to be evacuated in the first rescue helicopter. The last group was personnel who were injured but did not require immediate medical care. After a while, someone came up to me and said, 'Put your weapon down and relax.' I sat down with the group of personnel that did not require immediate medical care."

Davis's voice cracked, but not from emotion. He spoke as though his throat was dry.

"We can break for a minute, if you need a drink," I said. "Then we'll continue."

By that point, no one was taking notes. The investigation team members were mesmerized by the testimony they were hearing. They sat in rapt attention to Davis's account of his experience after the accident.

He uttered a low groan when he reached for the water bottle and took a quick sip.

"I am ready to continue, sir."

"How were you evacuated from the site?" I asked.

"Sir, I was evacuated on a Blackhawk helicopter. We flew from the crash site to Kandahar Air Base."

"What happened after arriving at Kandahar?"

"Sir, I walked onto the Blackhawk helicopter and walked off after landing at Kandahar. I was told to get into a waiting ambulance. I was driven to a non-trauma emergency room. A doctor came into the room and asked what happened to me. I told him I was feeling a burning sensation around my stomach, and that my hips were hurting. He told me to lift up my shirt. When he saw my stomach, he yelled for someone to bring a stretcher. I was prepped for immediate surgery. My colon and bowels were bleeding internally. The surgeon cut through my stomach to make repairs of internal organs. The surgeon also repaired my right oblique (muscle assisting in respiration and torsional movement of the torso). It had torn away from my abdomen wall. I also had a large cut on my right shin requiring stitches. When my muscle heals, I'll be back on duty, sir."

After questions from the other board members, I concluded the interview. I thanked PFC Davis for his time that day and his professionalism the night of the crash. Each of us personally thanked him and shook his hand. We stood in silence as he walked out of the room.

"Geez," I said. "That's one tough kid. He isn't twenty-one, and he's made it through an incredible selection and training process to become an Army Ranger."

"Are they all like him?" Adams asked.

"Some different in their own way," O'Leary said, "But the Army ensures they're cut from the same grade of boiler plate – resolute … hard … tough and dedicated."

"I can't believe his insides were ripped apart and he walked around a hostile desert catastrophe in the dark helping others, ready to fight off an enemy in the process," Kelly said. "He is an impressive young man."

I moved closer to Doc. Harper.

"Hey Doc, he plans to recover and return to his unit. Do you think that'll happen? He seems to be counting on it."

"If it were a matter of conditioning, I'd say he'll do it. No problem."

"But?" I asked.

"But … he's pretty beat up. Without access to his medical records, I don't know how serious his internal injuries might be."

"What do you think? This is his life. You heard him."

Doc Harper pursed his lips, stared at his shoes for a moment shaking his head. "I think his career as an Army Ranger is over."

CHAPTER THIRTEEN

SGT CHARLES CLAYBAKER

PFC Davis's interview had taken less time than we had allowed. We used the extra minutes to debrief and consolidate notes, while TSgt Adams saved her data and reset her recording equipment for the next session with Sergeant (SGT) Charles Claybaker. No one had a specific take-away from talking to Davis except to marvel at how he reverted to his training, even under extreme duress. But then, few outside Special Operations communities can appreciate how combat and stress for these soldiers is routine.

"Sir, I just talked to the First Sergeant," said Kelly. "We have a problem. SGT Claybaker has been confined to stay at his home by his doctor. He has been told he needs to remain in bed for the next week or two. He had a surgical procedure that needs to heal before he is able to walk. The First Sergeant says he still wants us to interview him. What do you want to do?"

"Find out if he will allow us to go to his home and interview him … just like we did for Luce." I answered.

"I'll be right back, sir."

"Hey everybody," I said. "We may have to drive to our next interview. Kelly is checking on it now."

"Sir," said Kelly. "He lives about ten minutes from the base and has agreed for us to interview him at his home."

"Ok. Let's pack up and get over there."

We drove the short distance to Claybaker's neat and well-kept home located on a street where each house was perfectly lined up in a row. The homes looked very similar in size and floor plan. The only thing different was the exterior paint colors and a variety of toys, bikes and sports equipment lying in the front yards. It was definitely a neighborhood that would attract military families desiring to live off base, as opposed to the small, cramped quarters provided for them at Fort Benning.

We approached the front door and knocked quietly.

When Mrs. Claybaker answered the door, we each introduced ourselves. She was very young, thin and pretty.

"Please come in," she said. "Make yourselves at home. My husband is anxious to meet you."

SGT Claybaker was lying in a portable hospital bed. He was covered with bandages and looking very frail. When he saw all of us piling into the house, he perked up and welcomed us to his home. He was in excellent spirits, considering his medical condition. I chatted with him about his recovery while the other team members arranged chairs, plugged in the recording equipment and prepared the living room for the interview.

"Sir, we are ready to start," said Winsett.

I read the requisite preliminary narrative. When he understood our mission and his obligation to relate truthful testimony, I covered the basics regarding his position in the Army and his unit.

He told us he had served in the Army for four years, three and a half of those being in the 3rd Battalion, 75th Rangers. He was a fire team leader with responsibilities of training, administration, and the general welfare of the soldiers he supervised. On the night of the mishap, he was assigned to the lead platoon. Their mission was to conduct the initial assault on the objective and then provide area security. He related his routine activities that day from the time he reported for duty, until he boarded the mishap aircraft.

I asked him about preparations prior to getting on the Osprey at the Ranger's base.

"Roger, sir. Once the aircraft landed, I made sure that all the combat multipliers [snipers, interpreters, and non-assault team passengers] were in line and ready to board the airplane. We conducted a quick pre-mission brief with the flight crew and boarded the aircraft. Everybody snap-linked tethers onto a rope that ran along the side wall of the aircraft and sat down. When we took off, it was funky."

"Funky? How?" I asked.

"I don't know any other way to describe it, sir. Several us were on interphone and able to talk to team members in the airplane. We were joking that the takeoff was weird and awkward. We said something bad might happen. I don't know why we all felt that way, but for some reason we had a feeling that something was not right. It might've been our nerves, considering this was the first mission on an Osprey for some of us. Before we knew it, we got the six-minute call from the aircrew and made sure everyone was awake. At six minutes, we check that our Garmins (hand-held GPS) are tracking correctly, put on our Night Observation Devices (NODs) [Night vision goggles attached to their helmets], and check our weapons are in the 'safe' mode … all that good stuff, sir."

He continued, "At the one-minute call, we got up on one knee, and the bird (referring to the Osprey) … like you could see the ground and we were moving really fast. I have been on some pretty interesting Blackhawk[6] flights where we are really going, but I have never been in anything going that fast and where we could see the ground coming up at us that quickly. Once we were at thirty to forty feet off the ground, I started seeing bushes and rocks coming by us really, really fast. I remember thinking to myself, 'my God, is this going to be one of those Chinook[7] flights where we land, and everybody gets knocked on their backs?' For some reason, the CH-47s always land hard, so everybody gets knocked down. Well, this time everyone got knocked down. I remember stuff getting thrown around. The vision looking out of my NODs turned blue. That was the last thing I remember."

He paused a moment to think, then continued, "When I woke up, guys were hollering and moaning. Stuff was on fire and dudes were starting to drag people out of the airplane."

"Please continue," I said.

---

6 Blackhawk – Medium lift helicopter carrying troops or equipment.

7 CH-47, Chinook – Twin rotor helicopter capable of carrying troops, cargo, or small motorized vehicle(s).

He looked at me kind of surprised, "Do I need to go any farther, or is that good?"

"I want you to share everything you remember," I said. "Were there any unusual noises or sounds in those last few seconds before you hit the ground?"

"Sir, one thing, I don't remember getting a 'prepare for crash' warning from the crew. I am not a pilot, but I imagine that at the one-minute warning, they would know if something bad was about to happen. They should tell the guys in back to brace themselves. We are hooked up to a rope that is rated for about 300 or 400 pounds. I weigh 175 … with my equipment, I weigh more than 260 pounds. That pushes the limits on the rope restraint. I don't know if it would have saved anybody's life, or my leg, but the airplane should have a bell to warn the passengers to brace for impact. I know the pilots are concerned about getting everyone on the ground safely. I know they were trying to save lives, and they sure the heck did, or I would not be here talking to you right now, sir."

"What is your first recollection following the crash?"

"Sir, I thought I was unconscious for one minute. I found out later it was more like ten to fifteen minutes. When I woke up, I saw that my legs were broken and dangling through a hole ripped in the side of the aircraft. There was a metal beam of some kind on my lap and belts of 50 caliber machine gun rounds were wrapped around my body. When I looked out, I saw that the front of the airplane was completely gone. It looked like it had been ripped away. I took my helmet off and tossed down my rifle. As soon as I did that, I realized another Ranger was under me. My body and the debris on top of me trapped him. When I looked at him, he grabbed me and asked. 'Who's that?' I told him 'it's me … Claybaker.'

"I threw the beam off me and some dude crawled over me," said Claybaker. "I tried to stand up. At that point, I realized the whole right side of my leg was destroyed. I let out a yell and sat back down. I tried to help the Rangers next to me. I helped one get his helmet off and lifted a rifle off the neck of another Ranger. I tried to break the 50-caliber links off me, but using smashed fingers on my hand, I couldn't. Two Rangers walked over to me and lifted me up and over the side of the airplane while I held on to my pant leg. My ankle was shattered. It was just flopping all over. It was moving freely like it was not attached to my leg. I tried to stand one more time and realized that my hip was separated. The two Rangers dragged me about fifty meters and dropped me near another Ranger. They went back to the airplane to help other people get out. Since I couldn't help with pulling people out of the airplane, I rolled over onto my stomach and put my rifle in position so I could provide security for the site. As I raised my rifle to a firing position, another Ranger came over to check on me. He wanted to make sure I wasn't going into shock. I had the Ranger splint my bad leg to my good leg while we waited for evacuation. Eventually, they put me and one of the Air Force crewmembers on litters. We were carried to a Black Hawk helicopter and evacuated to a medical facility for treatment, sir."

"Do you remember which crewmember was evacuated with you?" I asked.

"Negative, sir, I do remember his arm was severely injured. He was bleeding all over me and asking for pain relief. I remember telling him to 'calm down, we will get there.' I don't know who it was. I wish I did, sir."

"How is the recovery from your injuries going?" I asked.

"Sir, I bruised my left lung, and I cracked some ribs on my right side. I dislocated my right hip. I broke my right acetabulum[8]. I had a tibia plateau shear[9]. My ankle was broken into three pieces. I had traumatic brain injury. I've had hip, knee and ankle surgery. I still have moderate pain. My surgeon says it will take at least fifteen months to recover. I have numerous plates and screws in my knees and ankles. It is a day-to-day thing, sir. I will never be able to do any impact activities like running or jumping. My job is pretty much done. My battalion is looking to get me a desk job."

"Ok, SGT Claybaker. I have no further questions, but Lt Col O'Leary has a couple."

---

8 Hip bone where the femur ball fits into the socket.

9 Broken leg

"Sir," SGT Claybaker said. "I am sorry. I just wanted you to know, sir, that I am not upset and if I could go back, I would do the exact same thing. I would get on that aircraft and I would go on that mission. I wanted it to be on record that I am not bitter about anything, sir. I don't want you to get the wrong opinion."

Perhaps I surprised SGT Claybaker by telling him I was done asking questions. He had taken it wrong.

"SGT Claybaker, I'm … we're all extremely proud and impressed with your performance that night. Your actions after the crash were exemplary and in the finest tradition of the Rangers. When the other board members have completed their questions, I'll conclude the interview without prejudice toward you in any way."

"Roger that, sir."

"Lt Col O'Leary."

"Thank you, sir. When you got the one-minute call from the crew, what was the aircraft doing at that time – speed and altitude that you could tell?"

"Sir, at the six-minute warning, I could hear the engines rotate up toward the helicopter position. The aircraft was flying in a pitch-up (nose rising) attitude. I could see the ground out the back of the airplane. Later, I found out from one of the crewmembers at Walter Reed Hospital with me – he had a back brace and a very short haircut. He said the crew was trying to belly land the airplane. He said there are four things that must be right to land the CV-22. He said two or three things changed after the one-minute call. So, we were doomed at that point.

"The pilot tried to save the aircraft and all of us. Now, I didn't know it at the time, I was scared half to death. I wondered about the airplane's abrupt flare so soon after the one-minute warning. We were near the ground and going very, very fast, sir. Does that answer your question?"

I nodded and looked at the rest of the board. Everyone had scooted their chairs closer to the table with heads down, writing notes.

I leaned toward O'Leary sitting next to me. "I think he must have been at Walter Reed with the copilot. The copilot had a back injury. The tail scanner had multiple compound fractures of his left arm and internal injuries."

O'Leary nodded and penned a note. "You talked to another crew member in the hospital that told you how you were doomed. At the time, did you think you were going to crash?"

"Well, sir, I have never been in an aircraft crash before. I was kind of optimistic as to what was going to happen, sir. I was relating the experience to the CH-47 Chinook. Sometimes they land a little fast and skid a little bit. I thought that was going to happen, and it seemed like it was going to be okay when we landed. The airplane touched down fast and we all got knocked off our knees. For a second or two, it seemed like everything was going to be okay. Suddenly, the airplane started flipping and wings and airplane parts started flying all around. We banged around and then I went unconscious, sir."

"You spoke earlier about waiting to be evacuated," O'Leary said. "You were at the casualty collection point (CCP) near the aircrew member with the arm injury. We believe that person was the tail scanner. Did you talk to him?"

"Negative, sir. We were all in extreme pain. It seemed like his was excruciating, totally on a different level than the rest of us. He had open wounds that seemed very severe. I just tried to reassure him that every-thing would be okay. He was banged up pretty good, sir."

"I want to go back to the conversation you had at Walter Reed. The Air Force crewmember at the CCP, was that the same crewmember you talked to at Walter Reed?"

"No, sir, it was a crewmember who looked completely different than the one at the CCP."

"And you told us the crewmember said the pilots were trying to save the airplane?"

"Yes, sir, that is what he said. He said the pilots said that something happened between the one-minute warning and us hitting the ground. They were doing everything they could. It seemed like he was trying to tell me that it wasn't the pilot's fault. I kind of figured that out already. Pilots don't crash airplanes for no reason. So, he was just trying to reassure me, I guess, sir. I didn't need it, but it was comforting, you know, nice to hear that they were doing everything they could from one of the crewmembers."

"Did he definitely say that something went wrong after the one-minute call?"

"Yes, sir. I asked him what happened. He said that after the one-minute call something went wrong. They tried to save the airplane and belly land because they were coming in too hot … you know, and something went wrong. He did not say specifically what went wrong."

SGT Claybaker fielded a few questions from the remaining board members. When no one had further questions, I stepped around the table and shook SGT Claybaker's hand. I wished him well in his recovery and offered my personal cell phone number and email address should he remember anything else. While we spoke, the remaining board members queued beside me forming a line to individually thank SGT Claybaker for his time and selfless service.

We packed up our gear and drove back to Fort Benning. Another amazing young man. We were very impressed with his attitude, courage and determination. We discussed Claybaker's statement that the crew believed there had been an undetermined and serious malfunction with the Osprey inside the one-minute warning. He also testified, despite what occurred with the aircraft, he believed the crew made every effort to immediately get the airplane on the ground safely.

As we drove back to the army base, we agreed to schedule a follow-up interview with Maj Luce. Perhaps reminding him about the conversation that took place between him and SGT Claybaker at Walter Reed hospital would stimulate his memory of what happened during those last few seconds of flight.

CHAPTER FOURTEEN

FIRST TO THE ACCIDENT SCENE

We conducted three additional interviews at Fort Benning learning little new, and no remarkable information. Piecing together individuals' testimonies, we discovered each passenger's location prior to the crash. The two fatalities were secured on the same side of the aircraft, but not in proximity to one another. Their unrelated injuries indicated no relation to a single cause. The severity of wounds suffered by the remaining Rangers fit our expectations. Those positioned forward of the wing, closer to the cockpit, came through the accident with fewer injuries than those aft of the wing.

Aspects of their testimonies left us in humble awe. Sleep deprived young men, some of whom were awakened six minutes prior to landing, could not have performed more resolutely and professionally in the chaotic aftermath of the accident. Despite their injuries, they established a defensive perimeter at the site, while their comrades rescued survivors and recovered the fatalities from the burning wreckage. Once they realized they were not under attack, they designated a collection point for casualties and administered first aid as they were able.

Seldom confident the board had asked all the questions that might elicit information essential to our investigation; I made a habit of making one final inquiry.

"Is there anything else you think relevant and want to tell us?"

Each of the five Rangers had similar answers. Task force headquarters monitored every mission, and on that night, video provided the commanders with their progress in real time. They watched the Osprey accident. The joint operations center (JOC) Task Force Commander wasted no time dispatching rescue assets to the scene.

The other two Ospreys orbited overhead assessing the situation on the ground, coordinating with command and control for guidance on what they should do to help the downed airplane. Poor performing radios, a regular defect in the Osprey, delayed their landing. Approximately fifteen minutes after the mishap, they landed in open areas two miles from the accident site.

Medical personnel from the first Osprey to land were too late for one Ranger who suffered severe, but perhaps survivable, injuries. Had the medical team arrived earlier, or if the Osprey had landed closer to the site, some Rangers believed their comrade could have been saved. Frustrated soldiers, remembering the sound of aircraft orbiting overhead, would never grumble, but wondered why help took so long to arrive. In a word, they characterized the support to be unacceptable.

By the end of the day, we had interviewed the Rangers who had returned to Fort Benning for medical treatment, recovery, or physical therapy. The remaining survivors were returned to duty at their forward operating base, some flying a mission the night following the accident.

Capt Kelly maintained a list of those to be interviewed once we arrived in Afghanistan. If we failed to receive permission to travel to forward locations from Kandahar, we planned telephone interviews using the secure STU III.

During the drive from Fort Benning to Hurlburt Field, we engaged in a spirited discussion relating to SGT Claybaker's conversation with the copilot at Walter Reed. O'Leary pressed to close the loop on Luce's ambiguous testimony. He stared out the window, his jaw muscles pulsing.

"The only witness in the cockpit at the time of the accident confessed to remembering nothing of the event," said O'Leary. "Based on what we've been told, he may be hiding something. We should interrogate him again right away … in the next day or two at the latest."

"Sir, that may not be possible," Capt Kelly said.

She reminded us of our schedule with six 8th SOS crewmembers who had recently returned to Hurlburt. She had reserved May 12th and 13th to work with the safety board since they set May 12th for release of Part One of their report.

"Regardless of the effect on schedules, we have to know what went on in the cockpit during the final seconds of the flight," continued O'Leary. "We won't be able to piece it together from any testimony we get in Afghanistan. I'm not comfortable questioning witnesses over there with a lie in our pocket."

O'Leary shifted his attention to Doc Harper. "Are his head injuries severe enough to cause amnesia?"

"Luce may have a head problem," Harper conceded. "But I can't say it is from physical trauma. His inability to recall that last minute of flight might be from the overall shock of the accident ... traumatic amnesia. Or, he's withholding information for reasons of his own."

"His memory loss seems pretty selective to me. All the more reason we should question him right away," O'Leary said.

"Not necessarily. He's still in pain and on meds that may cloud his memory. I suggest we allow him time to recover, get off his meds, and then address the discrepancies in his testimony."

They looked to me for a decision. I considered both arguments.

"Our primary goal is to get to the truth," I said. "If Luce has more time to recover, maybe he'll be more forthcoming. Meanwhile, let's press ahead with the schedule Kelly and Adams have arranged. How is it going with our travel arrangements to fly to Kandahar?"

Adams had requested a block of seats for us to travel to Afghanistan on one of the rotators[10] departing Baltimore, Maryland, between May 15th and May 19th. Only a few seats showed available during that period with zero seats offered for many of those days. She figured a large unit move filled the vacancies as fast as space was released by the military travel coordinator at Scott AFB. Whatever day we secured transportation out of the U.S. would drive our week's schedule.

"To be out of Afghanistan by June 1st we'll have to travel as soon as possible because of the pact I've struck with the commander," I said. "Even

---

10 Chartered commercial aircraft regularly scheduled to depart from U.S. locations to fly military personnel to air bases in the Middle East

then, we'll have to complete seven to eight interviews each day to finish our entire list of potential witnesses. The sooner we can get there, the better chance we have to question everyone."

O'Leary, in true pit-bull fashion, refused to give up. "The copilot knows more than he's telling. I had a gut feeling after we spoke to him the first time. Knowing what he told SGT Claybaker at Walter Reed, I'm convinced he's holding back, if not lying outright. We should talk to him sooner than later. Please, sir."

Winsett agreed.

"He's on the list, sir," Kelly said. "We'll plan a follow-up interview as soon as schedules permit."

We arrived back at Hurlburt Field late in the evening and agreed to report to work at 8:00 a.m. During our morning meeting, we discussed the importance of our next interview: Lieutenant Colonel Darrell Schultz, AFSOC Branch Chief for the CV-22. In the command, all things Osprey flowed through his office.

He was the first Air Force person not involved in the mishap to arrive at the accident site. We hoped for conclusive information regarding the airplane's flight information recorder. Otherwise, we expected he would offer a dispassionate assessment of the scene before the wreckage had been destroyed by the A-10s. We also relied on his firsthand account regarding what had been removed from the rubble of what had once been CV-22, tail number 06-0031.

We departed the office at 9:45 a.m. for the conference room on the ground floor of the Hurlburt control tower. We unloaded our vehicles and arranged tables and chairs. Before Adams and Dolan had the recording equipment ready, Schultz walked in.

Slender, about six-feet tall, he wore a flight suit with his hat (typical for most aircrew) stowed, with his rank not visible, in the lower right leg pocket. Hair, wispy on top and thicker over the ears and neck, made him appear like a skinny rendition of Friar Tuck. He walked straight toward me and shook my hand.

"Good morning, sir. Great to see you again."

His comment startled me. "Have we met?"

"Not exactly, sir. I sit along the wall at the headquarters' stand-up briefings on some mornings. I have seen you there many times. I wouldn't expect you to know me, but I know who you are."

"You know Lt Col O'Leary?"

"Yes, sir. We've been stationed together."

He shook hands with O'Leary. While they caught up on mutual acquaintances, Adams and Dolan finished setting up our recording equipment. Schultz rounded the table to meet the remaining board members.

Adams made one final adjustment to her recorder and took her seat. "Sir, we are ready."

"Okay," I said. "Let's get started."

I covered the requisite preliminaries and administered the oath.

Schultz, an eighteen-year Air Force veteran, had served in his present position, Branch Chief for the CV-22, for ten months. He had participated in the 8th Special Operations Squadron's deployment to Afghanistan as one of the unit's three qualified flight leads. He had flown several models of the C-130 Hercules as a squadron and instructor pilot where his mission qualifications included Special Operations. After a two-year stint in the Air Force Reserve, he returned to active duty where he served as the Director of Operations for the 58th Special Operations Wing, the unit assigned to bring the CV-22 into the Air Force inventory.

"In 2006, I was reassigned as the Assistant Director of Operations of the 8th Special Operations Squadron," said Schultz. "I helped the unit transition from the C-130 Talon I* to the CV-22. I was transferred to my current job assignment about a year ago."

"You deployed as a CV-22 flight lead during Operation Iraqi Freedom," I said. "What were your duties and responsibilities during that assignment?"

"Sir, there were three flight lead pilots on that deployment. Flight lead pilots oversee their assigned mission each night. As a mission comes down, the flight lead pilot gets briefed on the basics of the mission. Each flight lead plans the mission; to the tiniest detail.

˙C-130 Special Operations transport aircraft modified with upgraded radar and other electronic equipment.

He would then brief the other pilots and flight engineers about the mission to make sure everyone knows the plan, and multiple backup plans, just in case something unforeseen happens. The flight lead pilots also acted as the liaison between the team (Special Operations ground forces) and the aircrew. They pretty much handled all aspects of the mission."

"Was Maj Voas one of the flight leads deployed with you?" I asked.

"Yes, sir."

"Was the mission on the night of April 8th the first combat mission for the 8th SOS after arriving in Afghanistan?"

"No, sir. Their mission was the third combat mission. The unit flew two combat missions on the night of April 7th."

"Did the crews discuss and share techniques for conducting low visibility approaches in the high altitude and low visibility environment in Afghanistan?" I asked.

"Yes, sir. As a group, we discussed techniques and procedures for conducting low visibility approaches at high altitude landing zones. We talked about the performance of the aircraft at the higher altitudes, and especially with the winds and the dark area that Afghanistan is, even when there is light out there, it just seems to be an unusually dark place. We talked about those things to make sure we considered ideas or changes to our procedures in order to conduct the mission as safely as possible."

Schultz then detailed the procedures the crews used in performing an approach in an environment where visibility with the ground was limited due to weather, fog, rain, darkness, or dust.

"Where were you on the night of the accident?" I asked.

"Sir, I was in the operations center watching the mission on a monitor. Initially, I saw the dirt cloud when the lead aircraft touched down. Seconds later, it became obvious the lead airplane had crashed. I immediately had a brief discussion with the Army commander at the joint operations center. He was already busy coordinating an effort to send a MH-47 Chinook helicopter to the crash site and asked me to fly to the scene as part of the Combat Search and Rescue (CSAR) team on the MH-47."

"Can you describe the crash site when you arrived?"

"Yes, sir. I sat in the jump seat, behind the two pilots. I had a good view of the area as we flew in. There were mountains off to the distance, but the area where the crash occurred was flat. We landed about three hundred meters to the northeast of the crash site. The left wing was still on fire as I departed the helicopter and walked toward the crashed airplane. It was upside down. The right wing had separated and was lying parallel to the fuselage. Two HH-60 rescue helicopters had landed thirty meters to the northwest of the crash site and were taking on litters bearing the injured and the dead. As I walked to the front of the airplane, I noticed the pilot (Maj Voas) and the flight engineer (SMSgt Lackey) had just been removed from the airplane. They were lying in the dirt about a foot from where their crew station would be."

"How were you able to identify the two crew members?" I asked.

"Sir, their name tags and faces."

"Did you walk the path of the aircraft from the spot where it touched down to where it came to rest?" I asked.

"Yes, sir. I walked the path with the senior Combat Search and Rescue non-commissioned officer. We walked to the spot where we thought the airplane initially impacted the ground. We walked along the airplane's path and commented to each other, attempting to recreate what we thought had happened. He took photographs and noted coordinates on his notepad. We could identify the main landing gear touchdown scars in the dirt and observed what appeared to be some nose gear marks. I kept looking for the nose gear, but never found it. We walked all the way to where the aircraft had stopped. There were lots of small fragments of the airplane along the way. A few of the recognizable pieces were the airplane windscreen and a pilot's seat."

"Once you made your way back to the airplane, what did you do?"

"Sir, I clarified who was killed in the crash. There were several radio calls made early after the crash that misidentified who was killed. I radioed back to Kandahar to ensure they had the right names. I spent about thirty to forty-five minutes going through the aircraft and securing weapons, ammunition, classified equipment, and documents. I gathered as much of the crew's equipment as possible. I got their survival vests, helmets, and oxygen masks. I also removed the Data Transfer Module (DTM)[11] from its cradle. CSAR personnel helped me cut cables to the flare buckets, just to make sure we did not have any inadvertent discharges. I pulled equipment off the airplane and placed it on a litter that I set aside. When I was finished removing equipment from the airplane, I had someone help me carry the litter to the MH-47 and flew back to Kandahar. Upon arrival, I coordinated for some of the unit personnel to help me transport the equipment to a storage bin and locked it up."

"As you departed the crash site, were you aware of the decision to bomb the Osprey, rather than recover it?" I asked.

"Yes, sir. I was aware of that decision."

"Who made that decision?"

"Sir, the Army Task Force Commander conferred with Higher Headquarters (HHQ) [in Kabul]. He basically told the Headquarters there was not much left of the airplane, that it was just a piece of metal. He was told to evacuate everyone off the crash site. He told me HHQ decided the area was too dangerous to leave personnel at the site to guard the wreckage, so they decided to destroy it. I told him I had secured all classified and crew equipment from the airplane. I had no problem with the decision, as I did not think there was much left to try to recover."

"Do you know when the site was bombed?"

---

11 DTM - Hand-held electronic device allowing crews to load flight planned data into the aircraft navigation systems

"Sir, it was about four hours after the crash occurred. Four bombs were dropped on the wreckage by two U.S. Air Force A-10 fighter airplanes. The wreckage was reported as 'destroyed' by the fighter pilots."

"Two more questions," I said. "I know you have been on the email chain discussing the confusion on whether or not the CV-22 was delivered with a flight information recorder installed. Do you have anything to add to the discussion? Did you happen to remove the flight information recorder from the Osprey?"

"Sir, I have nothing to add to the discussion. Our flight manuals will be updated with the correct information as soon as possible. When I went to the crash site that night, I was under the impression there was no flight information recorder installed."

With the interview complete, Lt Col Schultz stood, saluted, and departed the conference room.

While the team gathered notes and packed equipment, I took Winsett and O'Leary aside. "That was enlightening. He had a unique perspective of the rescue and recovery effort. Photos were taken of the ground markings at the accident site. We need to find the person who took the pictures. We need those photos," I said.

"One thing struck me as strange, maybe borderline bizarre," I continued. "You tell me. Did either of you notice anything peculiar about his demeanor when I asked about the flight information recorder?"

O'Leary and Winsett exchanged glances.

"I didn't see anything," O'Leary said. "But maybe I was taking notes at that instant."

I looked to Winsett. "What about you?"

"Sir, I'm used to reading witnesses when I question them," Winsett said. "I didn't notice anything. Tell me what you're talking about."

"When I asked the flight information recorder questions … I swear he smirked."

Winsett smiled and nodded. "Oh yeah, I did see that."

CHAPTER FIFTEEN

ACCIDENT INVESTIGATION BOARD MEMBERS

Inconsistencies in the testimony of Lt Col Schultz gnawed at me for the remainder of the day. More than the testimony itself, the fact that an officer might contrive facts for any other reason than the absolute truth bothered me more than the mystery surrounding the flight information recorder. I kept a personal journal where I penned a reminder of questions to ask maintenance personnel at both Hurlburt Field and Kandahar Air Base concerning flight information recorder data.

The office buzzed with activity as we prepared forms to be used in the transfer of evidence gathered by the safety board. Throughout each day, hardcopies of papers relating to the accident and our investigation passed over our desks. In order to keep the information organized we made a large vertical file holder and labeled the files "A" to "JJ," representing tabs required for the final Accident Investigation Board report. Each board member would be responsible for writing information, as required by regulations, for each tab of the report.

As I looked around the room, I reflected on how much time we had already spent together. Normally, after spending a few days with a group, certain dynamics would separate the group into factions. But this group defied all odds and dynamics. Everyone got along very well. There was a common mutual respect for each person, regardless of rank, and whether male or female. Everyone was totally dedicated to the job we had been assigned. All were extremely hard workers and skilled team players.

Winsett, who had become my willing ramrod … foreman … adjutant, of sorts, seldom worked at his desk for long without getting up and walking to garner the assistance of other team members. Many mornings, he would wake up early to run a mile or two and was still one of the first to arrive at the office. Winsett saved me countless hours during our first three weeks together. I made decisions of importance and he intercepted and dealt with mundane matters before they reached my desk. Truly a superb officer by all measures. He spent most of his time conferring with Capt Kelly concerning legal aspects of our investigation. He ordered the pace of our activities, and she carried the load of coordinating and scheduling interviews, travel and transfer of information from the safety board to the accident board.

Kelly hadn't buddied-up with anyone on the team, choosing instead to spend what little personal time she had staying in touch with her husband and three young daughters. Being assigned to the board could not have come at a worse time in her personal life. She had recently returned from a tour in Iraq with little time to recover from the demanding deployment before being assigned to the accident board. She dedicated her attention to business almost to a fault with a characteristic good cheer I deemed impossible to sustain. But, she did. She brought an air of happiness wherever she went. Her desk sat beside TSgt Nichole Adams, who, in addition to being the board's recorder, helped to coordinate transportation and any other duties assigned. Both were tireless workers. They never complained about anything.

Adams had acted as recorder for prior accident investigations and I imagine she had recorded more depositions and testimonies than both our attorneys had taken combined. She excelled in her work. Though her duties on previous boards had been confined to recording and transcription, I insisted everyone should have the opportunity to question our witnesses. While Winsett and Kelly ensured we asked the entire list of previously approved questions, Adams saved her unscripted inquiries for the end of each interview. She read nuances of incomplete answers and body language like no one else on the board. She was funny, smart, and always a joy to have around. She worked long hours and never asked for assistance dealing with her heavy recording equipment or maintaining supplies in the office. No task seemed too daunting for her. She also brought a mood of positive energy to the office. MSgt Dolan was always there to assist her with the bulky equipment brought to each interview. When we vacated a venue, he ensured no one had to wait for Adams, by immediately packing up her gear and carrying what he could to the van.

A week into our investigation, Dolan gave us the most valuable piece of information we collected – the flight information recorder was installed on all Air Force Ospreys. Though we had yet to make the discovery pay, we held out hope that if it didn't surface in wreckage recovered by the safety board, we would find the recorder intact when we arrived at Kandahar. Whenever we traveled, he always drove one of the vehicles while the rest of us busied ourselves with clerical work. I don't remember him taking a break to visit the barber shop. I assumed he kept clippers in his quarters and used the appropriate attachment to maintain his close-clipped hair. It always looked freshly cut. The only member of the team to do so, he kept his battle dress uniform (BDU) starched and pressed to Marine Corps specs. He and Doc Harper made sure their desks were placed beside one another. They seemed inseparable - in or out of the office.

Considering they were seldom seen without a hand-held device, I assumed the two shared an interest in certain video games. Time pressures placed on their typical day being less than most other members, they had time to engage in what sometimes could be raucous jocularity that Winsett or I had to stifle, on occasion, for the sake of office harmony.

Harper preferred being called "Doc," as opposed to "Lieutenant Colonel." He was a cordial gentleman, without the typical unapproachable demeanor of many doctors. He had a great sense of humor and was highly intelligent. He would ask fascinating questions during staff meetings and interviews. Being assigned to Hurlburt had shortened the line in a long-distance relationship he struggled to maintain from his assigned base in Clovis, New Mexico, since his girlfriend lived near Atlanta, Georgia. Board members seeking remedies for a cold or minor injury suffered at the gym, sought out Harper's advice without hesitation.

While Harper kept our staff physically healthy, TSgt Scott kept our office machines running without a minute of down time. After he set up our workspace, computers, and the snack bar, he made sure all ran to perfection. At the end of each day, he transferred information from our white boards to PowerPoint™ slides and made timestamped photos before erasing our day's work. He, too, was very keen and added great ideas during our daily discussions. No matter what the task, he would salute smartly and get it done. He was always one of my favorite non-commissioned officers at the headquarters office and was very happy to have him on the team.

I had more in common with O'Leary, a fellow aviator, than anyone else on the board. I cannot remember knowing anyone more even tempered. In appearance, his close-cut blond hair, Irish blue eyes, and slight build, more resembled an Olympic marathon runner than a combat pilot. I never underestimated his intelligence, character, or resolve. He always worked hard. Usually the second to arrive each morning, he always had coffee brewed before most of the team walked in the door. There were times when he would be fuming mad, yet he never raised his voice above a conversational level. He would have to tell me later he had been angry. He smiled often but it was rare to hear him laugh aloud. He earned the respect and admiration of the entire investigation team from the first day they met him. He is the one guy I would want to have with me in any combat situation. Nothing rattled him. He was an exceptional problem solver.

Every member of the board possessed an individual and collective sense of duty. Our group could not have functioned without it. We made what time we could in our schedule to accommodate visits from family members who found the time to visit Florida. No one took advantage of the time, nor did anyone place anything above our assigned mission to complete the accident investigation.

I flipped the page of my personal journal to the following day of May 12, 2010. I penned a note at the bottom of my substantial "to do" list. I hoped the safety board evidence being turned over to us would shed light on whether the accident was in fact caused by pilot error as reported by a number of news outlets. I was anxious to see evidence if it really was true. May 12th could be the most important day of the entire accident investigation. The safety board evidence could solve the mystery of why the accident occurred. I did not sleep well on the night of May 11th.

CHAPTER SIXTEEN

EVIDENCE TRANSFER

On Wednesday, May 12th, the team arrived at the office well before 7:30 a.m. Since we had blocked the day to transfer evidence from the safety investigation board to the accident investigation board, everyone grabbed coffee and waited for the phone call that would start the process. After a short meeting to cover the protocol involved in the transfer, most of us caught up with emails and waited in anticipation.

At 9:30 a.m. Winsett conferred with the safety board's legal representative and obtained the green light. He drove one of our vans to the 1st Special Operations Wing safety office where the transfer would occur. I absented myself from the actual transfer, to avoid a chance meeting with the safety board president and the appearance of clouding our two independent investigations. I remained at my desk and monitored the flow of evidence as it was transferred and delivered to our office.

Winsett signed for every piece of recording and snippet of paper amassed by the safety board. Once transferred, Dolan would place it in boxes and drive it to our office. Kelly maintained an inventory log as the material came through the door. Once I saw what we had, it was distributed to the appropriate members of the accident investigation team for review. I hoped Part One of the safety board report would be made available early in the process, but suspected the safety board would make changes, and updates, right to the end and release it last.

Doc Harper collected medical and dental records, along with autopsies of those killed in the accident. O'Leary piled transcripts on his desk and immediately started plowing through the thick stacks of paper.

When we received a box of aircraft wreckage, Scott took Dolan's place running back and forth to the safety office, while Dolan evaluated debris from the aircraft.

Dolan stood at his desk staring into a near empty cardboard box about the size of a countertop microwave.

"Is there any more from the airplane than what I see?" I asked.

Dolan lifted a mangled length of stainless-steel fuel line from the box. "Anything not classified is in this box. Lt Col Winsett signed for each piece."

He handed me the fuel line and pointed to small pieces of composite material. It was a piece of the aircraft skin, about the size of half a large pizza. It was gray on the outside and black on the inside, torn ragged like a flap twisted from the top of a cardboard box.

"Lucky I was there. The person handing it over didn't know what it was or that it was very hazardous. In this state, these pieces should be encapsulated," Dolan commented.

Using the length of fuel line, I poked at the two or three pieces lying in the bottom of the carton.

"Sir … that stuff is dangerous," said Dolan. "The composite material sheds tiny airborne particles that are highly toxic. I should seal this box immediately."

I stepped away and handed the tubing to Dolan. He put everything back and covered the box with two large garbage bags and tied them closed.

"I'll make sure this is taken care of, sir," said Dolan.

"I haven't seen the maintenance records or the download from the VSLED[12]," I said. "Has anyone seen information about engine performance or notes from the safety board referring to records they recovered?"

"Any notes about anti-icing or coanda** valves?" asked O'Leary.

12' VSLED (Vibration Structural Life and Engine Diagnostics) – Monitors engine parameters and vibration.

** Coanda Valve – Bleeds air off engine compressor to deflect exhaust to prevent burn damage to objects on the ground.

"If either of those valves were open, it could account for a loss of power at low altitude," said Dolan. "Did the safety board ever tell you how or why they collected these particular pieces of the aircraft?"

"No," answered Kelly. "They interviewed Lt Col Schultz and asked why he recovered the parts. He told the safety board his primary job was to protect and recover classified equipment. It's beyond me why these items were recovered from the site. There is a note saying when the safety board arrived in Afghanistan, one of the maintenance troops gave them this box of parts. I'll email Lt Col Winsett and have him ask a few more questions about the container. Strange assortment, I agree."

When the arrival of evidence slowed to a trickle, I stepped to my desk. Capt Kelly had left me a list of witnesses interviewed by the safety board, an inventory of classified items not included in the transfer, and ten cassette tapes.

"Sir, Lt Col O'Leary has hardcopies of the safety board interviews," said Kelly. "The remaining interviews are recorded on cassette tapes. They either didn't have time, or take the time, to transcribe them."

The tapes, rubber-banded together, were each inscribed with the date, time of the interview, and name of the person being deposed.

"Adams has a feel for this," I said. "Have her listen to these and make notes. Don't waste time transcribing unless she finds something important. If she has questions about testimony, she can confer with O'Leary."

I piled through the burgeoning stack of paper on my desk. By my arithmetic, the safety investigation board conducted a total of seventeen interviews and took statements from an additional twelve people that included the eight crewmembers (four in each of the other two airplanes) flying in the Osprey formation the night of the accident. They also gave us statements recorded from two of the surviving Rangers. I had no idea why they had recovered a seemingly meaningless collection of wreckage, or why no one on the safety board visited the accident site. If the safety board had arrived at a conclusion for what caused the accident, I saw nothing in my cursory inspection of the information given to us that indicated what it might be.

Absent from their list of personnel interviewed were the two crew-members who survived the crash – the copilot and the tail scanner. To date we had conducted fourteen interviews, which included the copilot, and planned a very ambitious schedule once we arrived at Kandahar. My list of potential interviews neared a hundred personnel.

Late morning the following day, we took custody of the last pieces of information, which included the much-anticipated Part One of the safety board report. They conducted their out-briefing with the AFSOC Commander on the afternoon of May 13th. The safety board members immediately departed Hurlburt Field to return to their jobs at various Air Forces bases and the Pentagon.

As paperwork flowed to our office, I continued to look for the "golden nugget" of information definitively identifying the cause of the accident. It continued to elude me, and the other accident board members. Dolan found maintenance data indicating the "health" of the accident airplane's engines on April 7th – one day prior to the accident. Measured against a brand-new engine direct from the factory operating at 100%, the left engine indicated an engine performance percentage (EPP) of 98.47%, and the right engine 95.83%. At 95% EPP, the engine would have been identified, and sched-uled by maintenance personnel to be taken off the airplane and replaced with a new or rebuilt engine. Both engines had performed at an acceptable level prior to the flight on April 8th, but maintenance records indicated the engine air particle separator (EAPS) on the right engine failed for a min-ute and a half while on the ground during a dirt landing on the morning of April 7th. A failed EAPS would usually cause an engine EPP to degrade more quickly than normal. The right engine could have been at, or below, the 95% EPP level, requiring the engine to be removed and replaced prior to the April 8th flight.

Frustrated but optimistic, we continued to conduct interviews and pore over safety investigation board evidence for another week. Late one evening, Winsett, O'Leary and I were working late in the office. As we cleaned our desks and prepared to depart, O'Leary suddenly called out to us.

"Sir, you have to see this," O'Leary said. "We must have missed something in the safety board's information. A news article written by Jamie McIntyre just popped up online and it's stating the Osprey accident in Afghanistan was caused by pilot error."

The headline alone raised the hairs on my neck.

"What does it say?" I asked.

"It says a person close to, or involved with, the accident is blaming the accident on pilot error," said O'Leary.

"Do you think the safety board leaked information?" I asked. "This is going to send a shock wave through the command. I wouldn't be surprised if this leads to someone getting court-martialed."

Jamie McIntyre, *War Magazine Online*, May15, 2010, Exclusive:
First V-22 Combat Crash Likely "Pilot Error"

> *An investigation of the crash of an Air Force Special Operations CV-22 Osprey in Afghanistan last month has concluded the pilot of the tilt-rotor aircraft flew too close to the ground, striking an earthen berm. The final report is likely to blame the mishap on pilot error, because the evidence suggests the V-22 was flying at a high speed, at very low altitude, in airplane mode, with its massive rotors perpendicular to the ground when it struck the berm. A source says the force of the impact sheared off both engines [nacelles] and both wings before the plane flipped over.[6]*

CHAPTER SEVENTEEN

ACCIDENT BOARD TRAVELS TO AFGHANISTAN

With a few keystrokes O'Leary sent the article to the printer.

"Three hard copies are coming to you."

Winsett handed me one, then sat at the closest desk. We read in silence.

O'Leary was the first to finish reading. He leaned back in his chair and looked at Winsett.

"I agree. Someone should hang for this, if it's true. From a legal standpoint, what do you think?"

"That's up to the General," said Winsett. "Are you considering taking this to the commander, sir?"

"I'd like nothing better than to see some weasel squirm in front of the AFSOC leaders for leaking very classified safety board information," I said. "But what if the weasel is the AFSOC commander or vice commander? What then?"

"He fires you and we start over with a new accident board president having invested three weeks in this endeavor," Winsett said.

I filed a copy of the article in the vertical folder marked, "Tab EE, Media," to be included in our final accident report.

"He could fire me anyway, regardless of who leaked the information. In either case, we risk the appearance of interfering in an investigation that might compromise our own. If AFSOC's interested, it's their duty to plug the leak, not ours. We can't change that. Besides, we have our own job to do, and as repugnant as the article might be, it's a minor distraction."

"I agree," Winsett said.

"Me, too," responded O'Leary. "From the interviews I've read so far, nothing points to pilot error as the cause of the accident."

"Let's call it a day and hit it fresh tomorrow," I said.

I slept little that night. I couldn't put away the fact that someone, probably an officer, had leaked classified information to the press. I would wait to see what response emerged from the command. With little or no reaction from AFSOC it would appear the source might be someone at a high level.

The wonderful aroma of fresh-brewed coffee welcomed me as I entered our building the next morning. TSgt Adams must have seen me on the sidewalk outside and greeted me at the door.

"Good morning, sir. I have news."

"What is it? Did Lt Col O'Leary find the cause of the accident and we're being released from the investigation?" I said kiddingly.

"No, sir … nothing like that," she answered with a puzzled look.

She looked disappointed. I didn't mean to appear flippant, but she might have taken it that way.

"Then what is it? I'm excited for any news, as long as it isn't bad."

"We have seats on the rotator departing Baltimore the night of May 17th. Capt Kelly has the transportation office working commercial reservations to get us to Baltimore."

"That's great," I said. "We have two items on the agenda for today's meeting – our events for today and preparations for travel to Afghanistan."

Once everyone arrived at the office, the room buzzed with the excitement of the pending trip to Afghanistan - the heart of our accident investigation.

"Good morning, everyone," I said. "We will be on the rotator departing Baltimore at 10:00 p.m. Monday night. This morning we'll confirm our commercial travel to Baltimore. Does anyone have any questions about the mobility gear, or other requirements as we prepare for travel?"

Everyone replied, "No, sir."

"In order to save money while we're out of the country, the command has asked us to check out of our rooms. The only reservation we will keep while away is for my room. We'll use it to store all the items we'll not be taking. You can drop anything Sunday night or very early Monday morning. Since TSgt Scott will not be traveling with us, he'll coordinate transportation to get us to the Valparaiso Airport. Plan on a normal schedule tomorrow, but since we've been at it for twenty-one days straight, we'll take one day off to get ready for the trip. Monday will be a long travel day, so rest up."

We concluded the morning meeting with a discussion concerning the abundance of information we had received from the safety board and the possibility of confidential safety investigation information being compromised by sharing findings with news outlets. Despite the absence of evidence indicating pilot error, aviation magazines continued publishing articles attributing the accident to controlled flight into terrain (CFIT). The crew, they asserted – "accidentally" hit the ground.

Before departing Florida, we coordinated interview times with the 8th SOS crews and maintenance personnel still in Afghanistan. Since both the Rangers and the flight crews worked at night, we planned our workday to coincide with theirs – beginning at 4:00 p.m. each afternoon and finishing at 7:00 a.m. the following morning.

On Monday, May 17th, we departed Ft. Walton Beach to fly to Baltimore, Maryland. After a seven-hour layover in Baltimore, our rotator departed as scheduled at 10:00 p.m. for the long journey across the Atlantic Ocean to Ramstein Air Base, Germany. During the flight, I read through a stack of articles and newspapers I had brought along. An article in the *New York Times* grabbed my attention. It chronicled the reasons a greater number of Special Operations personnel were being sent into Kandahar, and why the CV-22s were, perhaps, being rushed into the war.

Thom Shanker, Helene Cooper, Richard A. Oppel Jr., *New York Times,* April 25, 2010, **Elite U.S. Units Step Up Effort in Afghan City Before Attack**

> *Small bands of elite American Special Operations forces have been operating with increased intensity for several*

weeks in Kandahar, southern Afghanistan's largest city, picking up or picking off insurgent leaders to weaken the Taliban in advance of major operations, senior administration and military officials say.

The battle for Kandahar has become the make-or-break offensive of the eight-and-a-half-year war. The question is whether military force, softened with appeals to the local populace, can overcome a culture built on distrust of outsiders, including foreign forces and even neighboring tribes.

[Alissa J. Rubin contributed reporting from Kabul.] [7]

Mid-afternoon we landed and deplaned at Aviano Air Base, Italy. We stretched our legs for the two hours it took to refuel and change out flight crew members. After re-boarding we continued our east-bound flight with the sun setting behind us. In between naps, I picked O'Leary's brain about the CV-22, its propulsion systems and procedures.

Nine hours later, we finally started our descent. As I peered out the airplane window, a sea of sand materialized. Though I'd seen the landscape many times, the enormity of the unforgiving desert seemed beautiful from seven miles overhead. The jet made a couple of turns during which Al Udeid Air Base, near Doha, Qatar came into view. From my vantage the modern brick buildings, military vehicles, swimming pools, and paved streets looked like any Air Force base in the United States. Al Udeid Air Base hosted more than ten thousand Americans, one hundred Qatari Air Force, and numerous support personnel. Aside from the expanse of desert sand, the base seemed comparable to the beautiful base at Hurlburt Field.

We landed on schedule, grabbed our carry-ons, and left our checked bags on the pallet for a forklift to pick up and carry to the customs building. Military and local officials checked our passports, immunization, and training records. At the end of the line, we were each handed a map of the base and a ration card.

"What's this?" TSgt Adams asked.

"As a rule, alcohol is forbidden in Middle Eastern countries," Capt Kelly said. "On this base it's allowed with restrictions – two beers per person, per day. Wherever beer is permitted, a bartender will 'X' off a block on your ration card. After two 'X's', you're done until the following day."

"What's to prevent me from buying a beer using someone else's card?" Adams said.

"You've worked with attorneys too long," Kelly replied. "It's the system, just not a perfect one. Most appreciate the perk and wouldn't risk losing the privilege."

Beyond the reception area, customs and immigration officers divided us into two groups. An NCO accompanied personnel being assigned to Al Udeid to an area where they were processed to become part of the base population. Passengers like us, passing through the base while on our way to other locations, were directed elsewhere. A USAF travel coordinator collected copies of our orders and confirmed our final destination for travel.

"Sir, you and your team are scheduled to depart on a C-130 tomorrow afternoon at 4:00 p.m. Base transportation will pick you up at your quarters two-and-a-half hours prior to departure. Processing for your flight will include issue of body armor, weapons, and ammunition prior to boarding your flight. Once you've gathered your gear, proceed out the door to your left. You'll find a bus that'll see you to your quarters. The driver has the keys to your assigned rooms. Welcome to Al Udeid."

We boarded the bus with all our gear stacked on seats at the back area. While traveling to our rooms, we agreed on a time to meet at the recreation area to decompress with food and perhaps a cold beer.

I dropped my bags inside the door to my room, one of eight such duplex-like apartments clustered in the area. Centered in each group of buildings an open patio with two tables and chairs sat amid a lush, manicured landscape. I quickly changed into running shorts and a t-shirt and walked the half-mile to the center of the base. Beneath the red sunset, the roar of military aircraft arriving and departing the self-proclaimed, "Gateway to the Middle East" punctuated the otherwise peaceful evening.

When I arrived, most of the team members were already there and had commandeered a table under a large tent-like structure. Fast food trucks and trailers provided meals while two bars served drinks.

"We arrived on a good night," O'Leary said. "There is a karaoke contest later."

We passed a pleasant but early evening being spectators, not participants, in the night's program. On the walk back to the billeting area, everyone remarked that their rooms were very modern and comfortable. I could not think of a military base in the United States that was as nice as Al Udeid. The base was beautiful.

The following afternoon, transportation picked us up in front of our billeting rooms for the short ride to the passenger terminal. Except for personal items we carried aboard the aircraft, all other bags and gear were loaded onto pallets marked "Kandahar Air Base – Afghanistan." We made our way through the terminal to the tables where we had checked in a day earlier. The same people went through their departure checklists for each of us. Representatives from the base armory issued each of us combat gear to don prior to arrival in Afghanistan. After processing, we were directed to a waiting area.

Each of us wore helmets, Kevlar (bullet-proof) vests, and carried a weapon – 9mm pistol for officers, and M-16 rifles for enlisted and NCOs. In addition to our personal baggage, we also carried a canvas duffle-type bag containing chemical warfare gear. We appreciated the requirement of being issued combat gear but looked forward to disencumbering ourselves from the added weight, baggage and responsibility. O'Leary told us when we returned to Al Udeid to board our return flight to the United States, we would be able to leave all the extra combat gear. He also cautioned us to take care of the equipment while in our possession since it would be carefully inventoried.

The transportation sergeant approached us as we were relaxing in the waiting area.

"Sir, your C-130 is ready for you and your team. Please grab your gear and follow me."

We walked about two hundred yards across the flight line where the loadmaster met us at the C-130 crew entrance door.

"Welcome aboard, sir. We only have twenty-two passengers, so there is plenty of room in the cargo compartment for everyone, and your extra gear. Make sure everyone has ear plugs, because it will get noisy when the flight engineer starts the auxiliary power unit. Go ahead and take a seat … I will follow the last person and give all of you a briefing once seated."

For over thirty years I had flown many different models of the C-130. The airplane, its smell, sounds, appearance, and the passenger process rekindled fond memories of missions that had taken me around the globe more than once.

We chose seats and allowed extra space to spread out during the four-hour flight. The active duty flight crew based at Little Rock, Arkansas, offered me one of the two seats in the cockpit, a courtesy often accorded senior officers, but I chose to ride in back with the team. They were gracious enough to invite members of our group to visit the flight deck for brief periods during the flight.

After takeoff, we made a turn to parallel the Persian Gulf for one more look at the expansive Al Udeid base. Our course followed the Persian Gulf southeast past Iran, across the Gulf of Oman, then turned north across Pakistan and direct to Kandahar, Afghanistan.

Toward the end of our flight, I awoke to the sound of the flaps and landing gear being extended. We descended into total darkness; no lights illuminated on the airplane, or on the ground.

I looked at O'Leary, "Sure is dark down there."

"Bad guys attack the base almost every night. Darkness is the best defense for the base against a visually launched rocket or mortar."

The C-130 landed and taxied for nearly a mile to get to the ramp area. Once the airplane stopped, the engines were shut down and the doors were opened. Two forklifts slowly approached the back of the airplane to off-load pallets as the loadmaster gave hand signals to the driver. All the passengers exited from the crew entrance door at the front of the airplane and were immediately greeted by an awful stench in the air.

"Oh my God, is that gas … do we need our chemical warfare masks … or is this the way Afghanistan smells?" TSgt Adams said as she pinched her nose in disgust.

Since O'Leary had been stationed at this base for over a year, I looked to him for the answer.

"Not all of Afghanistan smells like this," he said. "Welcome to Kandahar, home of the world-famous poo-pond."

CHAPTER EIGHTEEN

KANDAHAR AIR BASE

Kandahar, the sprawling air base in southern Afghanistan, hosts military units from the United States, Britain, France, Netherlands, and other allied countries from around the world. Miles of barren real estate contained by more than ten miles of perimeter fortifications and a buffer zone with another fence, secure the base from direct enemy assault, but provide little protection from nightly mortar and rocket attacks.

From the air, the most impressive features of the base are the airfield and the civilian terminal where the Taliban made their final stand against coalition forces. The plethora of temporary and semi-permanent structures serve as work areas and living quarters for the military base residents. The most famous, but least popular, area of the base is the poo-pond.

The crew and passengers familiar with Kandahar paid little or no attention to the stench defiling the night air and flooding our olfactory senses. Those of us experiencing it for the first time covered our faces and did everything possible to avoid throwing up.

"What *is* that smell?" Someone from outside our group said as they exited the airplane.

"Smells like raw sewage," Doc Harper said.

O'Leary continued to explain, "The Doc's right. It is raw sewage. It originates from a cesspool the size of a small lake in the middle of the base where all the human waste is collected. Constructed to accommodate a population of ten thousand, the pond is stretched to the limits to accommodate sewage of more than twice the population it was designed for. Maybe engineers who constructed the first installment of the base placed it on the perimeter and the base grew around the sewage facility. Once it had been constructed, they couldn't move it. Sometimes wind provides temporary relief, but there is always a putrid stench that permeates everything. I hope our quarters aren't directly across the dirt road in front of the pond.

The view isn't pleasant either. For anyone who's interested, I'll give you a tour."

"Do you ever get used to the smell?" I asked.

"Nope. You just learn to deal with it."

We assembled behind the aircraft while an airman from transportation driving the forklift set the pallet with our bags onto the tarmac. The aircraft loadmaster removed the straps securing our gear, and we separated our stuff from what remained on the pallet.

The airman killed the engine and stepped off the desert-painted diesel. "Welcome to Kandahar, sir. Major William Smith and TSgt Kim Brinkley from the base legal office are on their way."

Before I could thank him, the major and an NCO approached me with hands extended. We exchanged greetings and introductions.

"Sir, it's great to meet you," said Maj Smith. "We'll host you and your team while you're here."

"Maj Smith, how do we remove our bags and gear from the flight line?" I asked.

"Sir, we have three vans for your use while you're here … should be along any minute," he said as he looked over his shoulder.

As if on cue, three vehicles caravanned onto the flight line. Except for a small horizontal slit, the headlights like every other vehicle in Kandahar, were mostly covered with tape. The lack of light on the base slowed flight line operations to a crawl. Part of the price paid to keep the enemy from having an easy shot at a vehicle, airplane, or group of personnel.

Maj Smith explained we would be driven to our rooms to drop our bags. He had arranged offices and a conference room where we would work and conduct interviews.

"When do you plan to start?" asked Smith

"Tonight," Capt Kelly replied.

Maj Smith checked his watch.

"Okay, we'll get you to your quarters. Drop your gear in your rooms then we'll drive you to one of the dining halls so you can enjoy a meal before you start a long night of work. Each of the North Atlantic Treaty Organization (NATO) countries operates their own dining hall so you'll find a variety of great food."

Army and NATO forces in High Mobility Multipurpose Wheeled Vehicles (HMMWV – commonly called Humvees or Hummers), Interim Armored Vehicles (IAV), Stryker Armored Fighting Vehicles, M3 Bradley Cavalry Fighting Vehicles, and M113 Armored Personnel Carriers crowded the dirt roads on their way off base for the night's missions. The congestion slowed our progress to a crawl. Dirt from the hundreds of knobbed tires trailed each vehicle and spewed enough dust to obliterate the night sky. Driving against the flow of traffic toward the center of the base further slowed our movement as we had to pull over and stop multiple times to allow wide vehicles to pass as they rushed to exit the base.

The van driver stopped at a corner with no street names, just signs pointing toward base landmarks, one pointing to the gym, and another pointing to the base recreation area - the Boardwalk.

The driver turned and handed me a manila envelope.

"Sir, your room is behind the wall to the left of us. Here's the key to your room … room number four. I'll take the lieutenant colonels to their quarters and be back to pick you up in fifteen minutes."

The deafening roar of dozens of diesel engines spewed exhaust into the air. The smell of diesel fuel and dust lessened the pungent odor of the poo-pond. I navigated a maze of sandbags in front of the building and opened the door into a hallway lit by four exposed light bulbs hanging from the ceiling.

I was comforted by enough light to see numbers written with a black marker on each door. Carrying three bags and wearing combat gear with a pistol on my hip, I labored past door number five and dropped my bags outside room four. I blew an exhausted breath and for the first time this trip, deemed I might be getting too old for this. Though I thought myself as fit as someone much younger, my body reminded me of my age.

I opened the door and flipped a wall switch illuminating a single naked bulb suspended from the center of the ceiling. Once inside, I shed my combat gear. I took a few minutes to gather my senses and resolve while sitting on one of the two sets of bunk beds. The room had unpainted cinder block walls, a cement floor and two unpainted wood closets. Primitive by hotel standards, but pure luxury by deployment standards. I was very pleased with my accommodations.

With my flight suit soaked in sweat and infused with layers of desert dust, I walked back out into the hallway searching for a latrine. Down the hall at the opposite end of the building, I located indoor facilities with three toilets, two showers, and three sinks. When I had deployed for Desert Shield/Desert Storm in 1990, I was a newly promoted Major. I lived in a tent, with nine other officers, several hundred feet from a latrine. This seemed like the Hilton in comparison.

I washed my hands and face and returned to my room for my gear. I donned my sand goggles and helmet, locked the room, and stepped into the night where combat vehicles wound their way through the base. Within minutes, a van pulled up and stopped. I paused for a moment shining my flashlight on the exterior of the vehicle then got in.

"This van is green with pink daisy decals," I said. "Not very military, I'd say."

"Sorry, sir, we get vehicles where we can. This one might have come from missionaries who left town or somewhere farther away. I don't know. You'll see a great variety of cars, trucks and vans on this base. Runs good though."

In the rear of the van, Doc Harper, Winsett and O'Leary chuckled.

"I'm not complaining, trust me," I said. "I'm glad to have dedicated transportation."

I looked over the seat. "Hey Doc, how do you like our wheels?"

"I love it," he said. "I'd like to work a deal to ship it home if possible … it'd make a statement driving around Cannon Air Force Base … provide a little color to an otherwise drab surrounding, wouldn't you agree?"

I smiled and said, "It definitely would. Where are we on our schedule?"

"We'll meet the rest of the team at the dining facility (DFAC)," O'Leary said. "We will be here long enough to try all of them. Tonight, we'll go to the North Line DFAC specializing in American food."

"Sounds good to me," I said. "Do the others know to meet us there?"

"Yes, sir, I talked to them a few minutes ago. They're five to ten minutes behind us. Their quarters are farther away."

We parked in a dirt lot outside the DFAC. Everything in Kandahar; the streets, the easements, everything except the poo-pond, was dirt. Walking toward the dining hall, O'Leary pointed to concrete blocks stacked along the walls arranged in a zig-zag pattern. The stacked blocks enforced with sandbags formed a path to the building. As we navigated the path, O'Leary turned and smiled at us.

"All the best restaurants on base have these rocket barriers," he said.

We'd been together for a while but not long enough for everyone to totally understand O'Leary's keen, but dry, sense of humor.

A double wall of sandbags protected the front door. It resembled the entrance to an igloo. Once inside, the bright lights made us squint. Open twenty-four hours, the modern facility served hot meals, sandwiches, and salad along with an exhaustive choice of non-alcoholic beverages. Accustomed to a round-the-clock combat workday, the staff served good food in a clean facility with enviable efficiency. American forces mingled with troops of other nationalities; everyone with a weapon on their belt or slung over their shoulder. The scene, in cosmic contrast to what we had left in Baltimore forty-eight hours earlier, reminded us we were in a zone unfathomable to anyone without the experience.

We finished our dinner and headed back into the dark and dusty night to meet up with our driver.

"Sir, it was great to meet you and your team. We'll check with you in the morning to make sure you have everything you need for tomorrow evening. One last thing ... if the base should come under attack, the

119

nearest rocket shelter is across the street and to the left of the small building. There's a dim red light above the entrance to the shelter."

"Yes, I see it," I said. "Thanks for coordinating our arrival and seeing to our needs. You've made our job easier. Have a good night. We'll see you in the morning."

We walked up a flight of stairs on the outside of the building. At the top, a door opened into a hallway with our workspace and conference room on one side and three small offices on the opposite side of the corridor. We stowed our chemical-warfare bags, combat gear, and weapons in one of the small offices.

Enough metal folding chairs to surround two collapsible rectangle tables in the middle of the room were stacked against one wall. The tabletops had seen considerable use. The paper-thin overlay showed abrasive wear and gouges into the particle board.

Being the first one into the briefing room, Winsett determined where each member would sit while TSgt Adams worked on setting up her recording gear. Kelly entered with our schedule for the evening; an ambitious five interviews with the first being via telephone with an Army medical specialist riding on Osprey number two in the three-ship formation the night of the accident and the first to land at the accident site.

The testimony of the first med-tech on the scene promised a clearer picture of the handling of the injuries in the minutes following the accident. Winsett, O'Leary, and I were also interested in any contemporaneous conversation he might have exchanged with the surviving crewmembers in the chaotic aftermath.

CHAPTER NINETEEN

ACCIDENT SITE MEDIC

The entire second floor space allocated for our use had been vacated except for a rudimentary assortment of furniture. There was a coffee maker, bags of powered creamer and sugar packets, as well as a variety of cereal bars in a small office, one of four on the second floor. Across from the offices was a conference room with three portable tables and ten folding metal chairs. Expecting a long first night, I dispatched O'Leary to the latrine for water to brew a pot of coffee.

He returned and reported that the foul atmosphere in the latrine was creating a commotion with the female members of the accident board. He informed me that having only one restroom with a single toilet for our floor could pose a problem, unless we devised a protocol for sharing the facilities. I met with the team and after a brief negotiation arrived at an acceptable solution.

When I returned to the office, Winsett and O'Leary huddled inside the door snickering and nudging each other with their elbows.

"You handled that well, sir," Winsett said.

"Well done, General," chimed O'Leary with his sly grin.

I shook my head while pouring a cup of coffee. I was pleased they felt comfortable enough around me to tease me. It felt like we were bonding as a team.

"You guys ready to get started?" I asked.

We carried our notebooks to the conference room where Adams had set up her recorder and completed her sound checks. Kelly placed our only phone in the center of the table and called the base operator to coordinate our call to the forward operating base.

"Our first interview is with Staff Sergeant (SSG) Paul Montoya, Alpha Company, Third Battalion, 75th Ranger Regiment," Kelly said. "He's due to rotate back home to the U.S. before we can talk to him in person later this week. He can give us thirty to forty minutes before having to brief for his team's mission tonight."

I leafed through the papers Kelly had set in front of me; the requisite pre-brief items, Montoya's short bio and a list of the questions we expected to ask.

Thus far, we had interviewed survivors of the crash and a few personnel remote or removed in space and time from the accident. The survivors we questioned had recovered from injuries or surgery, and all were under medical care that included varying degrees and doses of pain medications. We considered the testimony of SSG Montoya, one of the first Rangers on scene and the first medic to arrive at the accident site, to be crucial to knowing what happened in the immediate aftermath.

The night of the accident Montoya had been seated mid-ship in the second aircraft flying one mile in-trail. The fireball resulting from the lead Osprey impacting the ground filled the cockpit windscreens of the two Ospreys flying one and two miles in-trail. Unsure the lead had not come under enemy attack, the pilots initiated a go-around and entered an orbit away from the accident site. Both airplanes contacted task force headquarters at Kandahar for instructions and updated intelligence concerning the situation.

The Rangers had expected to land seconds behind their lead, but instead stared at an orange fireball and plumes of black smoke towering over the distant landing zone. In three to four minutes, not much more, their hand-held radios crackled with urgent pleas for help from survivors below. Expecting the pilots to immediately return to the landing zone, they secured themselves for landing.

Rangers, accustomed to running toward the sounds, smells, and pitch of battle, orbited above the chaos on the ground. Despite their expectations and pleadings to render immediate aid to their comrades, they watched for an excruciating fifteen or more minutes.

After a delay, the task force commander issued the order for the Ospreys to land and administer aid to the accident victims. When the pilots announced they were maneuvering to land, the Rangers' protests at remaining airborne while their comrades begged for assistance, turned to cheers. They checked the security of their restraints and waited for the wheels to touch down. Montoya's aircraft landed 800 to 1,000 meters from the smoldering wreckage.

With the Osprey on the ground, Montoya and his fellow Rangers fixed on the orange glow towering in the distance and ran through the dense cloud of desert grit generated by the giant rotors of the Osprey spinning overhead. Sand pelted their goggles. Dust filled their nostrils and clung to the back of their throats. Clear of the worst of the dust and in full battle gear, they sprinted over the sandy terrain using the inferno for guidance and illumination.

Positioned at the forward bulkhead of the mishap aircraft, Major Keith Carter, commander of the ground assault force, survived the crash suffering a broken nose and lacerations to his arms and legs. With blood streaming over his face and in complete charge of the scene, he ordered Rangers arriving from the second airplane to relieve the injured soldiers securing the perimeter. He directed Montoya and another medic to where casualties had been assembled.

The phone in the center of our conference table rang. The base operator had acquired a secure line. I checked the time while Capt Kelly dialed the number at Montoya's FOB. Dealing with the potential dust-up over the latrine had cost us precious minutes I hoped would not require an additional meeting with our first in country interviewee. We would have, at most, thirty minutes for him to answer several pages of questions.

The dial tone droned over the speakerphone until the line rang at two-second intervals, the quality sounding like a hive of discordant bumblebees.

"Alpha Company, this is First Sergeant Drennen, may I help you?"

"Hi Sergeant Drennen," Kelly said. "General Harvel and the accident investigation board calling for SSG Montoya."

"Yes ma'am, he's sitting right beside me waiting for your call. I'll leave the room until you're finished, if that's okay?"

"Staff Sergeant Montoya here, good evening, ma'am."

"Brigadier General Harvel is listening to this call on a speaker along with the rest of the board. We understand you must sign off by 7:40 p.m.?"

"That's correct, ma'am."

I read the preliminary requisite legal briefing, swore his testimony, and introduced the members of the team. His initial testimony revealed he had been in the Army for six years and performed duties that evening in his specialty as the company's senior medic.

Winsett grabbed paper from one of the copiers and using Montoya's testimony sketched a diagram of the crash site – casualty collection points, security perimeter, and their relation to the burning aircraft.

Doc Harper asked Montoya several questions related to his training and experience and that of other medically trained personnel assigned to his unit.

When he'd finished, I asked what Montoya had experienced after landing.

"Yes, sir. After we arrived, MAJ Carter directed us to the casualty collection points (CCPs) where we focused on the personnel with the worst injuries. While my other medic saw to one group, I concentrated on another that included the aircraft copilot and a few passengers. Three of those I treated showed no signs of serious hemorrhage and were breathing on their own. The fourth, a female Afghan interpreter, appeared lifeless. She had no pulse and was not breathing, so I moved to help with the other group of casualties.

"My other medic applied a tourniquet to the left arm of the aircraft tail scanner (SSgt Curtis) and asked for my trauma shears. The crewmember appeared conscious and speaking. I also examined two other Rangers complaining about labored breathing and joint pain. I found their injuries painful, but not life threatening. When I moved to Corporal Jankiewicz, the other medic was already attending to him. He had a faint carotid pulse but wasn't breathing. I broke out my King LT to intubate him."

"I'm sorry to interrupt," Winsett said. "For the non-medical personnel on the board or others who might read our report, explain your reference to King LT."

"Yes, sir. It's a tube that is inserted through the patient's mouth and extends past the throat – allowing air to flow through the larynx. Due to his severe jaw and neck injuries, I couldn't establish an airway, so I went straight to a cric."

"And explain that, if you would," Winsett asked.

"Yes, sir ... a cric [cricothyrotomy] is where I make an incision below the victim's Adam's apple and insert a tube into the patient's airway. I made a successful cric but couldn't get proper profusion into his lungs. Instead I got fluid and blood through the tube. I tried suctioning but when the tube wouldn't clear, I made the call that he was *expectant* and moved back to assisting the tail scanner."

"Would you explain the term *expectant*?" asked Doc Harper.

"Yes, sir, it's a situation where the victim is lifeless and there is nothing else I can do to save his life. When I got back to SSgt Curtis, Captain McKenna, our battalion surgeon riding in the back of the third Osprey, was seeing to him. Curtis had lost a lot of blood. He drifted in and out of loopy consciousness. He complained of being cold (from the loss of blood) and I wrapped him in a blanket. About that time, the first Casualty Evacuation (CASEVAC) H-60 landed a few yards away. We secured Curtis to a *spine board* and loaded him and SGT Claybaker aboard."

"And after the first CASEVAC helicopter departed, what did you do?" O'Leary asked.

"I went to the other survivors and checked to see if I could do more for any of them. You know, double checked for head injuries, and then prepared them for the next H-60. It showed up a few minutes later and all the survivors were on their way to the forward operating base, or Kandahar – depending on the severity of their injuries."

"How long did you remain on the scene?" Doc Harper asked.

"I was one of the last to depart the accident site. Bravo Company arrived on a Chinook and provided site security while we policed up weapons, ammo, and other gear lying all over the place. I tried the best I could to keep track of who departed on which aircraft and where they'd been taken. When I arrived back at my base, I went to the field hospital. SSgt Curtis was the only one in surgery at the time. I stayed several hours to assist in any way possible but remained out of the way as best I could. The medical staff put out the word for blood donations and got several Rangers, including the Joint Terminal Attack Controller (air force – JTAC) embedded with our unit. About that time or maybe later, the triage doctor took one look at SGT Claybaker and sent him to a surgery room."

Our allotted time with Montoya was coming to an end. I polled the board for additional questions. O'Leary had one.

"SSG Montoya … while treating the Osprey crew and Rangers, did any of them comment on what, if anything, happened or what they might have seen or heard in the final minutes leading up to the accident?"

"No, sir … not that I recall. At that point we had other worries."

"We understand," I said. "We appreciate your outstanding work that night. Thank you for your time and Godspeed on your mission tonight."

"Thank you, sir. Good luck on your investigation."

We terminated the call and discussed the sequence of events after the crash.

"So, Doc, how'd the younger Ranger medic do?" I asked.

"In my opinion …considering the realm of what might be humanly possible, he did everything he'd been trained to do and more. I'm very impressed with his medical knowledge."

"And what about Corporal Jankiewicz?"

"Tough call for someone in his position … I'll never second guess anyone under those circumstances, but you know as well as anyone how the rear echelon might see it differently. We'll get an autopsy at some point, but someone else will decide if he could have survived with immediate medical attention. I've never heard of a battlefield medic being held responsible for malpractice … a commander for negligence perhaps. A medic's loyalty to his specialty, and his comrades, is a part of this special medical culture. Jankiewicz is an unfortunate casualty of this terrible war. There's no doubt he had the respect and admiration of his fellow Rangers. They did everything possible to help him."

SSG Montoya had assessed SSgt Curtis to be the most critical of the survivors. Suffering from a serious loss of blood and multiple fractures, he was evacuated on the first rescue helicopter. The crew of the H-60 advised medical personnel at the forward operating base of the number, and nature, of inbound injured personnel. After a brief triage, the base surgeon rushed him into surgery that lasted twelve hours. He had defied the odds given him by Montoya and other personnel who had examined him. No one thought Curtis would survive his multiple injuries.

We quickly changed gears and started to prepare for our interview with the 8th SOS Commander, Lieutenant Colonel Shawn Compton. His testimony promised to be lengthy, based on the number of questions submitted by the board members.

While I filed Winsett's sketch with our other notes, an alert sounded over the base. The siren adjacent to our building wavered in a loud screeching tone effectively halting normal conversation. We looked to Lt Col O'Leary, relying on his experience in the theater, to give us advice. Before we could ask about the sound, a recording of a female voice with a British accent, spoke over the loud siren.

"Rocket attack … rocket attack … rocket attack."

"Do we need to put on our chemical warfare gear?" Adams asked. "Should we run to the nearest rocket protection bunker?"

The warnings got louder. The sound of faint explosions could be heard off in the distance. All eyes were on O'Leary waiting for his instructions.

CHAPTER TWENTY

THE SQUADRON COMMANDER

O'Leary and I quickly pushed the tables against the cinder-block walls and directed the team members to don their helmets and huddle under the tables. I turned off the lights and kneeled to get under the table with everyone.

"We could take shelter across the street in the underground bunker," O'Leary said. "But we'd be in the open for the two minutes it would take to get there. We're better off here. The alert won't last long."

"How long?" I asked.

O'Leary folded his knees close to his chest and leaned against the leg of the table.

"Most often … less than ten minutes … could be as long as fifteen though. Base security activates the siren when a rocket is detected. It's not uncommon to hear explosions ten to fifteen seconds afterward. It's short notice."

No one made a sound as we listened for explosions. The warbling siren and the constant automated voice made it difficult to hear anything else. Someone verbalized their thought that we were lucky to have our own personal doctor.

"I'm sitting next to you and no more immune to the effects of high explosives than anyone else." Harper said. "What if I'm the one requiring medical assistance?"

They hadn't thought of that. The exchange, though, eased the tension, then the siren stopped. The verbal warnings ceased, then the British accented voice broadcast, "All clear … All clear."

We crawled from the protection of the tables and stowed our gear. Some went for water, while others queued up at the end of the hall for the latrine.

The attack warning delayed our next interview with the 8th SOS commander who had probably taken shelter in a position between our office and the squadron building.

In the interim, I engaged O'Leary over the rocket attacks.

"How can they fire on the base every night without giving away their position?"

"They use the cover of darkness and launch from the bed of a moving pick-up or a flat-bed truck," he answered. "Without a spotter to call corrections, the rockets are an unguided area weapon designed to disrupt our operations by terrorizing the base population. To a certain extent, it works, and on occasion they hit something or someone. Once, one impacted into the poo pond. If it detonated, it didn't even create a ripple on the surface … could have been terribly uncomfortable, but not catastrophic. At times, the commander extends the base perimeter to push them farther away, but then the Taliban employ longer-range rockets. After sitting through a few alerts, it'll become commonplace, especially in the dining hall. You'll notice few people take cover, acting as if nothing is happening … more hungry than frightened."

AFSOC had chosen Lieutenant Colonel Shawn Compton, the first to command the 8th SOS, and the unit's initial cadre for their demonstrated leadership, management abilities, technical expertise, and their compatibility with other members of the squadron. When the Air Force spooled up the unit, no institutional memory existed for those initial personnel operating a new aircraft designed for a very complex mission.

They relied on training without the experiences of *old heads* that by tradition could pass subtle aircraft idiosyncrasies and wisdom gained through years of experience. In units with a history of operating a specific aircraft, knowledge and stories might be passed on in the ready room, or during a training flight debrief with an old-timer. More can be learned from those stories than could ever be gleaned from flight manuals or technical orders. The crews of the 8th SOS had the best training available, and crews with experiences in other aircraft whose lessons might or might not translate to the Osprey mission. New technology created a new mission where experience and "lessons learned" in a dangerous world did not exist ... yet.

A flying (or any military) unit functions like a family with the commander providing the overlying philosophy umbrella under which the unit operates. The commander's unit functions with the command and support structures, while seeing to the organization's overall welfare through the staff. The second in command, the operations officer, supervises the day-to-day operations and the individual crew members' relation to one another and their mission. The duo is a two-headed manager, sharing a common goal – the mission.

During our interview with the 8th SOS Operations Officer at Hurlburt Field, he spoke of unit policy and management of aircrews using the pronoun *us* versus *I*. We expected to confirm the same command dynamic at Kandahar. Every commander is responsible for establishing the overlying culture by implementing their philosophy through their staff and operations officer. In a short time, we would discover if the Osprey crews had the best information and supervision to prepare and conduct the unit's mission.

Lt Col Compton entered the room dusting off his flight suit pant legs. At six foot two, set on a medium frame with a balding and shaved pate, he projected the aura of confident ability confirmed by his record and stellar reputation. I welcomed him and introduced him to each board member.

"Thank you, sir," he said. "Sorry I'm late. The attack occurred just as I left the squadron building."

I offered him coffee, water, and a seat at the center of the conference table.

He removed a bottle of water from the lower leg pocket of his flight suit.

"I'm good to go, sir."

After a period of small talk, I read the same recitation I had provided during previous interviews – the requisite information and admonitions ending with the oath swearing truthful testimony.

He testified to being a seventeen-year officer. He had been the Squadron Commander for ten months. He provided the handbook one-liner describing his duties as ensuring the unit under his command remained combat ready and able to perform any assigned mission.

Our initial discussion during his interview related to a software update to the Osprey's computers installed when the aircraft arrived in theater. Major changes included an increase in the maximum power available and upgrades to the head's-up-display (HUD). Though the change also permitted an increase in cruise speed, it resulted in a decrease in specific range due to higher fuel consumption. The unit elected to operate the aircraft at what had been their normal cruise speeds to conserve fuel and preserve their longer range. Enhancements of the HUD provided better utility and presentation of information to the pilots with slight format upgrades.

Power available also increased. Advancing the thrust control lever past a soft stop in the throttle quadrant allowed the pilot to select an additional increment of power beyond normal maximum power: a power setting known as *contingency power* … for emergency use only.

"Have any of the crews used contingency power while the units have been deployed to Afghanistan?" I asked.

"Yes, sir, one has … the second airplane in the formation the night of the crash. The pilot experienced a high descent rate while attempting to land. Anxious to get Army medical personnel on the ground, he used contingency power to avoid a hard landing. That's the only situation I know of."

MSgt Dolan followed with a question. "Sir, did the airplane require maintenance after that incident?"

"Yes, it did. Any use of contingency power requires maintenance to borescope[13] the engines. Once the borescope was complete, no further maintenance was required."

---

13 Borescope – Maintenance personnel use a fiber-optic device to internally inspect compressor, combustion (burner cans), and turbine sections of an engine looking for possible stress or damage not discernable using external or other means.

We had covered the subject of go-arounds with the squadron Operations Officer but needed to make clear that one mind-set existed within the unit's senior leadership.

"Lt Col Compton, what is your philosophy regarding go-arounds in a combat situation? We've heard go-arounds are not free. Is that true?"

"Sir, when my crews analyze the target set, I tell them their job is to get teams in and out safely. I tell them not to sacrifice mission accomplishment by trying to salvage a poor approach. I don't believe go-arounds are free, but when we fly a mission where we're putting a team into a landing zone that's not co-located with the objective, a go-around has minimal impact on the overall mission. As the mission moves closer to the objective, and the team is closer to being in harm's way, pressure on the crew increases. A go-around in that situation may degrade or prevent mission success. Nothing is more costly than not getting the team to the landing zone safely. My crews know my philosophy … if you need to go-around, go-around. The ultimate goal is to get the team in safely."

"To your knowledge, were there any issues that could have been a distraction to any of the crewmembers who were flying the mishap airplane?" I asked.

"Sir, there was only one issue. Prior to deployment, the pilot's son required a tonsillectomy. We allowed him to deploy two days after most of the unit had departed. He stayed with his son for the surgery. The surgery went well. That's the only issue I know of."

"Now that you and your unit have been in Afghanistan for over six weeks, what are the differences between flying in Iraq versus Afghanistan?" I asked.

"Sir, the main difference is the environment – high terrain, high altitude, pitch black nights. This is the most challenging environment I've ever flown in."

"Where were you when you found out about the accident?"

"Sir, I was in the squadron flight planning room watching the live video feed of the mission. Something seemed amiss when the video no longer tracked the lead airplane. I stepped to the Joint Operations Center (JOC) for a clearer picture of the situation than I had watching the single screen in the planning area. For a moment, when the ISR video panned away from the lead airplane, we feared the A-10 was searching for the source of possible Taliban gunfire. We stared at the video of the site and the burning aircraft with no indication of the cause. After a minute, not much longer, survivors crawled, walked or ran from the burning wreckage and gathered fifty or so meters away or dispersed in defensive positions. The JOC attempted contact with the other two Ospreys with limited success. About fifteen minutes later, the second CV-22 landed a good distance from the crash site and the Army Rangers made their way to help their comrades. When the Army ground forces commander on the mishap airplane, Major Carter, radioed for immediate assistance, the JOC generated an update on the ground situation and dispatched CASEVAC (casualty evacuation) helicopters, HH-60s, to the crash site. A few minutes later, the third CV-22 landed and the Army Rangers aboard that airplane ran to the site."

Compton continued, "When we had established communications with the two Ospreys, I had them fly to the forward operating base to refuel and stand-by while the JOC Commander launched the CH-47 Chinook, from Kandahar. I requested a CV-22 pilot travel to the site on that helicopter. The JOC commander agreed. We monitored the rescue operation and forwarded reports regarding the status of personnel – who was injured, who was killed, and where the casualties were being taken."

I glanced at Adams to ensure she was able to stay up with notes and recording the fast-moving testimony before asking my next questions.

Lt Col Compton testified the unit stood down for several days after the accident in order to grieve the loss of their beloved crewmembers. Group and individual counseling consumed most of the first day, which included a ceremony conducted on the ramp when the Killed in Action (KIA) departed the base. The unit also spent time assessing possible causes of the accident and brainstorming solutions to enhance mission safety margins.

The commander and his staff effected several adjustments in power management, flight planning, and approach profiles that maintained acceptable margins of operational safety without degrading mission capability. The unit increased the limits of power available in the event of the loss of an engine during an approach. For planning purposes, the crews modified pre-flight computations for available power by using the highest temperature forecast, prevailing, or actual outside air at the time of the operational event. Using the highest temperature provided an additional safety margin for aircraft and engine performance.

The squadron also agreed to decrease the allowable maximum cargo loads and minimum fuel requirements to reflect conditions and altitudes experienced in Afghanistan and not represented in data computed during Osprey initial trials and flight testing in the United States.

Lt Col Compton authorized modifications to the flight profile for instrument approaches that required crews to start descending earlier thus allowing more time to assess conditions closer to the ground, and near the landing zone.

Three days after the accident, the squadron resumed a light flying schedule of basic transport missions to allow crews the opportunity to practice the newly adapted procedures relating to low visibility approaches. A couple of nights later, the 8th SOS resumed combat infiltration /exfiltration missions.

I yielded to Lt Col O'Leary who indicated he had questions.

"Lt Col Compton, you sat in the mission briefing with the crews before they departed on their mission on the night of April 8th. Do you remember if Maj Voas briefed the possibility of altering the direction of landing based on a change in wind direction? Would it have been something he would brief, if he thought it was a contingency he might have faced?"

"To be honest, I don't remember him briefing a plan for changing the direction of the run-in. We did discuss the fact there was a valley to the east of the landing zone that could be used for maneuvering in the event of egress or a go-around."

"Okay, what would you have expected Maj Voas to do if he needed to change the direction of landing with only three miles to go until arriving at the landing zone?"

"If it was three miles and the wind was coming from a bad direction, I would expect him to turn away from the target area to reset and change the direction of landing. If he encountered unexpected winds farther from the landing zone, he would have time to maneuver to a different heading to get to the landing area."

"Did you feel confident he and the other aircraft commanders understood the contingency you just stated and could execute it safely during this mission?"

"Yes."

"This is a hard question, but I have to ask it. You talked about the changes you have made in operating procedures since the mishap. All of those changes were smart. Looking back to the first days of the deployment, do you think some of the changes could have been put into place sooner?"

"I think you'll always second-guess yourself. We trained at similar altitudes and terrain in the Albuquerque, New Mexico, area. We expected conditions in Afghanistan to be no different. Our power margins and operating procedures were proven during the deployment to Iraq. We can't plan ourselves out of accomplishing our mission. We've considered our Afghanistan operations and realize we could change some of our parameters and still comply with our tasking. I was comfortable sending them out that night with the procedures we had in place. I would send the crew out again. But the changes we've made are acceptable risk mitigations for our template of missions."

When O'Leary finished, MSgt Dolan had a question.

"Lt Col Compton, is there a policy or procedure about destroying an airplane after a crash?"

"I don't know if there is a stipulated criterion. When I was told the airplane would be destroyed in place, it sounded reasonable to me. From what I could see on the video, the engines and nacelles were torn off the airplane, and it was upside down. The senior pilot I sent to the site reported the airplane was not flyable. When I heard that decision come down from higher headquarters, I didn't think twice about it."

"When was the airplane bombed? Was it three hours after the accident, or more?"

"About four hours."

TSgt Adams raised her hand, "Sir, I have a couple of questions."

"Go ahead."

"Sir, did you travel to the crash site to view what was left of the wreckage during daylight hours?"

"No, I did not. I flew to the forward operating base near Qalat to visit some of the wounded the next day. I didn't fly by the wreckage."

"Okay, sir, there was a group of Army personnel who went to the crash site the next day. Do you know who went out to the site?"

"The next morning there was a ground force based near Qalat who did a recon of the area. They sent photos of the wreckage to the JOC. They provided the photos to the safety board when they arrived at Kandahar."

"Yes, sir, we have seen those photos. Do you know why that unit was sent to the crash site?"

"I don't know. I think they may have been the battle space owner's troops stationed in the area. It would have to have been his decision to send the Army personnel."

"Thank you, sir. That's all I have … General."

Adams seldom engaged in the query of witnesses, but when she did, her questions were on point. Her experience on previous investigations limited her role to recording, but she exhibited a keen sense of time and space that made her participation essential. This time, she asked the commander something I had not considered.

The two legal members engaged the squadron commander in a number of questions about how the crews received weather briefings and forecasts. Compton revealed that the crew's ability to get the latest weather information had not been codified when the mission was launched. The procedure improved dramatically following the accident.

Doctor Harper asked about the location of medical personnel and why the troops sat on the floor instead of using seats that were designed for passengers.

Lt Col Compton explained that the ground force commander had sole responsibility for the positioning of his force on the aircraft. Seats installed on the CV-22 do not accommodate the mass of equipment carried by special operators. Floor loading also facilitates rapid egress after landing.

When Doc Harper had finished, I asked Lt Col Compton if he had additional information he cared to share with the board and handed him a list of our planned interviews.

He indicated he had nothing further to add and after checking the list of personnel, provided no additional names.

Before I terminated the interview, MSgt Dolan raised his hand.

"Go ahead," I said.

"Sir, have you ever heard of or experienced a (CV-22) compressor stall?"

"Not in this aircraft. I have heard of them, but I have not ever had a compressor stall. I've studied the condition as outlined in our emergency procedures section of our flight manual."

"Sir, have you ever experienced a sudden loss of power?"

"No, I have not."

Dolan laid his pencil on the pad of notebook paper in front of him.

"That's all I have, sir."

I excused Lt Col Compton and thanked him for his time. Though I had no reason to consider him other than an outstanding commander, he seemed less than forthcoming regarding certain facts. He didn't address engine maintenance procedures put into place after the accident, such as the requirement to conduct periodic and thorough engine washes to remove sand that contaminated the engine turbine section. He could have been more decisive about the recovery of critical components of the airplane before it was destroyed, especially the VSLED, which would have provided critical data concerning engine health during the entire flight. Recovering equipment and portions of the aircraft required for an accident investigation should have been given equal priority to securing classified documents, but little wreckage had been recovered in the hours after the accident, the whereabouts of which still remained a mystery at the time of the interview.

While debriefing Compton's testimony, we addressed MSgt Dolan's unscripted questions regarding compressor stalls and power loss.

"What prompted you to ask your last two questions?" I asked.

"Well, sir, the way he answered your question about go-arounds not being free. I know dozens of flying squadron commanders. Lt Col Compton set the most positive tone about go-arounds I have ever heard. There is no doubt his crews didn't feel pressure to land from a poor approach, or with tailwinds that were out of computed or operational limits. His answer to your question made me think the crew probably tried to go-around. I considered possible reasons the crew was unable to execute a normal go-around. I thought … sudden power loss or a compressor stall. I've worked airplanes with those issues, so I know it happens. I wanted to know if he had experienced those malfunctions."

"A couple things bothered me as well," I added. "When he went to the forward operating base the next day, he didn't fly over or land at the accident site … odd … especially since it was so close to the base. Seems unusual to me that although he could, he didn't check out the accident area in daylight hours. He could have verified aspects of the terrain, and the run-in course, but he denied taking the opportunity. I don't get it."

What wreckage survived after being bombed, remained at the site the following day. Army personal had taken photos which revealed considerable portions of the aircraft survived the crash and subsequent bombing. It was curious that no one expressed interest in seeing it in person … or discovering what the Army personnel loaded onto a flatbed trailer … or where any of the recovered wreckage went.

I never assumed troops would take it upon themselves to check out a large vehicle from the motor pool and trek across miles of desert and return with parts of a destroyed USAF aircraft without specific orders, or without the knowledge of someone in their chain of command.

I was determined to find out what happened to the recovered wreckage. There was someone in Afghanistan who had the answers … we would have to conduct an Easter egg hunt to find clues and get answers. I had a feeling we were being stonewalled. I considered expanding the scope of interviews, even if we had to talk to everyone working at the operations center on the night of the accident. If a secret remained out there, I was going to turn over every stone necessary to find it.

CHAPTER TWENTY ONE

MR. CURLY CULP

Kelly removed photos from a folder given to us by the safety board and arranged them by timestamp on the conference table. The morning after the accident, soldiers from a nearby forward operating base drove a diesel truck with a low-boy trailer to the accident site, collected pieces of Osprey wreckage, and took pictures.

Due to the aspect from which the photos were taken, the low resolution, and despite our best efforts, we could not identify the individuals involved nor could we discern the unit to which they were assigned. They piled smaller pieces on top of large sections of the fuselage and the cockpit windscreen. Without knowing the unit involved, we were left to guess where the wreckage had been taken.

I penned a note to myself to search for units based in the area near the accident site. While I wrote, MSgt Dolan pored over the photos and became more agitated with each photo.

"What's wrong," I asked?

"Sir, when we work with certain parts of the Osprey, we operate in a controlled environment wearing respirators and coveralls. Exterior surfaces of the Osprey and some elements of the interior are constructed of composite materials. When fractured or smashed the friable material, like asbestos, is toxic and poses a serious health risk. These guys, in these photos, are handling pieces of the airplane without protection. At some point, they can expect health issues. We should find out who they are and not just for an interview, but to warn them. If their commander sent them to the site, he didn't know the danger involved. If they took it upon themselves, the consequences are the same."

We agreed to take the photos to the Joint Operations Center, and to the forward operating base where the Rangers were stationed in hopes of identifying the people, or the unit, in the pictures.

"By the way," I said while looking over to Capt Kelly, "how goes our transportation to the accident site and the Ranger's base?"

"Not well, sir," Kelly said. "After tonight's interviews, I'll meet with schedulers from two helicopter units here at Kandahar. But so far it doesn't sound promising. I asked the legal office to intercede with Brigadier General Walsh, the 451st Air Expeditionary Wing Commander. They'll meet at 10:15 a.m. this morning."

"Brig Gen Guy Walsh?" I asked.

"I think that's right, sir. I can get his first name for you. Do you know him?"

"If it's Guy Walsh … yes, I do. We've worked together a few times the past couple of years. He's a good commander and a great officer. Let me know if I need to be involved. I promised not to throw stars (military rank) around, but this would be more unofficial. We need his support as soon as possible. Our allotted time in country is only days … not weeks. We need to work on this as a priority for today."

O'Leary raised his hand.

"Sir, my old unit trains Afghan pilots flying the Russian MI-17 helicopter. My preliminary discussions with them indicate they may be willing to help. I approached them about using a training mission to fly us to the Ranger's base and perhaps over, or to, the accident site. I suggested they could refuel and conduct local training while we complete interviews and a possible survey of the site. When we're done, they'll fly us back to Kandahar. If we're flexible and give them two or three dates, I think they may be a good option for us. If the other helicopter units are overtasked and undermanned, they may not have resources to support us."

"Great," I said. "The day before we depart for the FOB, we'll shift to a day schedule. After the last interview around midnight, we'll break for rest and show up the following morning at whatever time the supporting flying unit requires. We'll begin Ranger interviews in the afternoon, which should fit their mission schedule.

"Can you please find a couple days where we can be flexible with our schedule?" I asked. "We can't complete an investigation without interviewing the Rangers surviving the accident.

"Pursue support from one of our Air Force, or Army, units first." I continued. "See if they'll at least fly us over the accident site. It would be very helpful to assess the surrounding terrain. Lack of security might preclude landing, but we'll take what we can get. Failing that, let's coordinate a date and time that suits the MI-17 unit's schedule. Questions, anyone?"

"No, sir."

After completing telephone interviews with support personnel, we interviewed crewmembers flying in the three-ship Osprey formation the night of the accident. Their testimony confirmed our previous impressions concerning the professionalism, judgment, and flying skills of Voas and Lackey. We heard nothing but respectful accolades about the two beloved airmen.

We studied the events prior to the Ospreys departing Kandahar. We confirmed details of the initial mission briefing, flight planning, landing zone selection, weather forecasts, and the rendezvous/briefing with the Rangers at their base.

Nothing in the original weather forecast hinted at a reason to consider altering the mission profile. High clouds, light southerly winds, and seasonal spring temperatures (67° F) existed at the time the mission departed. Crews did not request updates to the original weather briefing after landing to pick up the Rangers.

The forecast notwithstanding, when the formation of three Ospreys approached the three-mile point to the landing area, the winds suddenly increased from a seven-knot headwind to a seventeen-knot tailwind as the wind's direction shifted from north-northwest to southeast. The tailwind limit for the Osprey to land is approximately ten knots. I asked each crewmember if they expected Maj Voas to continue the approach and land with a tailwind. We recorded their universal and unequivocal response, "Absolutely not, sir." Each crewmember expected him to spin around (miss the approach, go-around or reset) for another approach to land into the wind.

"They were our most experienced crew," they said. "They'd never land with a tailwind exceeding the aircraft limit … no way."

Crews in the two trailing aircraft expected a radio call to change the run-in heading or barring a radio call, they watched to see if Voas veered off the current heading and reset for an approach heading in the opposite direction in order to land into a headwind. Instead, the number two aircraft maintaining position a mile behind Voas, watched in horror as the lead Osprey impacted the ground and burst into a fireball.

In the debriefing following our crew interviews, O'Leary summarized our conundrum.

"Okay … inside one minute the winds are out of limits. Did Voas land through the adverse condition on purpose, or attempt to go-around? If he had intentionally disregarded the limit, the rest of the crew would have had to go along with it by agreeing or saying nothing. We have no testimony indicating that happened. The personal and professional character of the crewmembers involved suggest that's not the case. Personally, I think they attempted to go-around. If we consider the crew attempted a go-around but did not make a radio call to the other two airplanes, they either screwed that up, or the notoriously bad radios did not work properly. The Osprey radios were always a problem. What else would prevent them from executing a missed approach or making a required call to the formation? Task saturation? Somebody tell me."

"Are we concluding a cause right now?" Dolan asked.

"We're not there yet," I said. "We're just talking about 'what if' scenarios. Do you have something to add?"

"I'm not ready to say for sure yet, but I'm leaning toward an airplane malfunction," said Dolan. Realize that I'm a maintainer and I don't like thinking the aircraft engines may be suspect … but … that's all I'm going to say right now."

"Good enough," I said. "Hold that thought. We're not near finished with interviews. There's plenty of information to gather here in Afghanistan. We'll put it all together once we return back home to Hurlburt Field. Everyone, please keep an open mind. Fair enough?"

"Yes, sir."

Our final interview was with retired Lieutenant Colonel (Marine Corp - Retired) Ron "Curly" Culp, a twenty-three-year Marine employed now as a civilian contractor. His job title was *Maintenance Pilot*. He had logged hundreds of hours in Marine Corps Ospreys (MV-22s) as a pilot and instructor. His job at Kandahar required him to be readily available to conduct Osprey test flights after engine, flight control, or when other components were repaired or replaced by maintenance personnel. He also monitored aircraft reliability and reported to the manufacturer, the contractor, and the local unit about discrepancies he discovered.

Arriving at our conference room, he took in our meager surroundings in a split second. His hair was clipped in the Marine Corps' "high and tight" fashion. He smiled sincerely as he introduced himself to each board member. I don't remember any other expression during the entire interview – as jocular a Marine as I have ever met.

I checked the time – 5:00 a.m. He had worked the entire night yet appeared as fresh and alert as if he had slept eight hours, showered, and reported for our interview five minutes prior. Just under six feet and medium build, he appeared ripped even under his loose-fitting contractor flight suit. His uniform bore no insignias, other than a nametag with U.S. Naval aviator's wings and his name – Curly Culp embroidered in white letters against a solid blue background.

We plowed through the familiar procedure ending with him swearing to tell the truth.

"Do you have permission from your civilian employer to testify to the accident investigation board this morning?"

"Yes, sir."

"How long have you worked for your employer?"

"Sir, two and a half years."

"Would you share your personal assessment of the 8th SOS leadership and CV-22 support units?"

"Sure, sir. From the commander to the lowest ranking officer and enlisted, they're top of the mark. I'm from a world of discipline, custom, and courtesy (referring to his Marine Corps career). AFSOC is similar in that they operate with a singular goal – the mission. They're as serious as any squared-away Marine. I also think the Army warrant officers that transferred to the Air Force have added maturity, leadership, and experience to the unit and the CV-22 program."

"In a few days, we'll interview Rangers who survived the accident. We're interested if they heard any unusual aircraft noises or conversations from the cockpit during the last minutes of flight. If an engine had failed, or lost power, what warnings would the crew experience?"

"There'd be no mistaking an engine failure, sir. A computerized female voice, we call *Bitchin' Barbie*, would annunciate 'Engine Failure, Left/Right Engine' depending which engine failed. There's also a warning indication at the top of both Multi-Function Displays (MFD), and 'Master Caution' lights embedded in the glare shield in front of each pilot. To ignore an engine failure wouldn't only be difficult, sir, it would be impossible."

"If an engine failed a half mile from the landing zone, how should the pilot respond?"

"Sir, it depends on where you are landing, the conditions, and the weight of the airplane. Those considerations drive the pilot's decision. In their preflight, the crew calculates single-engine performance data, the maximum single-engine altitude based on weight and other factors. In circumstances such as the night of the mishap, where the airplane had a full load of Army personnel infiltrating to a landing zone that is above 5,000 feet, the pilot must maintain transitional lift. That is critical."

"For the non-aviators," I said, "can you explain transitional lift concept in layman's terms?"

"Yes, sir, I'll try. The Osprey can operate as a fixed-wing airplane with nacelles horizontal, and as a helicopter by rotating the nacelles to vertical. The regime in between the extreme aspects of the two modes incorporates degrees of each – transitional lift. In the operational envelope, the aircraft functions with varying elements of both the helicopter and the airplane depending on the speed of the aircraft, orientation of the nacelles, and power available. The MFD displays in green the acceptable parameters for positioning the nacelles in relation to the aircraft speed and power available, but the travel limit is not restricted to the pilot. He has the capability of selecting any nacelle angle, even one that might not be supported by the available power or the airspeed."

Culp continued, "Visualize a graph depicting the designed operational ranges of the aircraft as an irregular shaped envelope [box]. Then consider an additional, smaller envelope within that box that moves around inside – the envelope for power available, airspeed, and orientation of the nacelles. The aircraft won't sustain controlled flight outside the smaller box, nor will it fly if the smaller box departs the larger one, *outside the envelope*. Consequences of operating outside either envelope range from varying degrees of airframe or engine damage, or in the worst case, loss of control of the aircraft. Does that make sense, sir?"

I looked around the table. Everyone expressed at least equivocal understanding.

"I think we've got it. Please continue, Mr. Culp."

"Thank you, sir. The pilot should establish an immediate climb and transition into the airplane mode, because that is the safest realm with a failed engine. At the same time, he must remain within the aircraft's operating envelope."

Lt Col O'Leary interrupted, "Excuse me, sir, but Mr. Culp makes a great point. Everyone should understand the situation you describe. Would you expect the pilot to advance the thrust control levers to full power and try to maintain a slow climb while transitioning from helicopter mode to airplane mode while performing a go-around?"

"That's right," said Culp, "but, with some caveats because of the design of this airplane. The problem we face with the V-22, unlike any other airplane, is as you transition toward airplane mode, the pilot can advance the TCLs at a rate and position that would cause the aircraft to stall. In such a case, the airplane will lose altitude at a rate relative to the severity of the stall. That's not what a pilot wants in that situation. He has to coordinate the transition of the nacelles to the horizontal, advancing power to maintain level flight or a very slight climb while the airspeed increases."

"With the airspeed at eighty knots," O'Leary said, "and with the conditions you describe, would the airplane have enough forward speed to transition to the airplane mode?"

"Yes. But it would depend on the wind velocity and direction," Culp answered.

"Okay, for the sake of discussion," said O'Leary, "Let's say the crew was experiencing a seventeen to twenty knot tailwind. Could the pilot transition safely?"

"That would be dangerous, for sure," said Culp. "In that circumstance, the pilot should use extreme caution while adding power and driving nacelles forward to the horizontal, airplane configuration."

Doc Harper looked at O'Leary, "Great points. Can I change the subject here and ask a related question?"

O'Leary nodded.

"Mr. Culp, we've asked every pilot about contingency power. Some pilots disagree on what constitutes the additional increment of power. So, not being an aviator, I have two questions. Was the additional contingency power available before the software was updated after the airplanes arrived in Afghanistan? And, explain to us … what is contingency power?"

Culp smiled. "The answer to your first question is no. Additional contingency power was not available prior to the software update in April. As for your second question, contingency power provides the pilot with an additional increment of engine power, to be used only in emergency situations. Normal travel of the thrust control levers is about four inches, idle to full power. In an emergency, the pilot may override the mechanical stop at maximum power and push the TCLs an additional two inches ... to select contingency power, 117% of normal maximum power. Remember, contingency power is for emergency use only. After an engine is operated in the contingency power position, maintenance must at least perform a visual inspection using fiber optics to view the compressor, burner, and turbine sections. The added power reduces the expected life of the engine and, in the worst case, causes damage that would result in having to remove the engine and replace it with a new engine."

Mr. Culp provided detailed answers to every question the board threw at him and did so in terms everyone on the board understood. The session continued for another fifteen minutes until my opportunity for follow-up questions.

"Mr. Culp, you and our board member Lt Col O'Leary, are two of the most knowledgeable Osprey pilots in the world. Based on your experience, and what you have heard about this accident, tell us how a crew on a routine approach to an uncontested landing zone in an open area might fly an aircraft into the ground?"

"In my experience sir, I've never known a more unforgiving area of operations than Afghanistan. When I first flew the H-46 helicopter, or V-22, we did not have the situation awareness tools available to crews flying the CV-22 – Heads up Displays, Forward Looking Infrared Radar (FLIR), Multifunction Displays, or a flight engineer (the V-22 does not use a Flight Engineer) in the cockpit. Even on a perfect day with everything nailed, conducting infiltration and exfiltration missions in this place sucks. Landing in dirt, pilots experience total brownout. Add challenges of high altitudes, hot temperatures and constant changes in wind velocity and direction, crews must be alert every second. Nothing is routine flying out here. I could speculate forever about the possibilities in this environment, but it comes to this. In a half second the airplane can get away from the most accomplished pilot on anyone's manning document. Another unfortunate thing about this crash ... systems on board the airplane could have answered every (accident investigation) question you've asked. It should've taken less than ten minutes to download and review engine and flight performance data. But, from what I've been told, neither the flight information recorder nor the vibration/structural life and engine diagnostics hardware has been recovered. No aircraft should be developed, built, or deployed without digital devices to capture every detail of the aircraft's operation. We're grateful for the survivors. Maybe they have a sense of what happened. Whoever decided to destroy the aircraft should have waited until the wreckage had been searched for usable information. They got the people out, gathered classified information and equipment, and that's right. But we wouldn't be having this discussion if the command had posted a security team around the airplane and had removed everything that could resolve the cause of the crash."

O'Leary raised his hand.

"Sir, I have a follow-up question. Mr. Culp, did you make a recommendation to the joint operations center commander to recover those items?"

"Yes, I did. I arrived a little after one in the morning. The officer on duty pulled me aside and provided an update on what they knew at the time. He told me two crewmembers had been killed. I told him to send someone to lock up their rooms. I asked if anyone was making a list of items to recover from the airplane. I was told a list had been made to protect the classified equipment. I told him they needed to think about getting the crash survivable memory units (the FIR and the VSLED). I never knew if my recommendation got passed along. Throughout the chaos in the operations center, everyone still remained focused and businesslike, but grim."

With no more questions, we thanked him for his time. The board stood while Mr. Culp filed past and shook hands with every board member before departing. While the other board members packed up and cleaned the conference room, I walked out with Mr. Culp.

"You mentioned while flying the MV-22, you'd been through two other incidents. What happened?"

"Yes, sir. The year two thousand was a terrible year for the V-22 program. I was one of fourteen pilots selected by the Marine Corps and the Air Force assigned to the Multi-Service Operational Test Team (MOTT). We deployed to Yuma Marine Corps Air Station in Arizona for six months. While there we completed the Operational Evaluation (OPEVAL), the last requirement before initial production of the V-22. In one of our final tests, we launched four V-22s on a simulated combat training mission using scenarios involving infiltration of a force from Yuma to Marana, Arizona, and reversing the process in an exfiltration of the same force. I had worked with all the crews involved and had a personal relationship with the eight pilots. Arriving at Marana, the first two aircraft set up for an approach to land and offload their Marines while the other two (empty) aircraft loitered overhead waiting to on-load the same troops and return to Yuma.

Due to wind shifting to eight knots on their tail, the first two Ospreys began their approach high and fast, necessitating a high, non-standard rate of descent. The second of the two aircraft attempted to maintain formation integrity but overshot his lead and flew abeam them to their right. The pilot then banked to his right to increase separation but maintained a two-thousand feet per minute rate of descent when normal rate should have been three to five hundred feet per minute. We couldn't determine whether the pilot stepped on the right rudder to increase his turn rate, or in response to wake turbulence from the lead aircraft. Unable to correct the roll with opposite (left) control inputs, the aircraft continued to roll and impacted the ground nose-down and inverted, with the loss of the airplane and everyone on board. Witnessing the crash in the lead aircraft, the crew chief and copilot simultaneously yelled for the pilot to *wave off* (go-around). After a second or two of shock, the pilot advanced the thrust control levers to maximum power and rotated the nacelles toward the horizontal airplane mode. With airspeed less than fifteen knots, air over the wings could not generate enough lift to fly away from the ground. The V-22 slammed onto the runway and bounced. Impacting a second time, the aircraft slid broadside across the runway and came to rest on an adjoining taxiway. The incident left the aircraft totally destroyed, but the occupants survived with various injuries.

"You know, sir," Culp continued, "There are a lot of similarities between the accident at Marana, and the accident that happened here in Afghanistan a few weeks ago. Both were night missions. Both were carrying troops. The crews flew a little higher, and a little faster than a standard approach to landing would dictate. Both missions involved tailwinds challenging the crew at a critical time. And, both missions almost experienced a second airplane crash after the first Osprey hit the ground … kind of eerie as I think about it. Eighteen Marines lost their lives at Marana. Two Air Force crewmen, one Ranger, and one civilian lost their lives near Qalat. I'm not telling you how hard it is to lose friends, because I know you've lost them too. Another curious coincidence about the two accidents haunts me. What was the date of the Afghanistan accident, sir?"

"The crew departed the forward operating base on the night of April 8, 2010, Mr. Culp," I answered.

"The Marana accident occurred the night of April 8, 2000, exactly ten years prior."

CHAPTER TWENTY TWO

TURBINE GLASSING

I silenced my alarm without remembering if I had heard it. At 4:00 p.m. on Friday afternoon, caravans of diesel-powered vehicles idled or inched their way along the dusty road outside my quarters. In my blacked-out room, I needed my flashlight to locate the light switch on an adjacent wall. Even though we had been in Afghanistan for a few days, my wake-up routine remained unaltered whatever the time.

After a quick shower, I dressed and collected my gear. Before leaving my room, I sat on my bed and reviewed the list of people we would be interviewing. All except one on the schedule were personnel assigned to the CV-22 maintenance squadron. The other, a Rolls-Royce factory representative, specialized in engine related issues. The Osprey's performance in the Afghanistan environment loomed large in our investigation.

At 4:55 p.m. I strapped on my web belt with a 9mm Beretta pistol holstered and attached. I donned my Kevlar vest and strapped on my helmet. O'Leary, Winsett, and Harper planned to pick me up at 5:00 p.m. I stepped out into the sun, dust and non-stop noise of diesel engines. My hands covered my face and nose as I dodged an array of combat vehicles motoring past me. I found a secure spot away from traffic to watch for my ride.

Within a couple of minutes, the three lieutenant colonels arrived in our hippie van. I slid the door open and settled into the back seat.

"How are you guys?" I asked as I removed my sunglasses to wipe the dust off.

Winsett skipped the small talk and moved right to business, his first report of the day. "Change in plans, sir … we'll interview four maintenance personnel tonight instead of eight. With your concurrence, we should knock off early to make a 10:00 a.m. takeoff for the forward operating base tomorrow morning. Lt Col O'Leary's connection with the Afghan MI-17 training squadron came through. Isn't that amazing?"

"Great news … and quick. How did you do it?" I asked.

"Sir, they were ecstatic," said O'Leary. "The unit was eager to fly an actual combat support mission for training … one catch though."

"What's that?"

"I hope you don't mind, sir. They'll do whatever you want in exchange for a photo op with a USAF general."

"Are you kidding?" I asked. "They must be easily impressed. If that's all it takes, I'm happy to take a few pictures with them … no problem. Has Capt Kelly coordinated with the forward operating base yet?"

"Yes, sir," Winsett said. "They have a mission tomorrow night, but they'll be available for a few hours prior to the mission briefing."

We met the other team members at the dining facility. Everyone was stoked about the opportunity to fly on a Russian helicopter. I was excited to meet the Rangers who survived the mishap, the same Rangers who flew into combat almost every night. Few people know the perils they engage in on a routine basis and do so with universal dedication and conviction.

After dinner, we headed to the office to prepare for the night's first interview. Engine performance in the theater and maintenance procedures required to keep the aircraft flying topped our list of inquiries. Our first interview would be with Technical Sergeant (TSgt) Pat Dooley. He was assigned to the 801st Special Operations Aircraft Maintenance Squadron (SOAMXS) as a flight line expediter.

When he arrived, TSgt Dooley appeared nervous, or perhaps intimidated by the interview process. He stood a little over six feet tall, fit, with hair clipped short in a flat-top style. His muscled upper body appeared as though he might have pumped iron for some time. He stood in the hall near the open door, shifting nervously from one foot to the other.

I sent Kelly and Dolan out to the hallway to explain the process to him, hoping to relieve his nerves. I had come to rely on Kelly much more as time passed. She could coax a cast iron gargoyle off its concrete pedestal with her universal good cheer and energy. With her in charge of our schedule, we seldom wasted precious time. After a few minutes, he stepped through the door and stared at every inanimate object in the room. He made little eye contact with the board members.

"Sir," Kelly said. "This is TSgt Pat Dooley."

We shook hands, his touch clammy and tense. I dispensed with any sense of needless protocol to put him at ease and offered him water or coffee. He declined but forced a slight smile. I read the preliminaries and administered the required oath.

"For the non-aviation personnel on the board, please tell us what a flight line expediter's duty entails." I asked.

"Sir, I manage the flow of parts and supplies on the flight line."

"Were you on duty on the night of April 8th?" I asked.

"No, sir. I reported for duty at my regular time, 1:00 a.m. on April 9th. When I arrived, the accident had just occurred. The operations center was busy with rescue and recovery operations. I helped my supervisor as best I could."

"Thank you. MSgt Dolan is the investigations board's maintenance representative," I said. "He would like to ask a few questions."

"TSgt Dooley, after an airplane returns from a mission, engine data and parameters are downloaded from the VSLED. Maintenance will use the information to evaluate the health of the engines and other systems prior to launching the Osprey on its next mission. Is that correct?"

"That's correct."

"I have reviewed the most recent trend data for both engines of the mishap airplane. The left engine appeared to be performing normally. The right engine indicated signs of degraded performance. Would you please look at the data for the right engine and share your impressions with the board?"

TSgt Dooley studied the information for a minute or more.

"We'd perform a complete engine wash with this trend data. Afterward, we would have it fly and perform a power assurance check (PAC) to see if the engine performance trends improved. A 100% engine is a perfect performing engine. The engine performance will degrade slightly after every dirt landing."

Winsett slid me a note. *Was this done?*

I didn't want to upset TSgt Dooley by suggesting required maintenance procedure wasn't properly completed. I indicated we would get an answer later.

"I'm sorry, TSgt Dooley, please continue."

"Yes, sir, we would also check computer data for 'faults,' such as a coanda valve, or anti-ice valves being stuck open. If the valves are open, it will (have a negative) effect on the performance of the engine."

"You mentioned the coanda and the anti-ice valves," said Dolan. "Do those valves fail often?"

"Yes. That's a common failure that we see around three times a week. When the valves fail open, there is less air available for combustion. Engine performance would be lower than normal."

MSgt Dolan spoke maintenance language and asked most of the questions. He knew and understood issues with maintaining the CV-22, especially in a dirt environment. It's a complicated weapon system with issues unlike any other fixed or rotary wing airplane. When Doc Harper asked maintenance questions, no one on the board thought anything of it. He and Dolan had been inseparable since the first day the board met each other. The influence of their friendship showed in many interviews.

"If you would," Doc Harper said, "tell us how the local environment affects the Osprey? You have spoken about having to wash the engines more often. Is there anything that stands out about flying in Afghanistan versus flying at home in Florida?"

"Sir, this environment is tough on the airplanes. Large amounts of sand ingested by these engines results in glass accumulating on the turbine blades."

Winsett grabbed my arm and passed a one-word note – *Glass*?

Everyone stopped taking notes and looked at me and Dolan. Six weeks into the investigation and this was the first we had heard about sand turning into glass in the turbines.

Dolan shook his head and tapped his pen on his notes.

"You said glassing of the turbines. Would you describe exactly what that means for the board?"

"Sure. When sand enters the engine and heats up, it coats the turbines with a (an irregular) layer of glass. The result is an engine that has less and less power as the turbine and blades become more contaminated."

Dolan and squadrons maintaining the CV-22 had been familiar with the phenomenon, but to this point in our investigation, had not mentioned it as a consideration. Operations also seemed unaware that the constituents of the dirt, the desert sand in Afghanistan, are a near-perfect combination of magnesium, lime, a form of soda ash, and silica used in the commercial manufacture of common, everyday glass. Sand – due to a clogged or malfunctioning filter –could be ingested into the intake, compressed, and heated in the compressor section where it may cause abrasion damage to the blades. It is then super-heated in the combustion section, forming molten glass that passes into the turbine section. There it cools enough to collect on the blades and other components. The resulting distortion disrupts flow of exhaust and decreases power the engine is able to produce. Glass … had not been addressed before now, but we would make it a key subject as our accident investigation progressed.

Dolan looked to me before carrying on with his questions.

I completed a note and looked at the other board members.

"Please continue, MSgt Dolan," I said.

"You have told us about valves failing in an open position and glassing of the turbines. Have you seen any other issues contributing to loss or degradation of engine power?"

"No. Those are the only issues that I know of."

We asked a few more questions concerning maintenance procedures and then ended our interview. After TSgt Dooley departed, we discussed the challenges of operating the Osprey in such an unforgiving environment. I pressed Dolan about the glassing issue. He confessed to being aware of the problem but hadn't considered it a factor in this accident until Dooley's testimony.

Board members expressed concern about TSgt Dooley's comment after reviewing the last data downloaded from the mishap aircraft. He would have expected maintenance to have performed an engine wash and then reassess the engine power afterwards.

During the interview, we had asked TSgt Dooley to evaluate engine data downloaded after the airplane returned from its mission on the morning of April 8th. He answered our question based on maintenance procedures put in place after the accident. That is why he said he would have expected an engine wash. I chose not to explore his comment during the interview because in the weeks since the accident, maintenance procedures had continuously evolved.

VSLED data on the morning of April 8th revealed a failure of the left engine air particle separator (EAPS) after prolonged operation during an early morning dirt landing. After the accident, maintenance developed a more aggressive protocol for handling degraded engine performance and failure of the EAPS. Those procedures did not exist prior to the accident.

I asked O'Leary to have a flight engineer validate the CV-22 approach and go-around performance data based on the weather conditions the night of April 8th. I wanted to evaluate the difference between data with no valve problems, data with an anti-icing valve failed open, and data with a coanda valve failed open. Without recovering the actual valves or having the VSLED data after the accident, it would be nearly impossible to prove the valves had failed. After the accident, the aircraft had been bombed, the engines and the valves with it. Perhaps one or more survived in the wreckage that had been preserved the morning after the crash by the mysterious Army unit. But we would still have to find it.

We finished the four interviews and left the office by 12:30 a.m. Winsett let me off outside my building. Not a single truck, Hum-V, tank, or van moved on the base. It was eerily quiet. When the hippie-mobile pulled away, I stood outside my quarters and listened. The only sound I heard was the departing van. Though we'd not been out that time of morning, the silence nonetheless seemed very peculiar. I couldn't imagine a base the size and population of Kandahar being at a complete standstill – but it was. When we had reported for work earlier in the evening, the base buzzed with tens of dozens of combat and other vehicles crowding the narrow dirt roads departing the base. Now, in the middle of the night, midway into the wartime workday, ours were the only two vehicles on the streets. Not a shaft of light or sound pierced the stillness.

CHAPTER TWENTY THREE

FORWARD OPERATING BASE VISIT

To make a 9:00 a.m. show time the following morning, we agreed to rendezvous at 8:30 a.m. for a quick cup of coffee and light breakfast before driving across the base to the Afghan MI-17 operations building. It seemed odd to be walking toward the usual van pickup point in morning sunshine. The morning, like the afternoon, was dusty and bright. Our duty day had flipped sides of the clock and my body felt it. When Winsett stopped the van to pick me up, the three lieutenant colonels grinned as though they had just won the Afghan lottery.

I stepped through the sliding side door and took the closest seat.

"Ok. What's up?" I asked. "You can't be this happy to get a ride on a Russian helicopter."

"No, sir. Although, we are looking forward to that." O'Leary said with his ever so sly grin.

"Then what is it?" I asked.

"Well, sir … last night … after we dropped you off … we were stopped by base security police."

It had been years since I had found it necessary to intercede with military or local police on behalf of a drunken or otherwise disorderly airman or junior officer. I hadn't, nor could I recall, a single commander who had provided such a service for a field grade officer … let alone three.

"For doing what?" I asked.

"A few hundred meters after leaving you," O'Leary said, "A senior master sergeant blocked the street in front of us, jumped out of his car, and aimed his pistol at Winsett. He asked where we were going. We told him we'd just finished work and were returning to quarters, but he kept his sidearm pointed at Winsett anyway. Then, he asked why we had chosen to ignore the instructions to shelter in place after an active shooter broadcast sounded over the base loudspeaker system. We apologized for our inadvertent blunder and told him we did not hear the announcement. I begged him to lower the muzzle of his pistol and to please allow us to return to quarters. Eventually, the master sergeant accepted our explanation and agreed to follow us until we arrived safely back to our rooms."

"Sir, that's why the streets were vacant last night," Winsett said. "We must have walked out of our building after the announcement. I'm not sure why we didn't hear the warning. We thought we were going to be arrested."

I couldn't help but laugh.

"There's never a dull moment around the three of you," I said. "MSgt Dolan will be disappointed to have missed the excitement. But, now that you mention it, it was eerily quiet when you dropped me off last night. I remember thinking it was odd … but forgot about it until now."

We finished breakfast and drove to the flight line. Jet fighters, helicopters and drones sat clustered in rows by nationality and type along mile long asphalt ramps on both sides of the main runway. Operations buildings and hangars – temporary to permanent structures – separated the tarmac from the rest of the base. We crossed to the opposite side of the base and parked outside the Afghan MI-17 flight operations building. Everyone in the Afghan unit from the wing commander to the lowest ranking enlisted and their USAF advisors had turned out to welcome us.

I led the board along the line and greeted each person with a proper salute and handshake. After the informal formalities and posing for official and unofficial photographs, one of the Air Force lieutenant colonels assigned to the unit conducted a mission briefing for our flight. They had scheduled two helicopters to accommodate additional security personnel for me.

O'Leary, Adams, and I boarded the second MI-17 while the remainder of the board rode in the first helicopter. Four Afghan Army personnel positioned on our helicopter provided security during the flight and augmented local assets once on the ground at the forward operating base.

O'Leary sat next to me providing a play-by-play account of the entire flight. He considered the U.S. purchased MI-17 to be a reliable and cost-effective platform for the Afghanistan environment – simple to operate and built as tough as a tractor. Placards on basic cockpit instruments and throughout the aircraft were scribed in Russian. The Afghans didn't learn to speak or read the language. Their training provided only enough information to deal with the flight instruments and equipment to tie down cargo in the rear.

They also didn't spend precious time spiffing up their aircraft for our trip. In all honesty, it would have been impossible in that environment. They worked in an atmosphere similar to where and how they lived – an accommodation primitive by western standards. The crew configured the back of the helicopter with enough fold down, synthetic fiber red seats for our trip. The passenger door, forward and on the left side of the helicopter, was secured in the open position. We plugged our ears with Air Force issued foam inserts and used headsets to monitor communications inside the aircraft and with the air traffic controllers monitoring our flight.

The cargo/passenger compartment smelled of petroleum, but when the crew started the engines the smell of raw jet fuel and exhaust filled the atmosphere. The sound of the engines and rotors, once up to speed, sounded more like a growl than the whine of a U.S. made machine.

After lifting off, we headed northeast toward the forward operating base, planning to make a small detour to inspect the terrain near the accident site. Dust and desert dirt that plagued all aircraft operating in this environment swirled through the cargo compartment until we reached an altitude where the rotors ceased to kick up the dust. The open door provided a panoramic view of the Afghanistan countryside. Mountains added color and texture to the otherwise barren desert. Our experience with the bleak images on the ground contrasted our aerial view, which encompassed the entirety of the picturesque landscape. Only the crewmember in the rear, manning a machine gun pointed out the door, obstructed our view. For most of the flight, he moved about tethered by straps secured to the floor.

We flew north and parallel to the main highway connecting the cities of Kandahar and Kabul to the northeast, with the small town of Qalat about halfway in between. Were it not for the few scattered villages or an isolated compound dotting the desolate countryside, we could just as well have been flying over the daylight landscape of the planet Pluto. Inhabitants in the primitive setting survived with no paved roads or modern infrastructure to clutter the remarkable countryside. It was like going back in time and having a view of people surviving with only basic necessities.

Thirty minutes after takeoff, we flew over the accident site and made several circles to photograph the surrounding area and the point of impact from every aspect. O'Leary moved forward and asked the pilots to fly ten miles east, to replicate the same course the mishap aircrew had flown to the landing zone. Five miles from the site, we descended to one hundred and fifty feet above the ground, slowed, then hovered for a time over charred dirt that marked the scene of the accident. Six weeks afterward, the desert floor still bore the scars of the crash but revealed nothing to mark the presence or passing of CV-22, tail number 06-0031, except blackened earth slowly fading to a pale brown as wind-blown sand covered the site over time.

We snapped pictures along the route and from overhead the dark charred stain on the desert floor. Departing the site, we made a slow climbing turn toward the forward operating base. In less than five minutes, the crew started to descend in a shallow spiraling turn for landing.

We touched down in a large gravel area close to fuel bladders located several hundred meters from the main part of the remote base. After the crews shut down engines, we deplaned, gathered our gear, and assembled with team members from the other helicopter.

"Did you get some good photos?" I asked.

"Yes, sir, hundreds," Kelly answered.

Consumed with preparations for their night missions, the base spared no one to greet us when we landed. Dolan and Doc Harper hefted Adams' equipment and we walked toward a cluster of tents hoping for directions once we found someone to ask.

O'Leary remained at my side after we landed, discussing typical operations of forward bases, as well as a discussion of the accident site and surrounding terrain.

"Sir, without terrain or weather considerations," O'Leary said, "The approach should've been simple. If I were to choose a landing area for training a new Osprey pilot for their first dirt landing, I would choose an area like the accident site. It was level and very easy to access."

Located in Taliban territory and surrounded by a cinder block wall and concertina wire, the base seemed small, and a challenge to defend against a determined force. Manned by at least one Ranger, four guard towers bristled with automatic weapons on fixed bases prepared to rain withering rates of gunfire on any adversary foolish enough to assault the perimeter.

We walked about five hundred meters before reaching the group of tents we had seen from the helicopter pad. We navigated a winding maze of sandbags that created a path to the entrance to the first tent. I stopped short of the tent's entrance door and called to MSgt Dolan.

A cylindrical shaft, about two inches in diameter, leaned against the exterior of the tent. The ends of the rod appeared to have been broken rather than cut. Chards of sheet metal protruded along its edge and appeared to have been ripped from a previous shape, serving no utility in its current use – a temporary doorstop.

"MSgt Dolan … look at this. Can you believe what we're seeing?"

CHAPTER TWENTY FOUR

SHOCKING DISCOVERY

Sandbags piled five feet high defined our narrow path to the tent entrance. Stopping short of the door, I log jammed our progress. Dolan, toting half of Adams' equipment, squeezed past everyone from his place at the end of our pedestrian caravan to where I stood at the front.

I reached for the three-foot-long object, but Dolan grabbed my arm.

"Probably shouldn't touch that, sir."

The shape appeared to be made of aluminum, but chards of varying shapes protruded at random from the cylindrical core and looked like sheet metal. I stepped a half pace away and looked to Dolan for an explanation. As soon as he spoke, I realized the reason for caution. The jagged edges of the sheet metal-like material could slice exposed skin and if our suspicions proved correct, were toxic.

Dolan stepped closer for a detailed look.

"Sir, I'd put money on that being the ramp hinge ... or part of it ... from our CV-22 accident. If not a section of the hinge, it's definitely a piece of the accident airplane."

O'Leary eased forward, edging Winsett and Kelly to one side of the compacted dirt path. "I agree. If the rest of the wreckage the Army recovered isn't on this base, it's got to be nearby."

"Well," I said, "someone placed it here. It didn't fly here on its own. Let's go inside and ask how it got here."

In theater, hand-scrawled signs, if they existed at all, were used to indicate who or what activity operated or lived in what space. But, if bad guys ever broke through the base perimeter, signs also gave away operations areas and inhabitants' living quarters. We had no idea who, or what organization, occupied the tent we were about to enter.

I led our little troop through the door. By the time Army personnel saw Kelly, with three lieutenant colonels between her and a general officer, they called the area to attention.

"At ease," I said. "We're here to interview Rangers who were aboard the Osprey the morning of the April 9th accident."

Five desks lined one side of an otherwise large open area. Twenty or more metal folding chairs sat in no apparent order or purpose about the room. More of the collapsed chairs rested against two wooden boxes at the far side of the tent. To our immediate right, knocked-together shelving, loaded with energy bars of every description, sat atop cases of bottled water and a half dozen cases of Girl Scout cookies. Two strings of clear incandescent lights hung the length of the tent illuminating the space.

"Who's in charge?" I asked.

"Sir, I'm the battalion First Sergeant … Drennen. We're expecting you.

I checked his name tag.

"First Sergeant Drennen, we talked on the phone a few nights ago."

"Yes, sir, welcome to forward operating base Delta."

"First Sergeant, out in front of your tent we saw a piece of what appears to be Osprey wreckage."

"Yes, sir, a souvenir we copped from forward operating base Apache … about seven miles west of here. They have a dumpster full of parts from the accident. A couple of us picked pieces to take home to Ft. Benning when we rotate out of here."

The tiny hairs on the nape of my neck tingled and rose over the top of my scalp. A wave of goose bumps raced through my body.

Winsett stammered, unable to speak at the pace thoughts were racing through his head.

"Sir … sir … sir."

"I know," I said, "Captain Kelly …"

"I'm on it, sir … forward operating base Apache … we'll go there as soon as possible."

For the first time since we had been together, Winsett spiraled out of his controlled element. We had the day in our hand, and he couldn't cope not being in two places at once. He muttered while he made notes:

… "flight incident recorder … engines … have to see the …"

"All right everyone, we have a job to do today," I said. "We owe it to the Rangers who were on the Osprey. They're here to talk to us. Let's focus on completing interviews. Everyone ready?"

"Yes, sir."

"Where do you want us to work, First Sergeant Drennen?" I asked.

"Sir, we're not long on space, but if it works for you, I've cleared an area in the rear of the tent. We've set up two tables and if you'll tell us how you want to set chairs, I'll have someone arrange them for you. Major Carter will be here in ten minutes, if that suits you, sir."

"Perfect," I answered.

Dolan set Adams' equipment at the far end of the tent.

"We'll get the chairs, sir. These guys have enough to do."

We carried our bags and equipment to the area of the tent partitioned for our use and set up enough chairs for us and anyone we would interview. Winsett assigned seats for the accident board members while Adams worked her equipment.

We had been working nonstop for over a month. The Rangers we were about to interview were accident survivors and had returned to duty as soon as physically possible. These were the best first-hand witnesses we would interview until we could talk to the remaining crewmember - the tail scanner. Though few of the survivors had been able to monitor interphone conversations between the flight crew, perhaps one of them had a clue about a sound, or event, that would prove to be critical.

Stunned that we had discovered a piece of wreckage and the prospect of finding more, lifted our expectations dramatically. Despite our temporary euphoria, we remained wary of the possibility that some official or unofficial chicanery would prevent us from discovering the remaining wreckage, or the cause of the accident.

While we finished preparations for the first interview, Kelly and O'Leary busied themselves with phone calls. Kelly searched for an opening in our schedule and O'Leary looked for a line to the MI-17 unit back at Kandahar Air Base.

We had no hours during our remaining time in country to pack even a minute into our schedule. If I had to split the board to accommodate a trip to another forward operating base, I would. The pomp and security involved with traveling within a war zone as a general officer meant I wouldn't get to see the dumpster. My biggest concern was whether it was still at forward operating base Apache. Or, were the Army personnel at the base ordered to destroy it weeks ago.

CHAPTER TWENTY FIVE

MAJOR KEITH CARTER

A must-do visit to forward operating base Apache descended on our already packed schedule. I didn't see a half day we could spare, but since the safety board recovered a mere shoebox's measure of wreckage, we couldn't pass the opportunity to recover debris that might provide definitive, or at least significant, accident information. The board hummed with the prospective revelation.

Winsett immediately set about arranging chairs and tables for our first interview and assisted with the recording equipment.

In a group or on our own we had revisited sections of transcripts when time allowed, but Adams more than the rest of the board became the most intimate with our mounting volume of testimony. She sat through every initial session then dealt with relistening to the interview at least ten or more times in order to transcribe testimonies into a final written product. She asked if she might open the session with Army Major (MAJ) Keith Carter. I admired her enthusiasm and had no objections.

We had interviewed other Rangers from the mishap aircraft, most with light injuries who returned to duty soon afterwards. MAJ Carter's unique position as the commander of the assault force required him to be plugged into, and listen with a headset, all aircraft interphone and radio communications for the entire flight. Others we had interviewed had received relayed messages from him, or the tail scanner, during the flight. We hoped he would provide a sliver of evidence suggesting the cockpit crew was challenged by a malfunction of some type during the last minute of flight.

MAJ Carter entered the tent with most of the board ignoring Winsett's urging to be in their seats and ready to start the interview. Undaunted by the lack of formality, Carter walked straight to me and snapped a crisp salute.

"General Harvel, Major Carter reporting as ordered, sir."

I acknowledged with a salute.

"My apologies for our lack of preparedness," I said. "We've just learned parts of the Osprey wreckage may be at a nearby forward operating base. Please have a seat. We'll start momentarily. I know your time is limited."

I made introductions while everyone took their seats. After the formal preliminaries, acknowledgements, and swearing-in, Carter stated his unit of assignment – Commander, Alpha Company, Third Ranger Battalion, Seventy-Fifth Ranger Regiment, Fort Benning, Georgia. Responsible for his company's training and operations, he supervised the tactical and technical deployment of unit personnel, weapons, and equipment.

The night of the accident, he commanded the ground force assigned a target situated on the outskirts of the village of Qalat. He oversaw the planning, determined assets required, and coordinated with support units, which included the Osprey flight lead (Maj Voas). Before I ceded the questioning to Adams, I asked a few questions to set the time and place of the events of April 8th.

"You were the first to board the Osprey and sat behind the cockpit door. Did you notice anything unusual about the takeoff, or the first few moments of the flight?"

"Yes, sir. I sat directly behind the cockpit. The takeoff seemed normal. We transitioned from helicopter mode to airplane mode normally. I monitored radio calls on my headset and chatted with the crew over the interphone."

"Do you remember a time over target being planned for the mission that night?"

"No, sir. It wasn't important. The mission wasn't a timed operation. The mission was conditions-based. I told the pilot my only request was to get us there as quickly as possible. I needed the cover of darkness to conduct the mission."

TSgt Adams interrupted.

"Sir, I have a question."

"Sure, go ahead," I said

"Major Carter, sir, you were on headset monitoring the crew's communications. Would you take us all the way up to where the crew relayed the one-minute call to you and your team?"

"Absolutely. We got the required ten-minute, six-minute, three-minute, and a one-minute call over the interphone. At each of the advisories, I flashed hand signals, combined with verbal calls, yelling the warnings to my team. Team members acknowledged by repeating the visual and aural signals. We perform certain actions at each call. At the one-minute warning, we get up on one knee and hold the quick disconnect device in our hand in order to unlatch us from the airplane safety line. The airplane safety line is the only thing holding us in the airplane. It's a simple, but primitive, seat belt of sorts. We were then in position for a rapid egress in the event the landing zone was 'hot' ... meaning under enemy fire."

"What about after the one-minute warning?" asked Adams.

"For the next thirty seconds, everything seemed normal. With thirty seconds to go, I started feeling like 'wow' we're really going fast. Looking out the back of the Osprey, I could see the sand whizzing by. I didn't hear anything to indicate something was wrong, nothing out of the ordinary, except we were going very fast while close to the ground. I expected the crew would flare, land, and let us out, no problem. A few seconds later, something seemed wrong. All of a sudden, the pilot flared the Osprey dramatically. The fuselage went vertical. Out the back of the airplane, all I could see was sand moving by very quickly. I was like ... holy shit ... I'm staring straight down at the ground. I had never been in a helicopter, or airplane that flared like that. There was no indication from the crew that something was wrong. We were all trying to keep our balance on one knee. I needed to sit down to stabilize myself. I heard a countdown through my headset indicating our height above the ground. The countdown started at ten and stopped at seven feet when we hit the ground. My head hit the sidewall of the airplane. After a second hard bump, I lost my balance and was knocked unconscious. I woke up trapped under avionics equipment and pieces of the airplane. I looked to my right and saw a fire. An engine was burning, but the fire was not spreading toward the fuselage. I tried to push the equipment off me. I couldn't budge it. Some guys moaned; others screamed. My ankle was hurt, and I had a broken nose. Considering everything, I was lucky to have such minor injuries. People moved around and eventually the avionics equipment was lifted off me. A couple of my guys asked me if I was okay and helped me stand up. I exited the airplane and walked the perimeter of the crash site searching for other survivors. The airplane was upside down. I had no idea we had flipped over. I approached a couple of my soldiers at the back of the airplane and told them to get everyone who was able, to go back into the airplane and get everyone out. I surveyed the rest of the airplane. The cockpit was gone. I walked to where it should have been, and one of the pilots was nearby. He was still strapped in his seat, but out in front of the airplane. One of my soldiers helped him get unstrapped and rendered first aid. The pilot was talking to my soldier, so I thought he must be okay."

"Did you talk to the co-pilot at the crash site?" Doc Harper asked.

"Yes, sir. I made sure all my soldiers were accounted for. I was told everyone had been pulled out of the airplane. One of my sergeants relayed that we had one dead and one in very serious condition. I ordered him to get soldiers posted around the perimeter to guard the site. The co-pilot was somehow still in his seat, trying to call someone using his survival radio and I asked him, 'Hey man, does your damn radio work?' He told me it worked, so I told him to call for help. Enemy personnel could be maneuvering on our position. I was thinking we may have been shot down. The co-pilot made radio contact with one of the support airplanes using an emergency radio in his survival vest. He asked if enemy personnel were in the area. The airplane relayed that the area was safe – no enemy in the area. That was a big relief. I changed my focus to rescue operations now that I knew combat was not imminent."

"Did you manage the care and coordination for the personnel who were seriously injured?" I asked

"Sir, my soldiers had that under control. After talking to the co-pilot, I walked back to the airplane to look for the other crewmembers. I couldn't find the other pilot, flight engineer or tail gunner [tail scanner]. Returning to the airplane a second time, I found the tail scanner, still in his harness, hung from the floor which was now the ceiling of the upside-down airplane. I shook him a little and did not get a response. I assumed he was dead. I should have taken a pulse, but I didn't think about it. We arranged injured personnel into three groups. One group was personnel who did not have a pulse. Another group was the personnel we considered to be in critical condition. They would be the first to be evacuated from the site when able. The last group was people who were injured, but not critically. Everyone had been accounted for except the pilot and flight engineer. As I searched, I contacted with my troops in the back of the other two Ospreys using my hand-held FM radio. They had just landed and were moving toward our position as fast as they could run. I gave them a quick update on our status. I yelled to my guys that chalk two was near, and that chalk three was close behind. We continued to help the injured personnel to the best of our abilities. Within minutes, personnel from chalk two arrived. They took over first aid and relieved my guys, providing a security perimeter."

"Do you recall hearing anything from the crew?" O'Leary asked. "Did you hear any kind of automated airplane warnings during the last thirty seconds of flight?"

"Yes, sir. I did hear an automated female voice that kept repeating 'altitude low, altitude low.' I hear that warning almost every time I fly."

"Did you hear any types of bells, alarms, or beeper tones that could be indications of engine problems?"

"Not that I know of, sir. But I can't recall with any degree of accuracy at this point."

"Just to clarify, at the one-minute warning and for thirty seconds after that, everything

was normal. Is that right?"

"Yes, sir. All was normal up to thirty seconds after the one-minute warning. At [about] twenty seconds to landing, we were still flying very fast. I have only flown on the Osprey five other times. The other Osprey flights were much slower at that point in time. They came into a hover and touched down as a helicopter would normally land."

Capt Kelly raised her hand.

"Sir, I have a couple questions. Major Carter, what did you mean when you said the airplane had a hard time stabilizing at twenty seconds to landing?"

"The reason I said the airplane was unstable, is because me and the rest of my team had a hard time staying on one knee. The fuselage was moving erratically, and we were getting knocked around. I'm not using an aviation term. I'm just saying we had a difficult time staying up on a knee due to the erratic airplane movement."

"Was the airplane movement a rolling type motion? Or a pitching motion?" I asked.

"Sir, it was definitely a pitching motion. The fuselage seemed to go back and forth from horizontal to vertical. I don't remember a lot of side to side movement."

O'Leary broke in.

"Have you ever heard the cadence of calls they make on a normal approach that goes something like, altitude one hundred feet, fifty feet, down forty, down thirty, down twenty, and down ten?"

"Yes, sir. Then they say, 'clear left, clear right.' Yes, I've heard that before."

"Did you hear those calls that night?"

"No, sir. I heard a crewmember make a call starting at ten … nine … eight. At seven the callouts ended and we hit the ground. The crew member was very excited while making the callouts."

"Were you able to tell which crew member was making those callouts?"

"No, sir. I had just met the crew for the first time earlier that evening."

Doc Harper asked, "Tell me how the tail scanner was removed from the wreckage?"

"Sir, after chalk two arrived, I told them the tail scanner was the only person still in the back of the airplane. I thought he was killed in action. They went to get him out. While cutting the rope to get him down, one of them yelled, 'Hey, Major, he's still alive.' The medics from chalk two and the battalion surgeon from chalk three immediately rendered aid."

"What about the cockpit crew members?" asked Harper.

"Sir, I never found the cockpit, or the crew members. I was one of the last Rangers evacuated from the site. I wasn't there when the pilot and flight engineer were found. The next day I was told they were found by the combat search and rescue personnel. They were able to lift the fuselage and remove the pilot and flight engineer from what remained of the cockpit."

MAJ Carter had to prepare for a mission that night, but I had one last question.

"When we arrived, there was a piece of the Osprey propped against the wall of the tent near the front entrance door. We were told it was recovered from a stack of wreckage at a nearby forward operating base. Have you been to forward operating base Apache?"

"Yes, sir. I've been there a few times. Numerous pieces of the wrecked airplane are in a large dumpster. During one of our trips, we picked out a couple parts for souvenirs. Sir, have you seen the photos, or an inventory of the parts?"

"We had reason to believe there were parts of the Osprey somewhere. But, until today we had no idea where. We're going to forward operating base Apache as soon as we can arrange transportation."

"Yes, sir. You need to go soon. I saw one of the Osprey engines there."

CHAPTER TWENTY SIX

MISSION PLANNER

For the time, we had set aside informal talk about crew issues. During our not so idle time in recent days, our conversations concerned those factors affecting aircraft and engine performance. Since none of the participants, or opinions, dominated the deliberations, I allowed it as a healthy exploration of our investigation. Fearing to weight the dialogue in one direction or another, I refrained from entering the conversations.

The prospect of recovering critical parts of the Osprey from what had been salvaged from the accident site intensified the conjecture concerning anti-icing or coanda valves failing open, thus reducing engine power available. Engine failure was also a consideration. If the flight information recorder were to be recovered from the dumpster at forward operating base Apache, our investigation might accelerate to a rapid conclusion.

While waiting for the next interview to start, we asked the first sergeant for details about forward operating base Apache. He provided contacts for the base orderly room and the unit commander. Kelly wasted no time coordinating dates and times for a visit. With Dolan's assistance, she compiled a list of tools and equipment that might be required to disassemble, cut away, or recover parts from the wreckage.

While I pored over the questions for our next interview, O'Leary engaged three soldiers who had just entered the tent. He brought one of the Army officers to meet me.

"Sir, this is Major Robert Kocher. He's here on temporary duty to coordinate next week's missions for the Rangers. He was working in the joint operations center on the night of the accident. Do you think Capt Kelly has room on our schedule to interview him while we're here? We could wait until we return to Kandahar, or by phone from Hurlburt, but he's willing to conduct an interview this evening."

I stood up and shook his hand.

"You were on duty the night of April 8th?"

"Yes, sir. I reported to work at 4:00 p.m. that afternoon. I worked until shift change at 4:00 a.m. the following morning. I'm the primary planner for Ranger missions. It is my job to get our strike force to the target and back to their base safely after each mission."

"Major, if you would, coordinate your Kandahar schedule with Capt Kelly. Worst case, we'll do a phone interview from Hurlburt. When will you return to Kandahar?" I asked.

"Sir, I'm here tonight. I fly back to Kandahar tomorrow."

"Captain Kelly will advise you when we can work you into our schedule. We look forward to speaking with you."

The first sergeant waited behind MAJ Kocher with a young soldier standing behind him. "General Harvel, this is Specialist (SPC) Craig Hansen."

We shook hands.

"Have a seat. I'll read you some required stipulations. If you understand and consent, we'll swear you in, take your testimony, and you can be on your way. Agreed?"

"Yes, sir." Hansen replied

At twenty-two years old, SPC Hanson had been in the Army three years and a Ranger for nearly two. Due to the nature of Special Operations' close-in contact, he often did not see action while providing indirect fire leading his 60mm mortar[14] team.

"The night of April 8th, did you consider anything to be unusual at any time during the flight?" I asked.

"Sir, one thing I noticed was after the one-minute warning, we seemed to be going very fast. I couldn't distinguish anything due to the speed. I heard a thump and then the airplane began to shake a lot. It was a

---

14 A stand-off, indirect versus aimed fire weapon, employing mobile launched high explosive artillery type support.

firm landing. I was trying to keep my balance. Suddenly my feet went out from under me. I realized we were crashing. After that, it was mayhem."

The remark concerning the aircraft shuddering disturbed MSgt Dolan. I also noticed as Hanson talked, his speech seemed uncomfortable and labored. I didn't want to embarrass him by asking about it, though.

"Can you describe the way the airplane shuddered?" asked Dolan. "Was it like what you have felt in your previous Osprey flights?"

"Well, sort of. I have felt the airplane shake when it gets close to the ground. It rocks back and forth. But, this time, it felt different. It felt like the airplane was straining, trying to do something. It was shaking bad. I was thinking this is not good, and we hit the ground."

"What happened after you hit the ground?"

"We hit hard, and I remember doing a back flip. My feet came up and I tucked into a ball and grabbed my head with lots of flying debris hitting me. My helmet flew off. I don't remember being knocked unconscious. But I must have blacked out for a while. To me, it seemed like a few seconds. I have been told that no one crawled out of the airplane until three to four minutes after the accident. I remember hanging from the roof. Later, I found out the airplane flipped onto its back and I was actually hanging from the floor."

"How did you get out of the airplane?" Doc Harper asked.

"Sir, I unhooked from the tie-down strap and moved airplane pieces out of my way so I could crawl out. When I got out of the airplane, I stood up. PFC Tilley and I were the only ones outside the airplane. Both engines were on fire. We needed to get the others out before the fire spread into the Osprey. We both crawled back into the airplane to help the other Rangers."

"Did you see the tail scanner on your way out, or when you went back into the airplane?"

"Yes, sir. As I crawled out, he was the first person I saw. He was smashed up bad and tangled in a lot of debris. He reached toward me and asked for help. I told him I would be back as soon as I got some more help. PFC Tilley and I went back into the airplane and cut away straps and untangled our teammates. SSG McGuire freed himself and helped pull people to a safe distance. He set up the casualty collection points. PFC Tilley could only use one arm, but he helped Rangers get untangled. We pulled people toward the back of the airplane, and SSG McGuire helped them get to where the injured were gathered. I helped SSG Nigro. He told me he thought his arm and ribs were broken. I got him untangled, then pulled two large pieces of wreckage off SSG Tennill's leg. He was not moving or talking so I hit him on the leg, just to see if he was alive. He was. He got mad at me because of his broken leg. It took a couple of minutes, but I finally got him out too. SSG McGuire pulled him away from the airplane. The next person I saw was the female Afghan interpreter. She was dead. I pulled her out of the way and put her helmet over her face. The male Afghan interpreter was the next person I helped. He had a broken nose and was tangled in wreckage. I was able to get him free. He crawled to where SSG McGuire could assist him. I went back into the airplane and pulled more wreckage off a body. It was Corporal (CPL) Michael Jankiewicz. His head was severely injured. The only way I could identify him was by his name tag. It took me a few minutes to get him untangled and moved to the back of the airplane. Other Rangers rendered first aid as best they could. It hit me hard seeing CPL Jankiewicz in such bad condition. I thought he might be dead. I tried my best to save him. He was one of my best friends. I still think about him often."

"That must have been a tough time for you," Winsett said. "You did an amazing job helping to get people out of the airplane. What injuries did you sustain?"

"Sir, I had back, knee and jaw injuries. I still can't open my mouth very well. Compared to the others, my injuries were not too bad. I was off duty for about a month. I have been back with my unit for about a week."

We had limited time to speak with each Ranger, so we asked general questions hoping to elicit specific information we might not have had. SPC Hansen provided specific post-crash details of how people got out of the airplane. I thanked him for his extraordinary service and for taking the time to participate in the interview. He stood and saluted. I returned his salute and he departed. For the next few minutes, we discussed his impressive courage, dedication, and bravery under such extreme circumstances. An incredible young Ranger by all measures.

We took a short break and prepared for the next interview. Winsett badgered us about our limited time. He wanted to ensure each interviewee had ample opportunity to tell us what they saw, heard or smelled during the flight. We interviewed SSG McGuire, SSG Tennill, and SGT Blaylock. They confirmed the seating diagram we had created. They also confirmed others' testimony regarding the order and means everyone used to evacuate the aircraft. By the time we finished the last interview, Rangers outside spooled-up in pep-rally fashion, hyping adrenalin for the night's mission, a practice repeated too often in the life of soldiers so young.

Capt Kelly broke my train of thought.

"Sir, would you like for me to see if MAJ Kocher is still available to be interviewed?"

"I forgot about him. Thanks for reminding me. Do we have time before the MI-17s return to pick us up?"

O'Leary lowered his head, looked over his brow, and flashed me his tight grin.

"Sir, they're working on our schedule. They'll wait while we conduct this last interview."

"Ok. Let's see if Kocher's still available," I said.

As Kelly went outside to locate him, the rest of us prepared for a quick interview and talked about forward operating base Apache and our growing list of tools and equipment needed for the trip. Our discussion was interrupted when Kelly returned with MAJ Kocher in tow.

"Sir, we have ten to fifteen minutes before he has to attend a mission briefing."

"Thank you, Major," I said. "Let's get started."

I read the legal preamble, swore him, and went right to questions.

"We talked about your job and duties earlier, but now that we are conducting an official interview, I want to capture it for the record. You stated you are a mission planner for the Army Ranger Task Force. It is your job to get the strike forces on target and back safely. You were the primary mission planner for the mission on the night of April 8th. Did I summarize the information correctly?"

"Yes, sir."

"Almost forgot ... please state your name, rank and unit of assignment."

"Sir, Major Robert Kocher, Third Battalion, Seventy-Fifth Ranger Regiment."

"Without disclosing classified information, please tell the board about the process you went through to plan the mission on April 8th."

"Sir, we had been tracking the objective for a day and a half. We had him fixed to a certain location about five kilometers away from where we intended to land the Ospreys. I evaluated the threat, terrain, and the desires of the ground force commander. Due to the noise signature of the Osprey, the ground force commander elected to conduct an offset infiltration. After careful study of the area with an imagery analyst, MAJ Carter and I agreed that this would be a perfect mission for the Ospreys."

"Did you plan a time over target for this mission?" O'Leary asked.

"No, sir."

"How important was it for you, as the mission planner, to have the team arrive at the landing zone during a certain time period?"

"Sir, for the team to arrive within seconds or minutes of the scheduled time was not critical. Arriving within thirty minutes to an hour of the time would have been critical due to limiting factors of the other support assets. The ground force commander needed the cover of darkness for his Rangers to walk and/or run to the target area, and then to conduct a safe exfiltration when complete."

"Where were you when the accident occurred?" O'Leary asked.

"Sir, I was working in the joint operations center. I heard about the accident from the A-10s supporting the mission. When I investigated their report, our messaging systems went crazy with multiple reports. Within one minute of the accident, we confirmed the aircraft was down. We immediately re-located one of our surveillance sensors in order to use its camera to monitor the accident site. I asked other air assets if they detected enemy activity or suspected the airplane may have been shot down. They replied negative to both questions. I directed one of the officers on duty to alert the combat search and rescue team leader. I also had him notify the Medical Evacuation (MEDEVAC) unit to have their officer-in-charge report to the operations center immediately. I called the MH-47 unit and told them to prepare for an immediate launch to carry a platoon of infantry to provide security at the site. After hanging up my phone, I heard a commotion. Personnel in the operations center watched as survivors crawled out of the crashed airplane. We counted the number as they helped each other out of the wreckage. We then relayed the information to Army personnel aboard the other two Ospreys orbiting the accident site area. We monitored communications between the A-10s and the Ospreys asking if the area was clear of enemy forces. The A-10s declared the area safe. The Ospreys radioed they were evaluating landing sites. They planned to land within five to ten minutes."

"Did anyone in the operations center keep a log that recorded these events and what time they happened?" Kelly asked.

"Yes, ma'am. We always keep a log. Do you need a copy for April 8th and 9th?"

"Yes, that would be helpful."

"Was there any discussion in the operations center about preserving or recovering the airplane, or what was left of it?" Winsett asked.

"Sir, we decided to send a CV-22 pilot to the site on the MH-47. The Task Force Commander, Colonel Walrath, also went to the site. We agreed that a pilot on scene could ensure all classified information was properly recovered from the airplane. He would also advise COL Walrath whether a recovery operation would be feasible. After seeing the airplane, they determined that lifting the weakened fuselage would be difficult to impossible. The cockpit was totally flattened. Nothing appeared to be recoverable. The status of the wreckage was forwarded to Higher Headquarters (HHQ) in Kabul for a decision to preserve, recover, or destroy. HHQ ordered the airplane destroyed."

"After the accident, special operators issued a pause in flying the Ospreys. Describe the criteria for getting them back on your list of usable mission assets." O'Leary asked.

"Sir, we worked with the unit leaders to improve safety margins. We looked at passenger and cargo weights, altitudes, and temperatures to better utilize the Ospreys. The crews performed several day and night landings to improve their proficiency on low visibility approaches. They also changed their training, tactics, and procedures. I told them I would make sure they had a minimum of two hours for mission planning, instead of the previous one hour. They also changed the criteria for descending to approach altitude. Before the accident, they started the approach at three miles. After the accident, they would start the approach at five miles in order to give the crews more time to evaluate the wind speed and direction at the approach altitude."

Adams addressed the recovery of some of the aircraft wreckage.

"The morning after the accident, soldiers went to the crash site. Did you or someone from the operations center send them?"

"No, I had nothing to do with that. Those personnel were from the First Battalion of the 508th Infantry Regiment. They operate out of forward operating base Apache. They tried to help in any way possible. Unbeknownst to me, they moved a convoy and troops to the crash site at sunrise and recovered some of the wreckage. I haven't been to forward operating base Apache to see what they have, but MAJ Carter told me they have quite a few pieces stored at their base."

Adams wanted more specific information.

"Sir, exactly who went to the site? Do you have names?"

"No, I'm not sure. I do know it was two platoons from the First of the 508th. I'm sorry that I do not have names."

"Sir, do you know why they were there?"

"I think they were just curious. The intensity of helicopter traffic operating in their area drew them to the site. They were not invited or ordered to go."

I checked the time. MAJ Kocher was due to attend the mission briefing with the other Rangers.

"MAJ Kocher, I can't thank you enough for taking the time to share information with us. We truly admire and are very grateful for the work you and your teams are doing here."

He stood, shook hands, and rendered a salute before departing. We gathered our notes and rearranged the area to look like it did when we arrived. Army personnel were huddled in a nearby tent getting ready for their mission. Out of respect, we quietly gathered our gear and exited the tent. I glanced to where the Rangers had gathered. I couldn't imagine going on life-threatening missions every night and doing so with such positive attitudes. They were the epitome of tough, courageous, smart, and totally dedicated heroes.

We made our way toward the helicopter landing area. Silhouettes of two MI-17s stood against the dim moonlight. Crews outside the helicopters prepared for flight. As had become our custom, O'Leary and Winsett walked with me. Kelly and Adams followed close behind. We discussed the interviews and the phone calls that needed our attention as soon as we landed at Kandahar. Doc Harper and Dolan lagged the group, engaged in frivolous chatter, as always.

Approaching the helicopters, we separated into two groups to board. The Afghan Army personnel waited for me at the bottom of the steps and offered to help remove my backpack and load my gear. As I started climbing the steps, Dolan grabbed my arm and cupped his hand over his mouth so he could whisper directly into my ear.

"Sir, forward operating base Apache is only a few miles from here. It's possible we will not have another opportunity to travel there. I've talked to the other team members, and Lt Col O'Leary has briefed the crews. How about we make a quick stop? If the flight information recorder is in that dumpster, we can recover it and take it to Kandahar tonight. What do you say, sir? It's only a few minutes out of our way."

CHAPTER TWENTY SEVEN

SEARCHING THE WRECKAGE

Flying to forward operating base Apache would consume a few minutes of the remaining daylight. Then, if we had an hour to comb through the wreckage for anything usable, we would still be on our way to Kandahar before the night's missions departed. But … we had no tools or equipment to remove twisted metal and airplane parts from whatever we might find.

I backed down off the steps of the MI-17 and motioned for O'Leary to come toward me. "What do you think about making a stop to look at the wreckage stored at forward operating base Apache?"

He looked at me and MSgt Dolan with the wry grin that indicated he knew the answer. "Sir, as tempting as that might sound, this time of night it might not be a good idea to drop into any forward operating base unannounced. Most units are preparing for the night's missions and may not have the inclination or capability to handle last minute visitors. Remember … we're in a Russian helicopter. MSgt Dolan approached me with the idea. It may suit our purpose, but maybe not everyone else's. And, we had agreed that our investigation wouldn't impact operational missions. We have contacts at Apache. We should call first thing in the morning and schedule a visit when it's convenient for everyone. That said … the decision to fly there tonight is still yours, sir."

"No … you're right," I replied.

I looked at Kelly.

"I'm on it, sir, as soon as we land at Kandahar," she said with her typical jovial smile.

As much as I would have liked for the whole team to travel to Apache, I hesitated to ask for two helicopters to support two flights on whatever day we would negotiate. Though I did not want to burden the mission, the stars on my flight suit always seemed to be in the way. I put the matter to rest with everyone.

"It's been a long day. When we arrive at Kandahar, we'll discuss tomorrow's interviews over a late dinner. Questions?"

Everyone shook their head saying no. Despite our collective disappointment at being close to and unable to visit a prime objective, we loaded our gear and prepared for the flight to Kandahar. Within minutes, we droned through the Afghan sky with only the noise of the rotors over our heads. Most of the team sorted through notes from the day's testimonies. I visited with soldiers in our Afghan security detail, with the assistance of an interpreter. They seemed to appreciate the effort and the interest shown for their support.

The sound of the rotors changed pitch and the MI-17 banked left to start the descent. Against the dark sky, runway lights and ramp illumination separated the facilities associated with flight operations from the rest of the blacked-out base. It seemed small in the vast Afghan desert.

The crew maneuvered the helicopter toward the ramp and touched down in front of their hangar. With the rotor's energy spent, the crew gave us a thumbs-up, indicating we could grab our equipment and deplane.

We stacked our gear on the tarmac behind the helicopters and sent Harper and Winsett to retrieve our vans. While waiting, we exchanged pleasantries with the soldiers who had supported our mission over the long day. The Afghan student pilots and soldiers insisted I pose, once again, for pictures with them while O'Leary negotiated a future trip to forward operating base Apache with the unit commander.

The U.S. Air Force detachment assigned to train the Afghan pilots and support personnel held O'Leary in high regard. They seemed willing to do anything to help him. Again, I counted my good fortune having him assigned to the board. Before we departed the flight line, they committed to whatever schedule we would require getting to forward operating base Apache.

"Just give me a date and time, we'll make it happen," the commander said.

O'Leary looked at Kelly, "We'll have that information for him by tomorrow morning, right?"

"Perhaps within the hour," she said. "I'll call our Apache contacts as soon as we get to the office."

We departed the flight line for the Niagara dining facility. Over Mexican food, we discussed changes in our schedule for the next few days. Although our schedule was in disarray, we all agreed the opportunity to recover wreckage was critical. We would somehow get the most important of our remaining interviews done. I hoped to leave nothing behind when we departed Afghanistan.

After dinner we returned to our office, made phone calls, and filed the day's interviews for future reference. I emailed Maj Gen Dobrinski concerning wreckage we had discovered, and I requested our time in country be extended a few days past the 1 June deadline to work on wreckage recovery and interviews. I also advised him of the difficulty in booking travel from Al Udeid back to the U.S. Despite repeated and daily contact with the Air Mobility Command (AMC), no seats showed available for our planned departure date. I needed AFSOC to give me travel options. I wished for but had no expectation of receiving a positive reply. In either case, I prepared for the possibility that the request could make the commander fuming mad.

Noise in the adjoining office rose to an unusual level followed by Kelly begging my attention.

"Sir, can you come here for a minute, please? I have a Major Michael McCrossin, commander of the unit at forward operating base Apache on the phone. They're due to transfer out of Afghanistan next week. Their replacements arrive in the next three to four days. They will overlap for a few days and then start rotating their unit back home. He suggests we travel to Apache in the next day or two, while the personnel who recovered the wreckage are still there for us to interview."

O'Leary referred to notes on a legal pad.

"Sir, the MI-17s have penciled us in on one of the two training lines they're flying tomorrow."

"Sir, can we shoot for a "go" tomorrow morning?" Kelly asked.

"Yes, do it. Coordinate your arrival with MAJ McCrossin. I won't be going with you. Neither will TSgt Adams. When you're done, meet in the conference room to go over Winsett's checklist. MSgt Dolan, do you have a list of the tools needed for the trip?"

"Yes, sir. I'll procure the tools and safety equipment we'll need from maintenance ... tonight."

"Sir, with your permission, I requested legal representatives from the local office to accompany us. They'll be the ones to protect and arrange for transport of whatever we decide to recover. They'll be an extra set of hands to deal with and photograph whatever we find. Assuming we recover the flight information recorder and/or the vibration/structural life and engine diagnostics, I suggest we retain those items in our possession. Both of those pieces of equipment are game changers. Other than that, once we have supplies and tools, we're ready."

"Great, what's the show-time at MI-17 ops?"

"Show at 8:15 a.m. for a 9:00 a.m. takeoff," O'Leary said. "The afternoon training flight will pick us up at the forward operating base at 5:00 p.m. ... back to Kandahar by 6:15 p.m."

The next morning, I stopped for a quick breakfast and drove to the MI-17 operations building to see the team off. I found it uncomfortable to eat alone for the first time since we had arrived. Each member of the team had specific duties sending them to different parts of the base. I parked next to MI-17 Operations where I could see Dolan and Doc Harper loading bags and toolboxes into the helicopter.

"You guys ready for this?" I asked.

"You bet, sir," Dolan said. "If we asked for something and they had it, the maintenance squadron broke it out for us – no paperwork, no justification, no questions asked. Lt Col Winsett and Capt Kelly are still at the legal office. They'll be here in ten minutes or so. Lt Col O'Leary is in flight operations briefing the crew and catching up with a few more of his Afghan buddies."

I met O'Leary, the crew, and several tag-alongs walking out of the operations area.

"Good morning, sir," O'Leary said. "I have a couple more people to introduce to you."

We exchanged greetings while the flight crew completed their checks. Winsett and Kelly parked near the hangar.

"Looks like everyone's here," I said. "This is a very important day for us."

"I hope so, sir," O'Leary said. "We're excited. Perhaps by nightfall we'll have answers to a basketful of our questions."

"I'll be waiting here when you arrive this evening," I said.

The team filed into the helicopter and within minutes the rotors accelerated to full speed sending dust and exhaust fumes in all directions. I removed my hat and shielded my eyes from the onslaught. As the helicopter's weight rose, the main gear struts extended as it stabilized at five feet above the ground. I wanted to be with them as they searched through the wreckage but couldn't justify the requisites of having a general officer tag along with the team. As the helicopter disappeared into the Afghanistan sky, I returned to the office and spent most of the day coordinating interviews and trying to find seats for a flight back to the U.S.

Engrossed in my work, I lost track of time. I forgot that Adams was working in a room at the end of the hallway transcribing interviews.

"Sir, the MI-17 unit called," Adams shouted. "ETA is 6:10 p.m."

I checked the current time – 5:45 p.m.

"You want a ride to the flight line?" I asked.

"Yes, sir. I can't wait to see what they discovered."

We drove to the MI-17 hangar where maintenance pre-positioned equipment for the arrival of the afternoon training flight. The helicopter hovered over the runway then followed a maze of taxiways to the parking spot in front of the MI-17 hangar. We remained clear in the shelter of the hangar until the helicopter landed and shut down the engine. The rotors stopped and the side door slid open. O'Leary and Winsett hefted bags to the door and waited for the crew chief to extend the folding stairs.

"You see anything that might be wreckage in any of the bags?" I asked.

"Not yet," said Adams. "Wait. What is Winsett carrying off the helicopter?"

Winsett set a couple of heavy bags onto the asphalt and gave us a "thumbs up."

"They look excited, sir. I think they may have found the flight information recorder?"

CHAPTER TWENTY EIGHT

A SECRET TOO LARGE

The crew of the MI-17 helped Winsett, O'Leary, and Dolan unload bags and boxes of aircraft wreckage. Adams asked me three times how large a package the flight information recorder might be. I told her again it would be about the size of a large shoebox. I didn't have the heart to dampen her enthusiasm. If the recorder had been found, she would have been elated. I would have had a heart attack.

Winsett and O'Leary surveyed their cache piled on the tarmac. They slapped the legs of their BDUs, sending clouds of dust drifting into the evening desert breeze.

"Do I dare ask if there are treasures in any of this?" I asked, while cupping my hands over my mouth.

The smile on Winsett's face dissolved with his reply.

"Not the flight information recorder, sir, or the VSLED. What we brought won't account for much in our investigation. But the left engine is intact at the forward operating base. I cautioned the commander at Apache about allowing his men to pilfer any of what remained for souvenirs and told him to expect a team to remove the stuff soon. Oh … and you might be on the hook for a manicure when we get back to Florida. I think Capt Kelly broke a fingernail."

With our hopes of finding the recorders dashed, Winsett nonetheless seemed pleased.

"Great job," I said.

I purged my mind of all hope we would recover either of the two recording devices. O'Leary and Dolan had to have known as well, though some on the team entertained a theory that at least one of the two components were recovered and quietly transported to some unknown location.

I considered the likelihood of such a conspiracy to be remote, a secret too large and deceitful for any conscientious officer or enlisted person to keep.

The cargo/passenger compartment of the mishap aircraft had flipped end-over-end, landing atop the cockpit leaving the panel securing the flight information recorder compartment sandwiched between the separated sections of the aircraft. Not until the fuselage was lifted to extricate the remains of the dead crewmembers, would the panel have been accessible. Then ... someone with proper tools and the knowledge of its existence would have had to remove it.

Only one U.S. Air Force representative was dispatched to recover classified documents and equipment – Lt Col Shultz. According to his earlier testimony, the list of items he was tasked to recover didn't include the flight information recorder or the vibration/structural life and engine diagnostics card. Based on our discovery early in the investigation, the 8th SOS did not know the flight information recorder existed as an installed part of their Ospreys. With fires still smoldering an hour after the crash, I couldn't see him retrieving either of the two recording devices unless he was instructed to recover one or both items prior to departing Kandahar to travel to the accident site. No Army person on site would have had the inclination to remove the panels, or cut through the bent metal, to look for the engine data recording devices. Their priorities were focused on the rescue and evacuation of accident survivors.

Motivated by their curiosity rather than orders, Army soldiers from the 1st of the 508th trucked to the site early the next morning and loaded pieces of the Osprey wreckage onto their trucks. None of the photos they took that morning included any section of the fuselage. What we saw in the photos of the wreckage allowed no room for even a small section of the aircraft where the two recording devices would have been located.

I approached O'Leary who stood in a line of Afghan crewmembers and staff.

"Sir, the left engine is mostly intact," he said. "The outer sections of both wings, both nacelles and pieces of prop-rotor blades are still at the forward operating base. With limited space on the helicopter, we brought some of the smaller pieces in these bags. We left the rest, but we have plenty of pictures. You know, sir, I've been on a couple of accident investigations and examined wreckage at the scene, in an aircraft hangar, or under some temporary shelter, but this is the first time I've scavenged through debris at a remote location. Capt Kelly and Doc Harper were out of their comfort zone today, but they were extremely helpful. We could not have done any of this without MSgt Dolan."

Dolan returned borrowed tools to maintenance and alerted them as to what was required to transport the remaining wreckage, including the engine, to Kandahar Air Base.

Winsett's gloom over not recovering the recording devices disappeared when he related discovering the left engine. He showed me pictures of the wreckage taken by the Army unit the day after the accident. His group of photos included several pictures of the right engine as well.

"Sir, I found this interesting photo of the right engine," Winsett explained.

The photo showed Army soldiers using thermite grenades, high heat explosives, in an attempt to destroy the engine and prevent recovery by enemy troops. Operational missions prevented the Army personnel from returning to the accident site as planned the following day. When they finally did get back to the accident site a few days later, everything was gone. The site had been combed clean.

"Sir, the Army personnel we interviewed today told us there wasn't a chard of metal, a strand of wire, nothing but scorched earth. They figured the Air Force must have scoured the site and recovered the remaining pieces."

"The soldiers who went to the site the day after the accident … did you talk to all of them?" I asked.

"Yes, sir," Winsett said.

"Did one of you take notes of your conversations?" I asked.

"Yes, sir … Capt Kelly has notes."

"Thanks for making the trip. Rolls-Royce will have the opportunity to tear down the left engine. Their findings could be the key to identifying why this accident occurred."

During dinner, O'Leary showed me his digital photos, discussing the piles of aircraft parts and pieces. Perseverance and blind luck led us to the forward operating base Apache. Despite all reason, I dared not hope that by some cosmic quirk of fate the flight information recorder or the vibration/structural life and engine diagnostics might materialize. Except for dealing with conspiracy theories later, I put the possibility out of my mind.

We discussed how to regard and include comments from soldiers at Apache into our report. Since Adams did not make the trip to record testimony, Winsett suggested using Memorandums for Record (MFR). I assigned Dolan the task of writing the memo detailing the wreckage, and Kelly and O'Leary for conversations with the Army personnel. I asked Winsett to coordinate with the local legal office regarding the relocation of wreckage from Apache to Kandahar. Dolan sorted and marked each piece of wreckage as "essential" and "non-essential" for the purposes of our investigation. Adams raised a common and curious point regarding accident investigations and the evaluation of aircraft wreckage.

"Sir, does it seem kosher for the company that built the engine to be the company that evaluates it after an accident? To me, the process lacks integrity. Wouldn't the engine manufacturer do or say anything in order to avoid being blamed for an engine problem? Considering the liability involved, could they be trusted to disclose issues about a defective or malfunctioning engine? Shouldn't an independent third party provide an unbiased analysis?"

"Excellent points," said O'Leary. "I've been through this with a helicopter accident a couple years ago. It's routine … well, routine as accidents go, for the engine to return to the manufacturer. They have the equipment and expertise to conduct a detailed evaluation. The companies realize their integrity and reputation are on the line. At least one Air Force representative will be at the site to monitor the analysis."

Before we broke up for the evening, I suggested we meet for an early dinner the following day. I had coordinated six interviews; crewmembers from chalk two and three, and the most senior person we would interview – Army Colonel Dan Walrath, the Task Force Commander.

Kelly stood slowly, as if her back was sore from bending and lifting objects. She had a gleaming sparkle in her eye.

"Sir, I've been on accident investigations before and completed a tour in Iraq. I've flown over the scene of an accident once, but not in a Russian helicopter with an Afghan student pilot and U.S. Air Force instructor pilot. I don't know if a five-minute shower will remove the dirt out of my hair or the sand crusted on my skin, but I don't care. Being the first to find and sort through wreckage and talking to the Army soldiers we met today and the past few days, I wouldn't trade it for a week on the beach in Hawaii. My husband is home in our comfortable house working papers stacked a foot high and staying ahead of our kids. He is so jealous. I might spend weeks when this is over getting the sand out of my boots. If we never get to the bottom of this, it won't be because we didn't do our job. I'm proud of what we're doing, and I'll never forget it. Thank you."

"I understand I might be on the hook for a manicure," I responded with a smile in my voice.

She extended her hands, palms flat with dirt caked under her nails, one of which had been torn to the quick.

"I'll wear it with pride for a while, at least until we get back to Florida," she said.

The next afternoon I walked out of my quarters to meet our colorful van at our usual location. Within minutes, Winsett arrived with O'Leary occupying the front seat and Doc Harper in the seat behind.

I slid into the van and sat beside Harper.

"Everyone recovered from yesterday?" I asked.

"Yes, sir," Winsett said. "We coordinated with the legal office for transport of the wreckage. We still don't have seats on a rotator to get home. We may need your help to make something happen."

"I begged AFSOC for assistance a couple days ago," I said. "I haven't heard back from them. I'll check my email later this evening."

After a team dinner, we went straight to the conference room and prepared for our first interview with COL Walrath. As the task force commander, he monitored progress of every mission from the joint operations center. Within minutes after the accident, he had marshalled resources under his command to protect, recover, and provide for the safety of the personnel involved. By reputation, he expertly commanded his troops from the operations center and in the field, choosing to be with soldiers at every available opportunity.

Engrossed in preparations for the night's activities, we had lost track of time. COL Walrath knocked twice on the open conference room door and walked in.

We exchanged greetings, and before I could present the board, he rounded the table shaking hands with each team member. Dressed in the newest pattern of the Army camouflaged battle dress uniform, he stood a little over six feet tall. He was lean and muscular, with close-clipped hair salted gray at the temples. His schoolboy complexion made him appear very young for his rank and experience. His voice rattled in a low timbre that could have been considered gruff. During conversation prior to starting the interview, he told us that it was his twenty-second anniversary of being commissioned into the Army after graduating from the United States Military Academy.

As task force commander he exercised command and control of Special Operations Forces (SOF) in Afghanistan. On the night of the accident, he monitored multiple real time feeds of missions in progress from the operations center. The infiltration mission in Zabul Province near Qalat being only one of the many missions. He told us in the first few seconds after the accident, no one in the room realized what had happened, but when the dust cleared, the video confirmed the lead Osprey had impacted the ground.

His initial testimony validated information we had recorded from previous interviews. He established communications with the other two

Ospreys in the formation. He also established radio contact with the AC-130 flying in an orbit eleven thousand feet above the accident site, to determine if any enemy forces were active in the area. When the AC-130 reported no activity, he ordered the two Ospreys to land immediately, secure the area, and render assistance to the accident victims. He dispatched a combat search and rescue (CSAR) team to the site and reported the occurrence of the accident to Higher Headquarters in Kabul, Afghanistan. He launched a medical evacuation (MEDEVAC) unit then ordered a CH-47 Chinook to fly a quick reaction platoon of Rangers to secure the accident site.

They were airborne within sixteen minutes after the accident, with COL Walrath and Air Force Lt Col Shultz (Osprey pilot) onboard. Osprey maintenance personnel gave Schultz a list of classified documents and equipment to recover from the downed aircraft.

"Colonel, can you describe what you saw when you landed at the accident site?" I asked.

"Sir, I walked off the helicopter and saw a small fire to the side of the main wreckage. The night was pitch-black. Using the fire light as a guide, I linked up with Army soldiers from chalk two and three. They provided a quick situation update and walked me around the site."

"Were any of the personnel on chalk one still at the accident site when you arrived?"

"Yes, sir, Major Carter. Despite his injuries, he still oversaw and directed the rescue effort. I told him I would take over duties at the accident site as I helped him climb aboard a MEDEVAC helicopter. I helped with the recovery of the last two Air Force crewmembers from the wreckage (the KIA crewmembers in the cockpit). Lt Col Schultz provided positive identification of the two men. We placed them on litters and carried them to the waiting CH-47. After that, we recovered classified equipment and materials. I ordered soldiers to conduct a three hundred meter by three-hundred-meter search of the area to pick up loose equipment, weapons and ammunition. Lt Col Schultz had combat search and rescue personnel help remove classified radios, weapons, and charts from the airplane. Someone, using a special tool, cut the tail number off the airplane. Not sure why they needed it, but I didn't question it."

"What did you do with the equipment your soldiers and Lt Col Shultz recovered?"

"Sir, we loaded it onto litters and placed everything into the CH-47. We put the last of the injured soldiers and the remains of the two crewmembers aboard and flew to the nearest forward operating base (Delta).

"At Delta, medical personnel moved the wounded to the base hospital. Soldiers transferred the equipment to the chalk two CV-22, while human remains were loaded onto the chalk three CV-22. Once loaded with personnel and equipment, the CV-22s departed Delta to fly to Kandahar Air Base. After the CV-22s departed, the CH-47 returned to the accident site and picked up the remaining Army personnel working there. Once everyone was seated, the CH-47 took off and flew to Kandahar."

"Sir, while you were at the crash site," Winsett asked, "did you evaluate the wreckage to decide whether or not to recover it?"

"Yes. I called Higher Headquarters in Kabul for their input. I asked if they wanted to keep a security force on the site to protect it for a recovery effort, or if they wanted us to destroy what remained of the Osprey. They asked for my assessment. I told them all that remained was the shell of the fuselage. They ordered me to proceed with the destruction. I called the operations center and had the operations officer coordinate with the A-10 unit to have them bomb the wreckage. The A-10s completed the mission within the hour."

"Was there any discussion about preserving the wreckage, or at least parts of it for accident investigation purposes?" Winsett asked.

"No. That wasn't discussed. By 3:45 a.m. local time, combat search and rescue personnel and support aircraft had departed the accident site. Two A-10s, based at Kandahar, delivered four, five hundred-pound bombs on the accident site. Classified radios and other equipment had been removed and flown to Kandahar. The equipment, radios and personal

equipment of the crewmembers had been gathered and stored at Kandahar
… somewhere."

MSgt Dolan squirmed in his chair in apparent discomfort.

"Sir, was there a list of items you were directed to get off the airplane?"

"Yes. Lt Col Shultz had the list. I saw him refer to it as equipment was
being removed. As far as I know, he recovered everything."

"Sir, were you aware Army soldiers went to the site the next morning
and recovered pieces of wreckage?"

"Yes, I was. It was the 1st of the 508th. They're the unit in charge of the
battle space in Zabul Province. They notified the operations center about
wreckage they recovered. They also told us they had numerous photos of
the accident site."

I acknowledged TSgt Adams who had a question.

"Sir, did anyone express concern about preserving anything that
would aid an accident investigation?"

"Sure, it was considered."

Commanders at higher levels agreed with COL Walrath. To preserve
or recover useless wreckage for any reason was considered too dangerous.
The risk was too great and could endanger the lives of personnel guarding
the site during recovery operations. Yet the following day without orders,
soldiers motivated by their curiosity went to the site and spent several
hours recovering a truckload of debris. They returned a few days later to
retrieve more wreckage, but found the site swept clean. Not by the Air
Force, as they had believed, but by local Afghan citizens who had probably
repurposed the materials. Recovery of the right engine and/or the flight
information recorder would have helped our investigation substantially. If
directed, it could have been done in minimal time and with a small security force.

"When I made the initial call up the chain, it was one of the options I
presented," said Walrath. "I told them we could secure the site if necessary.
We discussed my assessment of the wreckage. I told them there was no way
the airplane could ever fly again. To me, it was just a piece of metal. It was

not worth keeping a security force at the site and exposing them to danger. So, to answer your question, yes it was considered. But, in the end, the decision came down to whether it was worth it or not – stationing soldiers at the site and potentially having guys killed guarding a piece of metal."

"I understand that, sir," said Dolan. What about the *black box* (flight information recorder)? Was there any discussion about it?"

"No. No discussion about a *black box.*"

O'Leary consulted his notes.

"Sir, did you set criteria whereby CV-22s returned to combat operations?"

COL Walrath validated what we had learned during previous interviews. In concert with the 8th SOS Squadron Commander, they reduced payloads … adjusted fuel loads … increased time available for crews to mission plan … established procedures for tailwinds and go-arounds, and revised data used for calculation of available power for go-arounds.

"Sir, did anyone propose or discuss the possibility of an engine failure or a power loss as a factor in the accident?"

"No. The CV-22 Squadron Commander didn't think, nor did it appear that the accident was caused by engine issues."

"Any more questions?" I asked as I looked at each board member.

"No, sir."

"Colonel Walrath, I remind you of the official nature of this interview. You may not discuss your testimony with anyone, without my permission, prior to the final accident investigation report being released to the public."

"Sir, I understand," he said.

With the interview concluded, we stood up and shook hands. I expressed our appreciation for his outstanding military service. We all knew COL Walrath would be a very high ranking general before his career was completed. He was impressive by all measures.

After he departed, we discussed the 8th SOS's determination the accident resulted from calculated power margins, tailwinds, and poor mission planning rather than an engine malfunction.

"Their reaction in the aftermath might explain why we've seen newspaper and magazine articles citing pilot error," Doc Harper said. "We seem to be the only ones considering mechanical or engine issues. Do they know something we don't?"

"Or, they only addressed issues they control," O'Leary added. "So far we haven't heard anything about engine issues originating from anyone in the 8th SOS."

"Keep an open mind," Winsett said. "We still have more interviews to conduct. Until yesterday, few knew an engine had been recovered from the accident site. We still have a long way to go before General Harvel writes his final opinion about the cause of the accident."

Kelly tapped me on the shoulder.

"Sir, there's an urgent phone call for you – someone from AFSOC wants to talk to you immediately."

CHAPTER TWENTY NINE

DR. LUKE PORSI - SOFME

Since leaving Hurlburt, Kelly had queried the Air Mobility Command's passenger service office daily, begging for space on airplanes scheduled to fly from the Middle East to the United States. We did not dare stay in country one minute into the month of June – violating our agreement with General Becker. He had served as a lieutenant in the waning days of the Vietnam War and his first assignment after helicopter flight school was South Korea. He had no Vietnam experience, but no doubt remembered periodic dustups concerning the abuse of combat pay and refused to underwrite the old practice.

With each passing day, confirming seats became more critical. I advised AFSOC (General Dobrinski) often, reinforcing my concern. When a call from AFSOC came through, I immediately excused myself and went to my office and picked up the phone.

"Sir, this is Lt Col Chuck Coulter at AFSOC. General Dobrinski's in the commander's office. Can you hold for a minute?"

"Sure. How are things there?"

"Same as always, sir ... very hectic ... hold on. General Dobrinski just walked into his office. See you soon, sir."

The line clicked when Dobrinski picked up.

"It's difficult to get hold of you. Did you get the email I sent a few hours ago?"

"No, sir, I haven't checked emails yet. We have a full interview schedule tonight. Something important, sir?"

"I think I answered the questions from the last email you sent. The boss wants you out of country before June 1st. Air Mobility Command (AMC) just generated a flight departing Al Udeid on May 29th. Call the passenger service unit at Kandahar… should be seats available for you and your investigation team. Hurry, they won't be available for long."

"Thanks for the heads-up, sir. We're on it. Just want you to know we will stop at Walter Reed to interview SSgt Chris Curtis on our way home to Hurlburt Field."

"That's fine. Call me when you arrive at Hurlburt."

I opened the office door and called for Capt Kelly.

"General Dobrinski called … said AMC has generated a rotator departing Al Udeid on the 29th. Can we break for a couple minutes while you reserve seats for us?"

She checked notes on her clipboard.

"Adams and I will take care of it, sir. Captain Luke Porsi, Flight Surgeon, Special Operations Forces Medical Element (SOFME) is our next interview. Doc Harper and MSgt Dolan are occupying him, or maybe it's the other way around. They're amusing one another… shouldn't be but a few minutes."

SOFME flight surgeons are rare and unique in the medical community. Their skills reside at the pinnacle of combat medicine. After completing medical school and residency, candidates attend a ten-month course studying battlefield trauma and evacuation at the Center for Sustainment of Trauma and Resuscitation (CSTARS) in Cincinnati, Ohio. Exercises and exams train and evaluate the physician's diagnostic ability and skill performing surgical procedures under the most austere and hazardous combat conditions. Final exams are conducted using sophisticated simulators replicating a multitude of injuries sustained in a combat environment. Patients (robot-like mannequins) capable of exhibiting an array of symptoms and reactions, are controlled by an instructor during training and testing. After the Cincinnati course, flight surgeons continue with many weeks of training at Hurlburt Field before being assigned to an operational unit. SOFME flight surgeons are trained to operate alongside warfighters on the battlefield.

Captain Porsi, five foot ten, lean and muscular, appeared too young to have finished medical school. For the thirty minutes we waited for Kelly and Adams, the remaining board members sat mesmerized as he shared fascinating stories of his medical experiences in the war zone.

Kelly interrupted our conversation.

"Sir, we have seats departing Al Udeid for Baltimore on Saturday the 29th. We catch a C-17 out of Kandahar at 2:00 p.m. on Friday the 28th. We reserved rooms for Friday night at Al Udeid. We'll work on Baltimore accommodations after we complete interviews in the morning. What a relief."

"For sure," I said. "Thank you."

Doc Porsi and his two-man medical team departed Kandahar on one of the Ospreys flying to forward operating base Delta to pick up the Army Rangers. They were scheduled to accompany the Rangers on the April 8th mission. After landing, Major Carter told Doc Porsi he could not accompany them on the mission due to space limitations in the back of the airplanes. The three Ospreys departed Delta with sixteen Rangers in the back of each airplane. Doc Porsi and his two team members watched from an area near the control tower as the Ospreys departed without them.

After waiting forty-five minutes, none of the Ospreys had returned to Delta as planned. Doc Porsi sensed something was wrong. He and his team immediately reported to the Combat Army Support Hospital (CASH) at Delta. Within minutes, MEDEVAC helicopters started arriving with Ranger casualties and two Osprey crewmembers ... tail scanner Curtis and copilot Luce. Doc Porsi and his team assessed Curtis' condition as he was carried off the helicopter. Curtis was near death, but conscious and very scared. They comforted him while the CASH resuscitation team stabilized him, concentrating on his most life-threatening injuries. Porsi helped wheel him to the operating room where a Navy surgeon, Doctor Carlos Godinez, scrubbed for surgery.

"Can you give us a layman's overview of the tail scanner's injuries?" Doc Harper asked after Porsi was sworn in to start the interview.

"Yes, sir … massive blood loss … fractures of the pelvis, both femurs, and compound fractures of his left arm. The last I saw, Dr. Godinez and his team had him on the table being transfused through multiple lines. They put out an urgent call for everyone on the base to donate blood. To control bleeding, the surgeon stabilized Curtis' fractures by attaching external splints and then explored his abdomen for signs of internal hemorrhaging."

Leaving Curtis in surgery, Doc Porsi and his team walked back to the helipad and assisted offloading the CH-47 with injured Rangers, equipment retrieved from the crash site, and … the human remains of Maj Voas and SMSgt Lackey. They placed the bodies into bags designed for transport and loaded them on the chalk three Osprey waiting nearby. They also assisted with loading equipment onto the chalk two Osprey. Doc Porsi was asked to accompany an injured Ranger as he was loaded onto chalk two. Once everyone was onboard, chalk two departed Delta and flew back to Kandahar Air Base.

The following afternoon, Doc Porsi was stunned, but very pleased to hear that SSgt Curtis had survived surgery at forward operating base Delta. He was flown to Kandahar for follow-up medical care once stabilized. Doc Porsi visited him in the Kandahar hospital where Curtis lay unconscious, drugged into a medically induced coma, with three limbs in traction … intubated, transfused, and covered with bandages on every square inch of visible skin. Rangers had left him for dead hanging in his harness from the floor of the inverted fuselage. If not for a soldier cutting him loose, another providing … but misapplying a tourniquet, and his incontestable will to survive … Navy surgeon Godinez wouldn't have had a patient in Staff Sergeant Christopher Curtis on whom to ply his extraordinary surgical skills.

Despite this being her first trip to anywhere close to a combat zone, and after hearing Doc Porsi's grisly testimony, Adams pressed the interview.

"Sir, did you see or speak with the copilot, Maj Luce, that night?"

"Yes. After we landed at Kandahar, I saw him being admitted to the base hospital. While waiting for treatment, I sat next to him for ten or fifteen minutes."

"Sir," asked Adams. "Did he talk to you about the final seconds of flight prior to the accident?"

"Ah … yes, he did."

CHAPTER THIRTY

SOLEMN FLIGHT HOME

Toward the end of our time in Afghanistan, we had developed what we believed to be a clear picture of events prior to the accident and the aftermath. The black hole in our investigation remained the final seventeen seconds of flight. Absent the digital monitors that preserved data essential to an accident investigation, we counted on the testimony of the only surviving cockpit crewmember, Major Brian Luce. For whatever reason, he had been unable or unwilling to share his memory of those final seconds of flight. During his treatment and recovery prior to arriving back at his home near Hurlburt Field, he spoke to Captain Porsi and perhaps others regarding the flight. The prospect of hearing even a secondhand account of what happened just before impact piqued the interest of everyone on the board.

"Doctor Porsi, did Captain Luce remember the seconds leading up to impact?" I asked.

"He did. He told me about the approach to the LZ. He said at four tenths of a mile and 40 knots the VVI[15] pointed almost straight down. The abnormal [2000 feet per minute] rate confused him. The next thing he remembered was sitting on the ground, still strapped in his seat with the airplane burning in front of him. His helmet had been torn off. With his mouth and nose packed with dirt, he had to spit sand to breathe.

"After a minute or two, he heard people talking and saw them moving around the airplane. He called for help and eventually a couple of Rangers came to his aid. They unbuckled his seatbelt and shoulder harness. He complained of pain in his back and knees. They rolled him out of the seat and laid him on the ground. One Ranger yelled for a litter. Two Rangers ran over to assist him. One of them read Luce the 'Last Rites.' Luce told me

---

15 Vertical Velocity Indicator –Indicates rates of climb or descent in hundreds of feet per minute.

he responded by saying, 'Whoa buddy, I don't think I'm ready for that just yet.' I had to laugh when he told me that story."

I caught Kelly's attention. We had discussed the value of re-interviewing Luce when he had recovered from the worst of his injuries, hoping he might have regained memory since we last spoke to him. The board was split on whether a second interview would be worth the time, but after Porsi's comments, I decided to make the interview a priority.

"Doctor Porsi," Adams asked, "In a few days we'll interview SSgt Curtis when we stop at Walter Reed hospital. Have you seen or spoken to him?"

"Yes, last week. His condition and attitude shocked me. He had sustained injuries that would have killed a normal human. He has also endured numerous surgeries with the prospect of more operations and rehabilitation in the months and years ahead. He has the most remarkable positive attitude. I've never seen a more determined patient. When you meet him, you'll understand."

When we completed Capt Porsi's interview, we thanked him and extended our parting good wishes. He wasted no time hustling out of the conference room in order to get back to his duties.

Doc Harper shook his head.

"Even at his age, I don't know if I could have survived the training he's completed. I wonder what the completion rate is for those entering the regimen he's undertaken. I would expect it's near that of Army Ranger School or Navy SEAL training. The physical training is as tough as any in the military. I'm not in bad shape, but my condition alone would disqualify me from serving as a SOFME surgeon."

We completed an additional four interviews during the night, one being with TSgt John Brown, CSAR. He had conducted a detailed analysis of the accident site that had not been shared with the Interim Investigation Board or the Safety Investigation Board. He provided photographs and information that proved to be another very pleasant discovery for us. He had measured every mark the Osprey made in the sand – main and nose gear touch down points, the distance the aircraft had skidded on its back, the distances the wings and engines had separated from the fuselage, and the interval of strikes the spinning proprotors gouged into the sand as the airplane flipped onto its back. His information would prove to be invaluable. Since they had the equipment, CSAR had cut the tail number from the aircraft at Schultz's request. During our time in country, we searched for the various pieces of the airplane removed from the accident site. It became readily apparent that the parts would stay "missing" since their value was deemed more appropriate as souvenirs by rogue unit members.

Interviews during the next few days provided very little new information. It did validate much of what we already knew. I considered the week we spent in Afghanistan to be productive beyond expectations. We conducted over fifty interviews, discovered wreckage few knew or admitted knowing existed, viewed the crash site from the air, and flew the route taken by the mishap aircraft.

We departed Kandahar on May 29th with twelve other military passengers. Some were redeploying or relocating to other bases in the Middle East. A few of the military personnel were escorting three flag-draped coffins secured in a row at the center of the C-17's cargo compartment. The coffins were enroute to the military mortuary located at Dover AFB, Delaware. The fact that Maj Voas, SMSgt Lackey, CPL Jankiewicz, and Reeta Sandozai had made the same trip seven weeks earlier, added to our already somber mood. Without discussion, we renewed our resolve to find the cause of the Osprey accident.

The prospect of having to brief families of the injured and dead after completing the investigation at first gave me pause. In the ensuing weeks, the sentiment had faded and disappeared altogether. The accident board members passed the flight time organizing notes, and in quiet reflection. When the engine noise of the C-17 Globemaster III decreased and the nose dipped toward the horizon, I relieved the pressure building in my ears as the airplane depressurized. As the airplane maneuvered onto the final approach course and intercepted the glide path to land, I could see the airfield through the windows on the left side. Anticipating the landing, the three escort officers shuffled papers to prepare for the transfer of the human remains to escort personnel who would meet the airplane once it was parked.

We taxied for what seemed a long time before finally parking in the transient area. After the loadmaster lowered the ramp to the asphalt and opened the rear door, the cockpit crew killed power to the aircraft. The four-hundred cycle hum from the generator supplying electrical power ceased along with the sound of every piece of electrical equipment. I had never experienced total silence at any airport. There was a reverential hush in the air. The two loadmasters deployed ramps that bridged the small vertical distance from the floor of the aircraft ramp to the tarmac.

It appeared that all work on the flight line had ceased, almost as if time were trying to stand still as it had for those who died in the crash. A sizable percentage of the base population stood at attention in military formation behind our aircraft. In front of them, three ambulances parked facing away from the tail of the C-17. When the closest of the ambulances backed beneath the tail and stopped a few feet from the aircraft, the escort officers walked off the ramp, met their counterparts, and conducted the administrative transfer of custody. Eight airmen marched in slow, deliberate cadence and lockstep over the cargo ramp onto the aircraft. They stood at attention, half of them on each side of the aft-most flag-draped case. The leader of the airman sounded orders breaking the silence. On his command, the bearers saluted, then carried the remains, again in slow cadence, from the aircraft toward the waiting ambulance.

A member of the Special Operations Support Team entered via the crew entrance door and spoke to us in a hushed tone. "Welcome to Al Udeid, sir. If you'll grab your gear, I'll see you to your quarters. We'll secure your checked bags for the night and they'll travel with you tomorrow. I have a bus in front of the aircraft so as not to disturb the ceremony. Keep together and follow me."

We boarded the bus, looking over our shoulder at the sacred ritual behind the aircraft. Adams for sure, and a few others, daubed tears. All of us were choked up with emotion.

"I thought the remains were to stay on the aircraft and depart for Dover," I asked, as I cleared my throat.

"The crews and aircraft will stage out of here, sir," said our escort. "The aircraft you arrived on must require some sort of maintenance or routine check. I don't know. The remains change couriers and will depart on another C-17 in about an hour and a half."

The following day, May 30th, we had an unremarkable flight to Baltimore, with a fuel stop in Canada. We landed, cleared customs and immigration, then secured carts to haul our bags to the front of the airport. Winsett and Kelly stood in line at the Avis counter while the rest of us stacked and organized our luggage. It felt good to be back in the U.S.

Within thirty minutes, we had loaded our bags and checked into a nearby hotel. After ten days in Afghanistan and a long flight, we needed more than a five-minute hot shower to feel clean. We met for an early dinner and discussed the pending interview with SSgt Curtis before calling it an early night.

The next morning, we met in the lobby at 9:00 a.m. The fifteen-minute van ride to Walter Reed hospital went quickly. In 2005, Congress and the Defense Base Closure and Realignment Commission (BRAC) slated the Walter Reed Army Medical Center (Walter Reed General Hospital until 1951) for closure. The 113-acre facility opened in 1909 with 80 beds and expanded to over 1,500 rooms before closing and merging function and facility with the Navy Medical Center in Bethesda, Maryland. In 2007, the hospital endured charges of patient neglect and deteriorating facilities. Despite the previous allegations and the fact the hospital would soon close, we saw no such degradation of service or condition of the property. In my opinion, our wounded servicemen receive the best medical care available. Everyone I visited seemed grateful and happy with their care.

As we walked through the main corridor, we passed patients lounging or reading in wheelchairs. Soldiers missing arms or legs and burn victims bandaged over most of their bodies seemed to be in good spirits. Despite the horrendous injuries of many, the atmosphere of the hospital was upbeat. We rode an elevator to the fifth floor, ward fifty-eight.

We stopped outside the door to SSgt Curtis's room. I knocked twice and pushed the door to a slightly open position and called his name.

"Yes. Who's there?" someone answered.

I tried to push the door open so I could ask for permission to enter the room. Someone, or something immediately blocked the door.

CHAPTER THIRTY ONE

STAFF SERGEANT CHRIS CURTIS

I peeked through the narrow opening of the door. There were four nurses attending to SSgt Curtis. They had rolling tables and other equipment blocking the door while they changed bandages and checked on his medications. I backed out of the doorway and told the other accident board members it might be a few minutes before we would be able to enter the room.

As the last surviving crewmember who was on headset and able to hear all crew communications, we hoped Curtis would remember the cockpit conversation during the final seconds of the flight. I hoped for a quote, or even a word, that might steer our investigation.

If we hadn't conducted an in-person interview that day, we probably would have lost the opportunity altogether. SSgt Curtis, once released from Walter Reed, would be transferred to Brooke Army Medical Center, Fort Sam Houston, San Antonio, Texas, for follow-up surgeries and extensive rehabilitation.

Finally, the room door was pulled partially open by one of the attending nurses. Doc Harper had moved to my side to try to figure out what was happening in Curtis' room. With the door opened a little wider, we could see medical equipment, a computer station, carts laden with medical supplies, and a wheelchair blocking the door from fully opening. I nudged Doc Harper.

"Look at Curtis," I said. "We may have scheduled our interview too soon."

"We'll see," he responded. "I suggest we consult with the attending physician to get more detailed information about SSgt Curtis' condition."

One of the med-techs popped her head out the door.

"Sir, we're almost done," she said. "Give us just a few more minutes."

"Sure," I said. "Take your time."

I huddled with the team in the hall.

"I didn't get a good look, but he may not be up for an interview. If this doesn't happen today, maybe it's for the best. Doc, will you find out what pain meds he's on, and see if we can talk to him? Adams ... not yet, but be ready to rebook our flight to Florida."

A nurse exited the room with the empty wheelchair. The three med-techs followed, pushing stainless steel carts and carrying fold-up tables. One stopped and conferred with Winsett and Kelly.

"Give us a minute, sir," Winsett said.

Doc Harper stopped a doctor in green scrubs and motioned for him to join the conversation with Winsett and Kelly. They walked into an empty room across the hallway from Curtis and closed the door. We all stood in the hall and stared at the door anxiously waiting for our team members to give us the news ... good, or bad. Within a couple minutes, Winsett emerged with Kelly, Harper, and the physician behind him.

"Sir, this is Doctor Anthony Pistilli," said Harper. "He's a trauma specialist and the attending physician for this ward. We've discussed SSgt Curtis' medications and condition. He is cleared to conduct the interview. Despite taking strong meds for his pain, Curtis is coherent. A warning though, some of his meds cause drowsiness. He might nod off at any time. Dr. Pistilli said he is very anxious to talk to us about the accident."

Carrying chairs into the room, I got my first good look at SSgt Chris Curtis. He appeared pale, gaunt and frail. Four IVs hung from a stain-less-steel tree, two of which were routed through machines metering the flow of medications. A plaster cast extended from his shoulder to fingertips holding his left arm away from his body. Orange colored Betadine anti-septic seeped through bandages covering the back of his head. With his legs bandaged, he had little to no range of voluntary movement. Despite his physical condition, his eyes betrayed no hint of the catastrophe he had endured. I saw only vitality, hope, and a tenacious will to survive.

"Hi SSgt Curtis. I'm Brig Gen Don Harvel. I've looked forward to meeting you."

"General Harvel, sir. I've looked forward to meeting you as well. I apologize for being in bed. I hope I'm able to help."

SSgt Curtis had endured numerous surgeries and therapeutic procedures since the accident. He had been on heavy medications that controlled, but not eliminated, his intense pain, but he seemed undeterred at the prospect of more surgery and months of physical therapy. He anticipated the day when he'd walk … then return to duty and fly again.

I read the legal preliminaries and ensured SSgt Curtis understood the purpose of our visit and the interview.

"Briefly tell us about your Air Force career," I asked.

"Sir, I have been in the Air Force for eleven and a half years. I started out as an avionics technician and cross-trained to be a flight engineer on the MH-53 Pave Low. When the MH-53s were retired, I was transferred to fly on the CV-22 as a flight engineer/tail scanner."

Sedated and immobilized by casts and bandages, we only had the body language revealed in his eyes and bruised face to, in part, evaluate the reliability of his testimony. I asked several basic questions to test his recollection of technical details and events.

"Please tell the board about the duties of a CV-22 flight engineer."

"Sir, we are the airplane's systems experts. We also help with navigation, electronic warfare, and maintaining the cargo compartment equipment and/or passengers. There are two flight engineers on every mission. One flies in the cockpit with the two pilots. The other is at the tail of the airplane seeing to the cargo, passengers, and working the fifty-caliber machine gun mounted on the ramp."

"On the April 8th mission you departed Kandahar as a three-ship formation and flew to forward operating base Delta. Were you involved in the face-to-face briefing conducted with the Army Rangers?" I asked.

"No, sir. I stayed at the airplane with the co-pilot," replied Curtis.

"Do you remember how many Rangers boarded your airplane?"

"Yes, sir … sixteen."

"Was there anything unusual about the weather or the takeoff?"

"No, sir. It was a nice night, just very dark. The takeoff was normal."

"Tell us about the approach to the LZ. Did that seem normal?"

"Sir, I remember descending to three-hundred feet. Everything was normal. As we prepared to land, the nacelles were coming up as we slowly converted to the helicopter mode. I looked outside and scanned the area behind the airplane. Suddenly, we just dropped. I didn't have a chance to say anything or say, 'Pull-up, stop-down, or go-around.' I heard conversation in the cockpit, but I didn't understand what was said. It happened so quickly. When I realized we were going to hit the ground, I dove into the cabin to get off the ramp[16]. It was violent."

"Did the pilots or flight engineer talk about the speed of the airplane, or a tailwind that may have suddenly appeared?" I asked.

"Sir, it felt like we were flying a little fast. But we were still on profile. I would have called 'go-around' if they were not within the approach parameters."

"How did you know the cockpit crew was flying fast?" asked O'Leary.

"Sir, the flight engineer in the cockpit calls out ground speed, distances, and altitudes. I knew our speed by listening to his continuous call-outs."

"Did you hear any of the cockpit crew call for a go-around?" Winsett asked.

"No, sir."

"What are some things that would make you tell your crew to go-around?"

"Sir, a rapid rate of descent at a low altitude … if something in the cabin didn't look right … things of that nature."

---

16 For a landing in hostile environments, the tail scanner mans the M2, .50 caliber Browning machine gun mounted on the Osprey ramp. Anticipating a hard landing, Curtis says he dove off the ramp into the cargo compartment.

"If you would've had time, would you have called for a go-around for the rapid rate of descent?" I asked.

"Absolutely. Yes, sir."

"What would the pilot's response have been if you called for a go-around?" Winsett asked.

"Sir, they would have advanced the thrust control lever (TCL) to full power and climbed away from the ground."

"What was the last thing you remember hearing from the cockpit crew?" O'Leary asked.

"Sir, I can't tell you exactly what they were talking about. But, I remember them talking all of sudden, right before impact. I heard a lot of talking, it was a high-pitched voice. I remember hearing the flight engineer. They were talking very fast."

O'Leary leaned forward in his seat and asked, "The voice you heard sounded abnormal?"

"Yes, sir. It was a very high-pitched voice. The conversation started when the ground started to rise very rapidly."

"Just to summarize, the airplane started a rapid descent, then you heard an excited conversation from the cockpit. After that, you dove off the ramp into the cargo compartment. Is that correct?" O'Leary asked.

"Yes, sir, exactly."

Doc Harper interrupted by asking, "You said you heard an excited conversation in the cockpit. Did the conversation give you the impression the crew in front were aware of the rate of descent?"

"Yes, sir."

"Can you remember any of the specific words you heard from the cockpit after the airplane started descending rapidly?" asked Adams.

"No, ma'am."

"Did you know if the CV-22 had a flight information recorder installed?" asked Dolan.

"I didn't realize it until a few weeks after the accident. It came up in a conversation with a flight engineer when he visited me."

"Did you hear the engines spool-up (accelerate) during the descent?" Dolan continued. "Did you hear anything abnormal?"

"Honestly, with the rate of descent and my heightened awareness, I didn't hear any spooling."

"Did you smell anything, like something burning?"

"No, nothing like that."

Winsett asked the next question. "You told us about the excited conversation in the cockpit. Have you ever heard the pilot get excited during any of the flights in the past?"

"No, sir. Maj Voas is very relaxed. He is not one to get excited. He's a very controlled individual. His tone is not loud at all."

"Have you ever heard him speak in the high-pitched tone before?" asked Winsett.

"No, sir."

"If the pilot noticed there was something wrong with the airplane, knowing what your crew briefed about power available that night, what would you expect the pilot to do?" asked O'Leary.

"Sir, he would immediately apply full power by advancing the thrust control lever. He would climb away from the ground to get up to a safe altitude."

"Do you think the airplane reacted as though he was doing the go-around procedure you just described?" asked Winsett.

"Sir, the wings were level. My belief is the pilot pushed the thrust control levers to full power. I did not detect the engines going *crazy* … what we call it when the thrust control lever is pushed through the full power setting … to contingency power (a power setting above full power – available in case of emergency only). I didn't detect any of that, and the engines seemed fine to me. I would imagine that the pilot went to full power and maybe nothing happened. That's my belief, sir. But you have to remember, I wasn't in the cockpit so I can't be one hundred percent sure."

"Tell me a little about your crew. Did your crew eat meals together?" I asked.

"Yes, sir. We were the only crew that ate together. All the other flight engineers ate together and the pilots ate together. Not our crew. The four of us ate and worked-out at the gym together. We were a very tight crew, sir."

SSgt Curtis' speech slowed and he nodded off for a few seconds several times. After an hour of answering questions, he seemed to be running out of steam.

"We are almost done," I said. "We'll hold the rest of our questions while you look at a short video. Are you feeling well enough to watch a thirty second video?"

"Yes, sir."

We gathered around Lt Col Winsett's laptop and played the video taken by the A-10 airplane. Curtis' concentration intensified as the video progressed. His eyes transfixed on the screen. When the Osprey touched down and the dust and fire blackened the video, he flinched.

"Play it one more time," he said.

Winsett restarted the video. SSgt Curtis grunted as he used every ounce of his energy to lift his head off the pillow. His eyes intensely focused on the computer screen as Winsett pressed the "play" arrow to restart the video.

CHAPTER THIRTY TWO

AFGHAN INTERPRETER

Curtis intensely watched the video a second time, then a third. When the screen went black after the final viewing, Curtis plopped his head back and blew a deep sigh.

"It's still difficult for us to watch," I said. "We've seen it dozens of times. Did you notice anything you want to talk about?"

Curtis swallowed hard and considered his reply.

"Sir … seeing the video, I remember hitting the ground and rolling like we were on a very rough runway. I thought … hey, we're on the ground. This can't be our landing zone, because we should be hovering. The airplane bounced around, and I blacked out. I didn't remember that until watching the video."

"What about the dust cloud and smoke?" I asked.

"Sir, it looks like it blew in the direction we landed. It appears we touched down with a strong tailwind."

Winsett quizzed him about what he heard in the moments before the crash. He acknowledged hearing the typical automated warnings flying an LVA, characterizing them as usual during a normal approach, with the qualification that his crew position placed him in the cargo compartment and not in the cockpit.

Adams engaged him regarding procedures a crew might use to update wind data somewhere during the approach. No provision in the aircrew checklist addressed the subject, but Curtis' personal technique, one taught at the CV-22 school at Kirtland, dictated he reevaluate the winds on the leg inbound to the landing zone.

After watching the video, Curtis suddenly appeared more fatigued. Unless he remembered something later, we had discovered everything he knew.

"Any other questions?" I asked while looking at each team member. With no further questions, I terminated the interview.

"SSgt Curtis, relax, we're through. We're flying back to Ft. Walton Beach this afternoon. Godspeed on your recovery."

Curtis thanked us. The board expressed their regard, each touching the cast on his shoulder and wished him well.

Hospital staff waited in the hallway.

"Thank you, sir, anything we can do for you?" asked the head nurse.

"No ma'am," I said. "But please take care of him. I've met few warriors with his survivor's mindset and humility. He is a special young man."

"We couldn't agree more, sir. We enjoy being around him."

We loaded our equipment and departed Walter Reed. During the flight to Florida, I queried Doc Harper about the possibility of Curtis and Luce regaining more of their memory as they had more time to heal.

"SSgt Curtis passed on every opportunity to give up," Harper said. "Many wouldn't have. Tethered and hanging from the floor … bleeding … in and out of consciousness … he could have surrendered but didn't. The tail scanner's job is to evacuate passengers in the event of an emergency, but helpless, he dangled in his harness begging for help. Smoke and dust reduced visibility inside the aircraft to near zero. Dirt caked in every pocket of his uniform. Smoke and raw fuel filled the air, burning his eyes and throat. He could've given up, but he didn't. I don't think he'll give up on trying to remember more of what happened. I have a feeling we may hear more from him. Luce, on the other hand is a different story. Still not sure about him."

We landed at Fort Walton Beach late in the evening. After checking into our hotel, the team retrieved luggage and other items stored in the hotel room we had retained through our absence.

After the wearisome weeks, I looked forward to moving the investigation toward a conclusion. I could not imagine a moment in Curtis' day or his regimen, where he might experience relief from his ordeal. If he refused to give up, neither would I. The next morning, the team met for breakfast.

"It's been a long trip," I said. "After breakfast we'll meet out front and carpool to Hurlburt Field. Capt Kelly, do we have an interview scheduled for tomorrow?"

"Yes, sir. A telephone interview at 2:30 p.m. ... the Afghan male interpreter who survived the crash."

"Get a good night's sleep." I said. "We hit it again tomorrow. Rest well. I appreciate your hard work during our trip to Afghanistan. Thank you."

I rose with my alarm the next morning. After a quick breakfast, we caravanned our three vehicles to the base. In anticipation of our arrival, TSgt Scott had brewed coffee and restocked our snack bar. We stowed our gear, powered up computers, and gathered around the conference table. Within hours after our return from halfway around the world, we fell into our routine of briefing the day's planned activities.

"I missed all of you," TSgt Scott said with his usual giant smile. "Sure has been quiet around here. I can't wait to hear about your trip."

"We have lots of news and plenty of stories." I said. "We'll share everything with you once we get our interview times set. Capt Kelly, where is our first interview going to take place this morning?"

"Sir, here in the office," she said.

"I have to be at headquarters for an hour or so this morning. When you get a minute, please schedule a second interview with the co-pilot. It's been a month. Maybe he's recovered enough memory to tell us about the last minute of the flight."

I drove to the AFSOC Head Quarters building and met with General Dobrinski, briefing him on the highlights of the trip. He expressed concern about finishing the investigation as soon as possible, pressing me for a date we might finish. I reassured him our first priority, aside from the few remaining interviews, was to finish writing the final report.

"Sir, two issues could slow our progress. First, the Rolls-Royce's analysis of the left engine. Using AFSOC's influence and resources might help to expedite movement of the engine out of Afghanistan. Second, we've completed interviews at such a quick pace, we have overwhelmed the capability of my court reporter's ability to transcribe them. Without one or two more people to help with the backlog, our final report could be delayed a month or more."

Dobrinski leaned back in his chair. He turned toward me with an angry frown.

"I'll see what the boss wants to do about the engine. Meanwhile, check with maintenance down the hall. The minute you have it, I want the engine's estimated time of arrival in California. As for additional court reporters, we'll try to get extra help by the end of the week. Anything else?"

"No, sir."

I left his office and walked to the AFSOC maintenance section at the far end of the building. The maintenance commander's administrative assistant greeted me when I approached her desk.

"Good morning, sir. How may I help you?"

"Good morning. Any engine experts in today?" I asked.

She pointed to an aisle created by cubicles arrayed in rows.

"Yes, sir. Master Sergeant Coby True is our resident expert … last desk on your right."

MSgt True stood when I approached his desk.

"Morning, sir. May I help you?"

Surrendering only enough detail to enlist his aid with some priority, I briefed him about the accident investigation and recovery of wreckage and one of the engines in Afghanistan.

"Have you heard about the engine?" I asked.

"Yes, sir. The commander briefed it at the morning stand-up last week. Since we're not tasked to retrieve the engine, I figured we'd become involved once it arrived at Rolls-Royce."

"General Dobrinski wants a timeline," I said. "He wants to know when the engine will arrive in California, how long it will take to accomplish the tear down and evaluation, and when we'll get their final analysis report. 8th SOS maintenance should have crated the engine for shipment from Kandahar Air Base. We'd like an estimated departure date and time. Please notify them we're pressed for time and to expedite shipping."

"I'll take care of it, sir. I've shipped engines to Rolls-Royce many times. I'll call you the minute I get an estimated time of arrival for the engine."

At the AIB office I prepared notes for the upcoming telephone interview with the Afghan interpreter, Mr. Mohammed Naheed. I knew little about him, except that he had an excellent rapport with the Special Operators with whom he worked. We had discovered nothing about Mrs. Reeta Sandozai, the female interpreter killed in the accident. Difficult or impossible under the circumstances, I would have liked an off-the-record visit with Mr. Naheed to explore what motivated him and other Afghan citizens to imbed and work with U.S. troops.

He kept a residence in the U.S. and I was unsure of his legal status. I couldn't see him and his family making a home here without some sense of kinship for our country. The state department paid the contractors, and I assume the interpreters, a good salary … one possible motivation. Political differences with the Taliban may have influenced some who supported a less rigid religious or more secular state. The opportunity never arose, and Mr. Naheed remained the only Afghan interpreter I ever had the chance to interview.

When I arrived back at the office, everyone was consumed by phone calls and emails. Over the weeks, we had become adept at conducting efficient interviews. We spent little time writing questions and attaching blank pages for notes. Before I'd been at my desk ten minutes, the rest of the board were finished with their work and had arranged the table for our interview.

"Sir, are you ready for the call?" Capt Kelly asked.

"I am ready."

I sat in my usual chair at the conference table. Capt Kelly used the phone in the middle of the desk, dialed the number, and pressed the speaker phone button. After a few rings, a gruff voice answered.

"Mr. Naheed, this is Capt Kelly. We spoke earlier. The accident board is here listening to you on speakerphone. Can you hear?"

"Yes. Hi Capt Kelly. I hear you very well."

"Before we begin, Brig Gen Harvel must advise you of certain matters. Once he's finished, he'll administer the oath whereby you will swear your truthful testimony. Then we'll ask you questions relating to the accident on the morning of April 9th."

I read the legal narrative, administered the oath, and initiated the questioning.

Naheed testified to working for World Wide Language Resources (WWLR) where he taught dialects of Farsi and Pashto to military and U.S. Foreign Service personnel. He also embedded with Special Operators when missions required interpreters. At other times, he facilitated conversations between Afghan leaders and U S. forces by translating official and casual conversations.

"What were your duties on the mission of April 8th?" I asked.

"Sir, I was assigned to translate for the Army Ranger ground forces commander."

"Was that your first mission flying on a CV-22?"

"Yes, sir."

"We've been told that Mrs. Reeta Sandozai accompanied you on the mission. Was she along as an interpreter?"

"Yes, sir. It was her first mission. She had arrived at our base five days earlier. We spent those days training. She was happy to be working for WWLR. She was smart and professional."

"Was the flight on the CV-22 different than other helicopters?" Winsett asked.

"Yes, sir. It is a loud airplane. The Chinook and Blackhawk helicopters are quieter. We can have conversations while flying to the target. On the CV-22, we could not talk to each other. The aircrew gave us all the warnings verbally and visually. We relayed the warnings by holding up our fingers. When we heard the one-minute warning, I got up on one knee and prepared to rapidly depart the airplane."

"Can you remember anything else that may have happened after the one-minute warning?" I asked.

"Sir, I remember getting bumped around, hard to keep my balance. I sat near the cockpit. I heard someone in the cockpit say, '… hey that …' in a very loud voice. I don't know who said it, or what happened after that. I was unconscious for a short period. The first thing I remember is Captain Erick McFerran (interpreter coordinator on chalk one) asking me if I was alive. I remember telling him 'Yes, I am alive.' He pulled equipment off me and then grabbed the shoulders of my uniform and pulled me out of the airplane. He told me I might have a broken nose. He said, 'Please don't die on me. We have called for a helicopter to evacuate you.' Captain McFerran was very helpful."

"What injuries did you sustain from the accident?" Doctor Harper asked.

"Sir, I had three lacerations on my head, a broken nose, a broken right shoulder, a broken rib, and a collapsed lung."

"Does your doctor think you will be able to return to work at WWLR?"

"Yes, sir. I love my job. I was at home with the people who worked with me. I loved working with the soldiers. They are great. I can't wait to get back."

After we completed the interview, I thanked Naheed for his time and for his service. He provided little information about the last minute of the flight. No one knew what to make of the "… hey that …" coming from the cockpit, other than to assume something might have been wrong. Hearing that twenty-three-year-old Reeta Sandozai had been a casualty on her very first combat mission jolted our emotions.

During the final ten minutes of the interview, and through our discussion afterward, my cell phone vibrated endlessly. When we returned to our desks, I scanned my missed calls and found a dozen calls from Capt

Pierce, my executive officer. I hadn't checked in with her when I traveled to the Head Quarters building earlier in the day. I immediately dialed her number. She answered without a greeting.

"Sir, where are you?"

"I'm here, at Hurlburt Field."

"Yes, sir. I know you're back. Are you at the accident board's office?"

"Yes. Why? What's up?"

"Sir, call the 8th SOS Maintenance Supervisor immediately ... there's a serious problem in Afghanistan."

CHAPTER THIRTY THREE

AFGHANISTAN CUSTOMS DEPARTMENT

Before departing Afghanistan, we had made a herculean effort to complete our work. The day we departed, I looked over my shoulder while boarding the C-17. I wondered if the discovered Osprey engine would ever get off the base and travel to the United States.

After a short conversation with the local 8th SOS Maintenance Chief, he gave me a name and number to call at Kandahar Air Base. I checked my watch. It was midnight in Afghanistan, the middle of the duty day for most of the deployed personnel. I hung up and sighed.

"Something wrong, sir?" Kelly asked.

"Yes. Something has gone wrong at Kandahar. Can you dial this number on the conference table phone while I get my notebook please?"

"Yes, sir. Right away," Kelly responded.

"When you connect, put it on speakerphone. We all should hear whatever it is."

While Capt Kelly dialed, the board gathered around the conference table and waited. The distinctive Afghanistan dial tone buzzed while the number connected. After a series of clacking noises, someone finally picked up.

"8th SOS Maintenance, Captain Keith Nystrom speaking."

"Captain Nystrom, this is Brigadier General Harvel. AFSOC Head Quarters asked me to call you."

"Yes, sir. I'm glad they tracked you down. We have a serious situation with the Osprey engine we are trying to ship out. We desperately need your assistance, sir."

"Sure, how can I help?" I asked.

"Sir, per your request we recovered the left engine from forward operating base Apache and crated it for transport. When we delivered it to the Afghanistan Customs Department (ACD), it was refused for shipment. They insist the engine must be power washed to remove sand, dirt, and other debris prior to being accepted for shipping. We've done all we can on this end. They refuse to budge. We're at a stalemate. Please advise how we should proceed, sir."

In most third world countries, red tape that to us seemed arbitrary, or outright corrupt, would have been snipped with a bottle of single malt liquor or carton of American cigarettes. In a Muslim country, I couldn't, given my position, recommend such a shortcut. If it were possible, I assumed our local people would have considered it. We would work the issue through proper channels.

I looked around the table and asked, "Ideas, anyone?"

Dolan leaned in toward the phone.

"Captain Nystrom, this is Master Sergeant Dolan. The engine can't be power washed. It must arrive at Rolls-Royce in the condition as you recovered it from Apache."

"Roger that. We understand, but we're lost for a solution," said Nystrom.

"Sir, I'm on the ACD website," Winsett said. "They have a short-form request to appeal a problem with their service. They appear willing to accommodate special circumstances. I can download the form and fax it to you after I have filled it out. I'll also attach a cover letter with General Harvel's signature block on it. What's your fax number?"

"Captain Nystrom, we'll get this to you within the hour." I said. "There'll be a completed ACD appeal with a letter attached to clearly explain the reason the engine must be preserved in its present condition. It's after midnight there, can you deliver the documents to ACD first thing in the morning?"

"Yes, sir. I'll see to it personally. What's a good contact number for you, in case they reject the appeal?"

I gave Nystrom my cell number. Winsett and I worked the appeal and a letter explaining the accident investigation process, stressing the importance of preserving critical evidence. Once completed, I faxed the letters to Nystrom. I also scanned the documents and emailed them to MSgt True and Maj Gen Dobrinski to keep them up to date.

During the investigation, we maintained files containing substantiating documents relating to each section of the report. Until now, we had put papers into the boxes. Now, one-by-one, or in short stacks, we removed the documents and spent the rest of the day transferring data to the first draft of our accident report. Air Force Regulations provided clear guidelines for what information the report must contain. I was responsible for writing the *Opinion* and the *Executive Summary* stating my opinion of what caused the accident. The opinion must be based on substantiated findings, or a proven cause.

Adams had her hands full transcribing recorded testimony. She listened to testimony recordings dozens of times to ensure the accuracy of every word recorded – a tedious and time-consuming endeavor. An interview lasting an hour might take her three days to transcribe. Any assistance Dobrinski could marshal would be very much appreciated.

"Sir, Major Luce just called," Kelly said. "He's available to interview at 9:00 a.m. tomorrow morning. Sergeant Scott reserved the base operations conference room."

"Thanks … Winsett, please make sure we bring the video. We didn't show it to him during his previous interview. Maybe it'll trigger his memory."

I hated to add one more interview to Adams' workload, but I was not comfortable completing the investigation without giving Luce one last chance to recall the final seconds of the flight. We had a definitive picture of events leading up to those final seconds, and what happened afterward. But we had very little to paint the picture of what went wrong to cause the Osprey to basically fall out of the sky.

We still hadn't tapped one asset at our disposal; a full-motion CV-22 simulator located on base. I had flown and instructed in Air Force and airline simulators enough to know their capabilities. I penned a few notes detailing what conditions we could program into simulator flight scenarios and carried them to O'Leary's desk.

"What are the chances we could steal a few hours of sim time?" I asked.

"I don't know, sir. I'll call the simulator scheduler and ask. What free time they have available may be on the backside of the clock. Would you mind flying the simulator in the middle of the night?"

"I don't care," I answered. "We'll need a simulator instructor to load in data for us. Let's start with these scenarios and devise as many different situations as possible. To save time, let's start each scenario at one minute out from the landing zone. We'll record what happens if one engine failed… two engines failed … tailwinds … coanda and/or anti-ice valves failed open … compressor stalls … landings and go-arounds from one minute from landing. We'll evaluate all the data and determine what is closest to what actually happened to the crew on the morning of April 9th in Afghanistan."

"Sounds like a great idea, sir," said O'Leary. "I have another follow-on idea. Once we narrow down the malfunctions, how about asking the 8th SOS for a qualified aircrew. We'll put them into the simulator and record their reaction to a few malfunctions we determine may have contributed to the accident."

O'Leary's eyes widened. He was excited about this idea.

Doc Harper eavesdropped from his desk. Intrigued by the simulator prospect, he edged closer to the conversation and sat on the corner of O'Leary's desk.

"You probably won't be able to schedule a simulator before tomorrow, will you?" Harper asked.

"I doubt it," O'Leary answered. "Why?"

"We interview Luce tomorrow. If he's still in a traumatic or a contrived state of amnesia, why not put him in the simulator and have him fly the same approach to the landing zone the crew flew the morning of the accident? It may be a great memory jogger."

CHAPTER THIRTY FOUR

SIMULATOR CRASH

After Doc Harper suggested we put Luce in the simulator to fly the same approach as the night of the accident, I included Winsett in the conversation. He brought Kelly into the discussion and Dolan joined as well. Adams, intent with transcribing testimony, looked up from her work and seeing everyone huddled around O'Leary's desk, removed her headphones.

"Did I miss something?" she asked. "What happened?"

"Doc Harper just proposed we put Luce in the simulator." O'Leary said. "If he can't remember the final seconds of the flight, perhaps flying a couple approaches to the Afghanistan landing zone will stimulate his memory."

"Good idea…bad idea … legal issues?" I asked.

Winsett conferred with Kelly for a moment.

"Sir, we see no legal issues, but Luce must understand he's still under oath and anything he says or does in the simulator is testimony and becomes evidence. We should have either Captain Kelly or me in the simulator. Is that possible?"

"Sure," O'Leary said. "There's room, no problem. We're on the schedule for two hours tomorrow afternoon, after Luce's interview. Does that work for everyone?"

"Perfect," I said. "If he recovers from his two months of amnesia beforehand, Lieutenant Colonel O'Leary and I will use the period to test several hypotheses concerning the crash."

Winsett rubbed his hands together seeming to relish time out of the office in a state-of-the-art simulator.

"With your permission, sir, I'll accompany you and record what Major Luce might say. I'll rely on your knowledge for his performance, though I'd remind everyone, the object is to jog Luce's memory and take testimony, not to assess his flying skills."

O'Leary excused himself to take a phone call.

"Great, it's settled." I said. "We interview at 9:00 a.m. tomorrow. Without digital monitors for evidence, we're relying on Luce to shine a light into the black hole in our investigation. I hope this works."

O'Leary returned from his phone call scribbling a note on a wrinkled bit of paper. "Sir, the simulator scheduler confirmed our time for tomorrow afternoon. Our instructor has the profiles we plan to fly with Luce and is anxious to help. He also offered us 8:00 a.m. to 10:00 a.m. tomorrow morning. If I may sir, we could fly Luce before the interview then if the experience revives his memory, we interview with the entire board right afterward."

"I like that … a lot." I said. "Make sure Luce is available and set it up. We shouldn't need more than an hour in the sim. Kelly, we should be ready to interview at 9:30 a.m.

"Yes, sir," replied Kelly.

Luce had no conflicts and agreed to meet us at the simulator at 8:00 a.m.

The following morning, I met O'Leary and Winsett in the hotel lobby where we drove to the simulator building across the runway from the main base at Hurlburt Field. The 19th SOS, schoolhouse for AC-130 gunship training, used most of the space in the two-story structure.

Situated on the ground floor, the CV-22 simulator occupied a large, open space (bay). Crews briefed and debriefed in several small rooms outfitted with visual aids and training materials adjacent to the simulator area.

Entering the building, we greeted the scheduler who introduced us to Mr. Henry Brucker, a civilian flight instructor employed by the contractor who operated the simulator. Over coffee in the lounge area, we discussed what we expected from the session. Maj Luce hadn't been in an airplane or the simulator since the night of the accident. We planned the first event to be a normal daytime approach to the same landing zone his crew had flown the night of the accident – the same altitude, weather, aircraft gross weight, and fuel load. Succeeding approaches increased the complexity by varying weather conditions and aircraft malfunctions. We would debrief, if necessary, afterward with the rest of the board. Since Brucker would be controlling inputs to the simulator, we discussed profiles we wanted to fly and how we wanted him to record results.

During our discussion, Luce walked into the lobby wearing a flight suit and appearing in good physical condition. Lacerations we had seen on his face the first interview had healed and his tan indicated he was spending time outdoors. He walked without signs of knee or back issues and approached us with his hand extended.

"How are you, sir?" he asked.

"No, how are you, Maj Luce? As well as you look, I hope."

"Sir, I'm doing great. Physical therapy is progressing well. I spend about three to four hours a day working out at the gym. Not running cross-country yet, but I do run a couple miles on a treadmill. It feels good to get back in shape. I hope to be back on flying status in four to six weeks."

"Congratulations, that's good news," I said. "Thanks for coming in so early. Sounds like you're doing well enough for an hour of flying in the simulator."

"Yes, sir, but remember I'll be rusty. It's been a while."

"We understand," I said. "We're not here to evaluate your proficiency. What we do in the sim today has no bearing on your requalification in the aircraft, but you're still bound by the oath you took prior to your first interview. What you say or do will be a recorded part of your testimony. We'll warm up with a couple of daytime approaches followed by two night approaches. With succeeding approaches, we'll introduce more complex situations at the same landing zone in Afghanistan. You will be the pilot flying so take whatever action you deem fit. Fly the best you can. After four approaches we'll be done. The rest of the investigation board will be waiting for us in the base operations conference room and we'll shoot for 9:15 a.m. to start your interview. Fair enough?"

"Yes, sir, I'm ready to fly," Luce said eagerly.

We climbed a short set of stairs to the entrance of the flight simulator. The cockpit replicated, in every detail, the actual aircraft forward of the bulkhead. From the instructor's console aft of the cockpit, Brucker controlled all aspects of the simulator operation. With a few keystrokes, he could locate the simulator and visual screens to any point on the earth where crews might conduct Special Operations missions. He could also select any one of hundreds of airports stored in the computer database. He commanded an array of malfunctions affecting aircraft systems and flight characteristics to permit crews to practice and demonstrate proficiency dealing with normal and emergency procedures.

O'Leary sat in the left pilot seat, Luce sat in the right pilot seat, and I observed from the flight engineer's position. Winsett stood at my side.

Brucker demonstrated the visual capability by showing us the final approaches to Hurlburt and Hickam Air Force Base, Hawaii. The brief demo seemed to exceed Winsett's expectations of what simulators could do.

"Pull up the visual for Afghanistan and load the approach to the landing zone on April 9th," I said.

"Done," said Brucker.

Within seconds, the Afghan terrain approaching the landing zone we had seen while flying in the MI-17 appeared in the simulator windows. The simulator was in the "freeze" mode. We were in the air, but not moving. It allowed us to take in the surrounding area and was like looking at a high definition television with the picture stopped.

"So, this is what it looks like in the daytime." Luce said.

"Correct," said O'Leary. "We're three miles from the landing zone and two-hundred feet in the air. The landing zone coordinates are in the computer. When you're ready, we'll take the simulator off freeze. You're on a daytime low visibility approach (LVA). Winds are calm. Are you ready to fly?"

"Okay, sir. I'm ready," Luce said as he focused on the flight instruments.

Brucker hit a switch and took the simulator off freeze. We were now flying. O'Leary coached him through the first approach and landing. Luce performed well, especially since this was the first time he had flown in a couple of months.

"Good hands," O'Leary said. "Nice approach and landing. Now we'll reposition back to the same point and fly the same LVA. This time you'll have a ten-knot crosswind. Here we go."

Luce flew the approach with O'Leary performing normal copilot duties. He flew another nice approach and landing.

"Not too bad," Luce said as he wiped the sweat off his hands onto his flight suit.

O'Leary took notes and coordinated the next profile with Brucker.

"Yes ... very good," said O'Leary. "The next approach is a night LVA. Check your winds once the simulator is taken off freeze. I'll be your copilot and your flight engineer. Ready for a night approach?"

Brucker turned off the visual. The view in the windscreen went dark ... just like night. "This reminds me of how dark it was the night of the accident," Luce said.

O'Leary made a note on his chart and said, "That's the idea. Mr. Brucker has reset us to the same position where you started your last approach. Ready?"

"Sure, let's give it a try, sir," said Luce.

As the simulator came off freeze, Luce initiated a slow descent, but made no comment about the seventeen-knot tailwind. At one hundred feet above the ground, Brucker failed the right engine. All hell broke loose as multiple visual and aural warnings sounded loudly. Surprised by the sudden loss of power Luce reacted, but slowly. After the brief false start, he managed the engine failure correctly.

"I'm going around," said Luce.

He advanced the TCL to full power and raised the nose to get the Osprey flying up and away from the ground.

"Boy, she's heavy," he said as he continuously fought to get the nose of the airplane up without losing airspeed.

O'Leary read the AFTER-TAKEOFF checklist aloud. He reached forward and raised the landing gear lever, starting the landing gear retracting into the airplane's wheel wells.

"Gear up. Clear to transition, visual inspection of the cabin complete. Transitioning," Luce said as he slowly converted the Osprey from helicopter to airplane mode.

O'Leary placed his hands on the airplane controls.

"I have the airplane … good," said O'Leary. "You arrested your descent and got the airplane into a slow climb. The airplane could fly up to a safe altitude and proceed to forward operating base Delta for an emergency landing. Checklists are complete."

Mr. Brucker froze the simulator and reset the it back to the point three miles away from the landing zone.

"Okay we're ready to fly one last approach," said O'Leary. "Make sure you check the winds once the simulator comes off the freeze mode. If you have a malfunction, react as you've been trained. Mr. Brucker, are you ready to let us fly?"

"Yes, sir," said Brucker. "Here we go."

With the simulator now in full motion, Luce initiated a slow descent and flew a textbook approach to one hundred feet above the ground. At that point, Brucker inserted *Dual Engine Compressor Stall* into the simulator profile. We could all hear a slight engine power reduction as the compressor stalls occurred.

Luce pushed the TCL to maximum power and nervously paused.

"We're descending too fast," he said. "Maximum power."

He advanced the TCL past the soft stop at full power and went to the hard stop … contingency power limit. The simulator generated sound of engine noise remained unchanged. Within a few seconds there was a loud and blaring crash noise from the overhead speakers. Screens on both instrument panels turned bright red. Hydraulic pressure feeding three large actuators controlling the motion of the simulator fell to zero, settling the simulator to the floor stops within a few seconds. Red lights aft of the cockpit bulkhead lit the interior. The flight simulator had crashed. The vertical velocity exceeded 1,600 feet per minute as the Osprey impacted the ground at a steep angle. The word "CRASH" was clearly visible on the display unit in front of each pilot. All eyes were on Maj Luce as he sat as motionless as the simulator.

CHAPTER THIRTY-FIVE

SECOND INTERVIEW WITH COPILOT

Crashing the flight simulator appeared to have shaken Luce. But not enough that he didn't ask what happened. He unstrapped, got out of the pilot seat and stood at the back of the simulator in silence. The last time he had been in the seat of an Osprey, the flight ended with him lying in the dirt of the Afghanistan desert watching the airplane burn in front of him, surrounded by mayhem and destruction.

While Luce exited the simulator, O'Leary penned a few final notes and unbuckled his seatbelt.

"Mr. Brucker, that's it for this morning," said O'Leary. "I made additional notes on the profiles we'll fly during our scheduled period later today. Thank you for your assistance."

O'Leary stuffed papers in his briefcase and gathered his gear. I asked Brucker if he would review the list of scenarios we planned to fly that afternoon. He slapped a rolled-up stack of papers across his hand and reassured me he would review the profiles and have the simulator ready when we returned.

As we walked to the parking lot, I told Luce we would meet him at base operations.

O'Leary and I talked about the simulator flight as we drove across the base.

"I thought it was unusual Luce didn't ask what happened on the last profile," said O'Leary. "Not the usual attitude of a pilot wanting to know the cause of an accident, not so unusual if he wanted the cause buried."

Absent an engine failure, which would cause visual and aural warnings, the indication of a rapid rate of descent would have been the crew's only indication of a normal approach going bad. No one we interviewed mentioned automated warnings associated with engine failure, only terrain alerts. Our list of possible mechanical failures included both one, and two engine compressor stalls. We evaluated a dozen or more engine power malfunctions in the flight simulator later in the afternoon. O'Leary and I considered Luce's flying performance to be more than adequate given his extended break from flying. Luce made the correct, instinctive decision to add power - all the power available. There was no way Luce could have flown away from the ground with a dual-engine compressor stall. Luce's simulator performance reinforced our unspoken belief that the crew didn't just ride the aircraft into the ground.

When we arrived at the base operations building, the other team members had the interview room set up and ready for us to start. By the time I entered the conference room, Luce had walked halfway around the table greeting each of the board members.

"The perspiration showing through your flight suit tells me you're thirsty, Maj Luce," I said. "I brought you a cold bottle of water."

"Thank you, sir."

Winsett handed me an abbreviated legal narrative and walked to his seat across from me.

"The board's ready when you are, sir," said Winsett.

"Maj Luce, if you need to take a break at any time, please let me know."

"Yes, sir."

"For the record, I remind you, you're still under oath. Though this is our second interview, what we cover today will be considered along with your previous testimony. Do you have any questions before we begin?"

"No, sir."

"Great. We have a video for you to review. One of the A-10s support-ing your mission on April 8th provided this image. Do you consent to view the video and offer comments?"

"Yes, sir. I'd like to see it."

Winsett sat his laptop in front of Luce and played the twenty-second video. Since the board members had seen it dozens of times, most concentrated on Luce's reaction when he watched it for the first time. Luce's expression changed little while the mishap aircraft descended over the three large wadis. When the Osprey touched down and burst into flames, Luce winced and lowered his head while the cloud of dirt and smoke drifted in the same direction they had attempted to land.

"We have plenty of time, if you'd like to see it again," Winsett said.

"Yes, sir. Please."

Luce leaned into the computer screen and viewed the video again. He had been in the simulator for a little over an hour flying approaches to the same landing zone where the Osprey accident occurred. Nothing in his expression indicated he had come to a renewed realization. He either had to add to his previous testimony or repeat what he had said beforehand. I asked him the question.

"After flying approaches to the same landing zone as the night of the accident and after reviewing the video twice, share with the board any recollection you'd like to add to your previous testimony. What did you see, hear or experience during the final seconds of the early morning flight on April 9th?"

"The … watching the video … wasn't how I remembered it. You know, of course, I don't remember the last few seconds of it anyway. I was surprised to watch … watch the video and to … what kind of struck me was just at the end. Right before the impact was, you know, watching the descent of the airplane. So, I don't know. I guess it surprised me. It makes sense, you know, we were dropping like that. But I guess it didn't really make sense until I saw it."

Luce appeared nervous. He kept saying "you know" once or twice in each sentence. After recuperating for two months, he had spent over an hour flying approaches, simulating various weather conditions and aircraft malfunctions to the same landing zone as the night of the accident. He viewed the video of the crash taken from an airplane circling above the landing zone two times and still claimed to have no specific recollection of why the airplane suddenly started falling out of the sky.

I stared at my pen lying on the blank pad in front of me. I breathed, but in shallow gasps. I looked at Winsett. He pushed his eyebrows high on his forehead and cocked his head. He had no ideas. I looked at O'Leary. He leaned over the table, shook his head and returned my gaze. He couldn't believe it. The silent feedback from the rest of the team ranged from disappointment to anger.

I considered ending the interview after the one question. I hesitated for a moment to weigh my options. This would be our last go with Luce. If we continued, maybe he would remember something … or … if we were being played, maybe he'd blunder and give up a sliver of information we had not heard before. I decided to make one last attempt to discover the truth.

"Go back to preparing for the mission. Were you involved in route planning on April 8th?"

"No, sir. This was my first mission of this type. I've been involved in the route planning for exercises and training missions, but this was the first operational mission I'd flown."

"Even though you have limited route planning experience, would you consider the forecast winds at the landing zone and use the information to plan a route from the initial point to the landing zone to land into the wind?"

"Yes," said Luce. "Yes, sir. That's, you know, you get the weather. I was not present, you know, when the aircraft commander, Maj Voas got the weather briefing. You know, the crew went different directions to prepare for the flight. Looking at winds, you know, if you can line up the final approach to be into the wind, that's ideal. And then, you know, the other big factor would be the terrain features going into the landing zone. You would ideally plan to be into the wind, you know, within, you know, probably forty-five degrees either side of the nose. There wasn't a lot of elevation change on our mission that night. You know, the big problem with the Osprey is descending and decelerating at the same time. So, you know, if you can find the flattest path in there that still lines you up into the wind, that's what they would plan."

I asked Luce three more questions about how they were alerted for the mission and what the crew did the day prior. We knew the answers. In fact, we had asked him the same questions during his first interview. I couldn't ease him into a comfortable dialogue where his stream of consciousness morphed into a lucid memory of the seconds prior to impact.

Doc Harper used the same tactic of using different points in time, as did Adams, Winsett, Kelly and Dolan. Luce provided facts buried in nervous, gibbered vocabulary punctuated by the frequent, and irritating, use of "… you know …" for any time frame we asked outside the crucial last eighteen seconds of flight. When asked about his recollection of the final seconds, he spouted complete gibberish. I allowed the questioning to continue, but after a few minutes, my mind retreated to a point where I heard Luce's voice but not the words. The possible key to solving the mystery of the accident sat three feet in front of me and I felt there was more information he could share.

Adams and Winsett reminded him of conversations he'd had at Walter Reed with SGT Claybaker and SSgt Curtis regarding the accident. Confronted with the testimony of two other survivors, he admitted to visiting with both of them on several occasions. But he denied having conversations regarding the cause of the accident.

It became very difficult to continue listening to the interview. Luce couldn't remember, or refused to admit he remembered, what happened or why the airplane had descended at an abnormal rate prior to impact. He had nothing to add … nothing. We had done all we could. Before enduring more nonsense and continuing to waste valuable time, I ended the interview.

"That'll be all, Maj Luce. We're done. I remind you of the official nature of this interview. You may not discuss your testimony with anyone without my permission prior to the accident report being completed and released to the public. This concludes the interview."

Maj Luce stood and worked his way around the conference table shaking hands with the board members. Before leaving, he shook my hand and thanked me. Even after shaking a half-dozen hands, his palms felt cool and clammy. In silence, we all glared at the door closing behind him as he exited.

TSgt Adams broke the silence by stating, "Sir, to me, he seemed really nervous."

Everyone turned and stared at me.

"Yeah, I agree," I said.

"When I transcribe his testimony, sir … ah … he said '*you know*' a lot. You want me to redact the hundreds of times he said it?"

"No, leave them in," I replied. "All of them. I want the record to reflect exactly what he said this morning."

"Yes, sir."

I checked the time and released everyone to go eat lunch. I asked O'Leary to join me while we planned our afternoon simulator flight. Except to order our lunch, neither of us spoke until we arrived back at our office.

"Did Luce seem nervous to you?" I asked.

"Yes, sir, he did. It was weird … he didn't seem nervous during the first interview a few weeks ago at his house. Maybe the simulator flight rattled him? Or, maybe he knows more than he wants to share. Not sure we'll ever know."

"Well, we still have that black hole," I said. "I'd hoped for better information. If the crew didn't screw up, maybe they had an engine power malfunction? Perhaps a unique malfunction that didn't have enough time to annunciate an aural warning. Without the flight information recorder or any other engine instrument history, how can we find evidence of a compressor stall, an open bleed air valve, or another malfunction that would have reduced available power from one or both engines?"

O'Leary flipped to a page in his notebook.

"Wait a minute, sir. I should have thought of this earlier. I think I have a solution."

CHAPTER THIRTY SIX

INGENIOUS IDEA

O'Leary opened his binder, took a page out, and slid it across the table to me. It was a handwritten page of engine malfunction scenarios O'Leary had prepared for our simulator period later in the afternoon. I counted thirty-eight profiles.

"We'll never get through these in two hours," I said. "Should we prioritize what we can get done during our simulator period?"

"No, sir, we should do all of them," O'Leary replied. "If it takes one or two additional simulator periods, so be it. I'm willing to come out for any period they make available for us. Even if it's at midnight."

O'Leary defined conditions we would require for each of the profiles - weather and aircraft data being constants. We used an environment identical to what the mishap crew and aircraft experienced the night of the accident – aircraft gross weight 45,500 pounds … temperature 68°F … fuel load 4,000 pounds … landing zone elevation 5,300 feet … winds northeast at 17 knots … right engine 96%, left engine 99% (based on the latest recorded engine performance capability downloaded from the airplane on the morning of April 8th).

"Looks good to me," I said. "No, it looks better than good. It's perfect. Now, tell me about this great idea you have. I'm intrigued."

"Sir, I'll explain my idea after we get more data from our simulator flight. I want to make sure my idea is valid. I'll share my idea when we finish our simulator session this afternoon."

"Okay. We all look forward to the discussion with you."

"Sir, I wrote these flight profiles as I thought of them. They're in no particular order. With your permission, it'll be easier for Mr. Brucker, and we'll save time if we cluster similar malfunctions together. I'll have them organized by the time we depart for our simulator session."

"Good enough," I said. "When you're ready, I'll be in my office."

I sat down in my office to check emails. I scrolled to those from Afghanistan and saw I had an email from Capt Nystrom.

> *Sir, Great news! The Afghanistan Customs Department (ACD) released the engine for shipment to the United States. We had to change the covering on the outside of the crate. We also had to attach your letter, and their waiver for the shipment, in the documentation folder attached to the crate. The engine is still at the ACD. I will notify you as soon as it departs Kandahar. Very respectfully, Captain K. Nystrom.*

I printed the email and walked it to Winsett's desk.

"Look at this ... the engine has been released for shipment from Kandahar."

"That's great news, sir," said Winsett. "We sure needed it."

The news eased the gloom lingering over the board members after the disappointing Luce interview, but only a little. We never thought that either engine had completely failed. But one or both engines may have suddenly lost power. Perhaps Rolls-Royce would confirm the left engine was operating at low power.

O'Leary came to my desk carrying his briefcase and hat.

"Sir, you ready to go?"

Winsett drove us to the simulator building while O'Leary briefed the initial series of profiles. Mr. Brucker met us as we entered the simulator building. He had the weather, location, and aircraft data loaded into the flight management computer. The simulator was on "freeze" at two hundred feet above the ground and three miles from the landing zone.

O'Leary keyed his interphone switch so all of us with headsets over our ears could hear him.

"The first series of scenarios addresses situations I think are improbable - failure of either or both engines. Mr. Brucker, initiate the malfunctions when we are thirty seconds from landing on each approach."

"Got it," Brucker said. "Whenever you're ready."

"Let's fly," O'Leary said enthusiastically.

Hydraulic pistons controlling motion clunked and the simulator rose off the floor. We were flying. O'Leary reduced the thrust control lever to slow the airspeed and thumbed a small switch on the thrust control lever to tilt the nacelles toward vertical (helicopter position) for landing. He corrected for changing winds and lowered the landing gear. Thirty seconds prior to planned touchdown, the rpm on both engines rolled back rapidly and a computer-generated female voice repeated loudly, 'ENGINE FAILURE … ENGINE FAILURE.' Warning lights on the glare shield and the display screens in front of each pilot annunciated L ENG and R ENG in bright red letters. The airplane nosed into a steep descent and crashed violently.

O'Leary looked over his shoulder at Winsett and said, "For the record … that rules out dual-engine failure as a probable cause of the accident."

For the next hour and a half, we plowed through O'Leary's list of possible malfunctions – exhaust deflector, coanda valve, anti-icing valve, compressor stalls. Winsett recorded cockpit indications and the success or failure of pilot inputs to control the aircraft and possibly fly to an alternate airfield to land safely. Perspiration stained O'Leary's flight suit. Winsett, light years away from his element, seemed stressed at first with the gyrations of the simulator. But, after the third crash his stomach settled and seemed eager for the next profile. The hour and a half went by quickly.

"Sorry gents," Brucker said. "This'll have to be the last approach. The next crew is waiting outside."

I checked my list. We had attempted only a third of our planned profiles. We would need at least one or two more simulator periods to finish collecting data. As we walked out of the flight simulator building, I asked O'Leary if he was happy with our simulator period.

"I'm almost one hundred percent sure the crew did not have an engine failure," O'Leary replied. "The computer-generated warnings are broadcast on overhead speakers in the cockpit and over the interphone. As you heard, the speakers are loud. MAJ Carter who was seated near the cockpit and SSgt Curtis on headset would have definitely remembered hearing the warnings."

Winsett and I agreed.

While driving back to the office, O'Leary suggested we use the imagery in our possession to address the white puffs trailing the aircraft as seen on the video of the accident. Perhaps it was a clue to identify the crew was dealing with an insufficient power issue limiting their capability to execute a go-around. I thought for a moment about O'Leary's idea.

"Save your idea for the evening briefing with the entire team," I said. "They have to hear this."

Dolan greeted us when we walked into the office.

"Sir, good news … the engine has departed Kandahar and is scheduled into Al Udeid in less than three hours. The itinerary afterward is still open, but lots of people are watching to make sure the engine gets on the next available airplane to the U.S. We'll get an email as soon as the outbound flight is identified. That's the short story of my six emails waiting in your inbox."

I gave Dolan a thumbs up.

"Give me fifteen minutes," I said. "I need to check phone messages and emails, and then we'll have our afternoon staff meeting."

The time we spent on the final report consumed more hours each succeeding day. We relied on having two daily staff meetings to keep everyone informed about each person's work. I kept the morning meeting at 8:00 a.m. The afternoon meeting was more flexible, but usually held between 5:00 p.m. and 6:00 p.m. Most everyone continued working after the afternoon staff meeting and would depart the office at 8:00 p.m. or 9:00 p.m.

I assembled everyone for our staff meeting. O'Leary and Kelly were in the middle of phone calls. Both held up two fingers. They'd be free in two minutes. Mimicking one another's hand signals amused them. The rest of us settled into our seats and waited.

"While we have a minute," I said, "Adams, I have some good news. Two court reporters have been assigned to help you - one from Travis Air Force Base arrives Thursday evening, the other from Wright-Patterson AFB arrives tomorrow afternoon. Scotty, (SSgt Scott's nickname) can you find desks and make space for them to work here?"

"Yes, sir. It'll be set up by tomorrow afternoon," he replied.

"How many interviews have you transcribed?" I asked, while looking at Adams.

"Sir, I'm on number twenty-two. I still have more than eighty to go. Thank you for getting help. I thought I'd be at this until Christmas. Oh yeah, I meant to ask you about the testimony I'm currently transcribing - Major Luce's second interview. I counted over nine hundred '*you knows*.' Are you sure you don't want me to redact those?"

"No, keep them. Don't change a thing. I want the testimony to be recorded exactly as we heard it."

Kelly and O'Leary finished their calls and joined us.

"Did we miss anything?" Kelly asked.

"Two court reporters are on the way to help Adams," I said.

"Great," Kelly said. "I've been tracking our progress. We have twenty percent of the interviews transcribed. With the added court reporters, we could be fifty percent complete by the end of next week."

"Dolan ..."

"Sir, I have copies of the aircraft maintenance records for my section of the report. Everyone was updated on the shipment of the engine from Kandahar. I will let you know when it ships from Al Udeid. That's it."

"Doc Harper ... "

"Sir, I finished human factors today ... I see no other problems. I am continuing to gather information for my section of the accident report."

"Lieutenant Colonel Winsett ..."

"Sir, I've reviewed completed sections and redacted information from the transcribed interviews – names, call signs, bases, tactics and Special Operations procedures. I recommend we start preparing you for the briefing you'll have to present to the command once the report is finished. Have you ever heard of a 'murder board', sir?"

"No, what's that?"

"Sir, we hold mock presentations. The commander and his staff will ask pointed, if not contentious, questions. We'll anticipate what they might ask, and you can practice your responses. Have you given much thought to the briefing you will have to give, sir?"

"To be honest, no. Once I write my opinion, I'll work on the presentation. Thanks for the heads up about murder boards. I'll need everyone helping to prepare. Plan the first practice in two weeks. Lieutenant Colonel O'Leary ..."

"Sir, we finished the first period of simulator test runs. Lieutenant Colonel Winsett and I will compile the data and email it to each of you. Today, we discovered the crews were operating with very little margin for engine failure situations. The airplanes would be able to maintain level flight but would have been unable to climb higher than one to two hundred feet above the ground. That said ... once the pilot elects to go-around, the aircraft may descend slightly while the engines spool-up to full power. Two factors affect the airplane's capability during a go-around – the altitude at which the go-around is initiated and the rate of descent. Lower altitudes and higher rates of descent may make a go-around difficult to accomplish without hitting the ground. Another condition affects aircraft performance but is not accounted for in calculating performance data. The accelerated degradation of engine performance while operating in a dirt environment puts crews in a dangerous box not considered when performance data is calculated prior to flight."

"Very good," I said. "We're still compiling simulator data. Updates will follow. Today, for me personally, marked a low point in our investigation. With your collective assistance, we've discovered everything that could be learned about the accident. Everything except what happened during the final seventeen seconds of flight to cause the Osprey to rapidly descend. Absent a credible witness in the cockpit and no recorded digital data, we're left to surmise what happened. I thought we'd have to rely on empirical evidence with no proof of engine "health," so I look forward to getting the report on the left engine after analysis from Rolls-Royce. Lieutenant Colonel O'Leary also approached me with an idea that gave me a grain of hope. I'll let him explain."

"Thank you, sir," said O'Leary. "We have a video of the accident. Everyone's been over it dozens of times, but I suggest we look at it with a more technical eye. I'm convinced that an Air Force imagery expert may have the technology to slow the video so that, frame-by-frame, we can count the revolutions of the proprotors. With the elapsed time displayed on the screen, we should be able to determine an rpm. Once we have an rpm, we can convert the figure to calculate an engine percent of performance. We already know the airplane did not have 100% engines. The left engine was approximately 99% and the right engine was approximately 96%. I have contacts at the Air Force Safety Center who can connect us with experts to accomplish the analysis and calculations. We also have another source that will provide the same information, but in a different way. Photos taken by Combat Search and Rescue (CSAR) at the accident site show scars gouged in the sand where the tips of the proprotors plowed the earth when the aircraft flipped onto its back. The CSAR team was very thorough in collecting information. They gave us a measurement of the distance between the gouges made by each proprotor as it hit the ground. By using the airplane's touchdown airspeed, engineers should be able to calculate the rpm of the proprotors based on the distance between mark number one and mark number two in the sand. What do you think?"

The board sat silent, some because of the brilliance of what they heard, and others because they had no understanding of what O'Leary said.

Adams raised her hand and said, "Okay ...so when the engineers analyze the data, then give us their report, how will it help us?"

"We'll know if either or both engines were operating in a normal range, 95% to 100%, or if the engine performance had degraded to a much lower than normal power percentage," O'Leary replied.

Adams thought for a moment. "OK … what a great idea. Perhaps this information can finally solve the engine power mystery. But, do you think the Air Force Specials Operations Commander and the Chief of Staff of the Air Force will be receptive to such an unusual way to collect engine performance data?"

CHAPTER THIRTY SEVEN

NATIONAL SUPPORT TEAM

Adam's question could not be answered until the final report was submitted. We were still not sure whether the data would even prove to be substantial.

By the end of June, we had exhausted our list of people to interview. Through the Fourth of July weekend and the following week, board members worked long hours completing their respective sections of the final accident report.

O'Leary contacted friends at the Air Force Safety Center at Kirtland AFB, seeking engineering assistance for evaluating the accident video and photo evidence we possessed. They recommended we send our data to the National Geospatial-Intelligence Agency (NGA) National Support Team (NST). NGA employed over 14,500 personnel assigned at their headquarters in Fort Belvoir, Virginia, and another large facility in St. Louis, Missouri. The two large facilities and numerous liaison offices worldwide provided support to combat operations of U.S. and selected military services of allied nations.

Though their main mission is analysis of signal and satellite data for intelligence agencies and the Department of Defense (DOD), we hoped they would entertain our request to examine the accident video and photo evidence provided by the combat search and rescue team.

Neither O'Leary nor I had heard of the organization, but we trusted them to expertly deconstruct our evidence into data that might add clarity to our investigation. O'Leary made the contact and forwarded the video and two photos taken at the accident site to the NST based at Wright Patterson AFB, Ohio. One photo showed gouges in the dirt made by the rotating proprotors when the aircraft flipped onto its back. The other picture depicted the tracks made by the landing gear and the gouge the ramp of the airplane made in the soft desert sand. Precise measurements indicating the markings' relation to one another accompanied each photo.

We wanted to discover or verify several pieces of information: the forward speed of the aircraft from approach to touchdown, the rpm of each proprotor, the nacelle angle(s) and pitch of the Osprey at touchdown, drift angle, analysis of the white vapor or smoke trailing the aircraft, and any other information deemed important for our investigation.

Two prominent engineers, John Vulgamore and John Hemker, each with more than twenty-five years NST experience, accepted the project.

A week and a half later, Vulgamore emailed the results of their analysis. When it arrived, O'Leary printed copies, and the accident board gathered around the conference table in anticipation.

"We have the results from our request to the NST," I said. "Take a few minutes to digest the copy in front of you. Then we'll talk about what it means. Don't let the numbers and calculations peppered throughout the report overwhelm you."

I had read it once on O'Leary's computer before we printed the hard copies. I read it again while the other board members attempted to make sense of it. Dolan pursed his lips and nodded while he read. He paused at intervals to circle salient numbers with a red pen. Winsett had spent enough time in the simulator that he didn't seem deterred by the jargon or the numbers. Doc Harper tilted his head side-to-side and marked a few passages he might discuss when we arrived there. Adams and Kelly read a few lines, looked at one another and shrugged their shoulders. After reading the email twice, they pushed the papers toward the center of the table.

I waited until everyone had finished reading.

"Adams, would you like to start the discussion?"

"No, sir, not unless you translate it first."

"I know it's difficult to understand," said O'Leary. "Let's go through it line by line. The NST started out by first calculating the speed of the aircraft during the last seventeen seconds to touchdown. They enhanced the video taken by the A-10. They measured and compared the distance the aircraft traveled over the ground to the time stamp on the video. They calculated the final touchdown speed to be approximately seventy-four knots. They also confirmed our observation … the aircraft definitely pitched up when near the ground in order to clear the last of the three deep wadis under the flight path."

O'Leary continued. "Then the NST used a highly technical analysis tool called photogrammetry, to slow down the video and count the revolutions of the proprotors during the final seconds of flight. They calculated the proprotor speed to be between 308 and 317 rpm. The engines of an Osprey in the conversion mode would normally be at 100% power. We already knew the engines of the accident aircraft had degraded to 96% on the right engine and 99% on the left engine. If both engines were performing normally, the proprotor speed would have been 381 rpm for the right engine and 393 rpm for the left engine. The NST experts calculated the engines of the mishap aircraft to be operating at approximately 78% and 80% … much lower than the engines should have been."

We all flipped to the second page of our reports and O'Leary continued to explain.

"The NST also performed an analysis of the picture that depicted the rotor marks in the sand. By measuring the distance between the rotor marks, they were able to calculate an rpm based on the airplane's touchdown speed of seventy-four knots. The spacing between the first and second rotor marks in the sand was eight feet. NST calculated the rpm to be 311, which equates to 78% engine power. Again, much lower than normal. They also estimated the pitch attitude of the aircraft at touchdown – less than 14 degrees. The pitch attitude was within acceptable flight manual limitations for landing. That's an important fact because it shows the pilot was likely aware touching down with a pitch attitude greater than 14 degrees would have resulted in the open ramp violently hitting the ground prior to the main landing gear tires touching down on the sand."

We all flipped to page three and O'Leary explained. "Using the photo showing the impressions the main gear and ramp left on the sand, they determined the aircraft touched down tracking straight along the axis of the fuselage, despite the crosswind. This proves Maj Voas was making rational inputs to the flight controls to make a perfect landing. Since the NST was strictly concerned with data analysis, they offered no possible cause of the accident. They also did not speculate on the cause of the white puffs of smoke or cool vapor trailing the aircraft prior to touchdown."

O'Leary put down the report and looked up.

"Any questions?" he asked.

"Yes," said Kelly. "What does it mean?"

"Under normal conditions in the conversion mode, the flight control computers will govern the proprotor rpm at 100%," O'Leary explained. "In the event of a dual engine compressor stall, the flight control computers would command a lower rpm, like what the NST calculated. In a single-engine failure situation, the flight control computers would attempt to maintain the rpm by maximizing power on the good engine and sacrificing proprotor blade pitch, causing a rapid loss of lift and altitude. The crew would also hear an automated verbal warning of 'ENGINE FAILURE' repeated numerous times. Although no one testified to hearing, or seeing an ENGINE FAILURE warning, the rpm calculated by the NST fell well below the threshold for the system to sense an engine failure. But, the possibility of a malfunction of both engines operating at reduced power, such as a compressor stall or surge, is likely. In that case, the crew would have experienced the 78% to 80% rpm phenomenon while the engine(s) attempted to relight and accelerate back to the normal 100% rpm range."

"I'm still not sure what all of this means," exclaimed Kelly, as she dropped the papers on the conference table and slumped in her chair.

"Put simply," said O'Leary, "compressor stalls can cause the airplane to go into a high rate of descent. The natural tendency is for a pilot to add full power to arrest the rate of descent. The procedure for recovering from a compressor stall is the exact opposite. The flight manual emergency procedure dictates an immediate reduction of power to allow the engine to recover rpm … set flaps to zero degrees … rotate nacelles to vertical … and if ground contact is imminent, advance power to maximum. The NST analysis, combined with the flight manual information and procedures, validate what we've learned during our simulator flight sessions. If the Rolls-Royce engine tear-down data validates the NST data, we will have concrete evidence that a dual-engine compressor stall was the primary contributing factor for this accident."

No one said a word for over a minute. Everyone was processing the information. The accident investigation team members silently looked at each other then looked at the NST report. The importance of the report was slowly sinking in and being understood. The information was critical to the investigation.

I never considered writing my final opinion of the accident without the left engine teardown analysis report from Rolls-Royce. Dobrinski called me later in the day to tell me AFSOC was in a hurry to get the report done. The command was feeling pressure to brief the families about the accident findings. When I mentioned I was still waiting for the Rolls-Royce report, he indicated the command might not be willing to wait much longer.

"Finish the report without the Rolls-Royce tear-down report," said Dobrinski.

"What …," I replied. "Are you sure?"

I couldn't believe what I had just heard.

CHAPTER THIRTY EIGHT

ALMOST DONE

I explained to General Dobrinski that I could finish the report, but data from the Rolls-Royce analysis of the left engine could end up either substantiating or significantly altering my findings. He assured me he understood, but there were other "extenuating" factors.

"You may or may not be aware I met with Mrs. Voas earlier today," he explained. "I expected her to be angry and upset, but she's more frustrated and frightened. She's anxious about her life without a husband and upset with the delays and rumors surrounding the release of the accident report."

"Sir, we're eager to finish, but at the same time we're reluctant to leave anything on the table," I replied. "I understand the burden rumors and unsubstantiated news stories can have on the families. I ignore them. I know it's difficult for the families to do that. In a year, or two, no one will remember and hold the rumormongers or media accountable. They'll remember the accident investigation board report and the true facts we've uncovered during the investigation. My name will be on the report, and I want the information to be truthful and correct."

"I think she's anxious to get at least one thing off her plate," said Dobrinski. "She shared with me she is going to have to sell her home. She's also in the middle of planning her husband's memorial service to be conducted at Arlington National Cemetery. She's under a great deal of stress. When you finish your report, coordinate her briefing date to make sure there is no conflict with the memorial service. Can you give me a rough idea of when you'll be done?"

"Sir, it will take at least two more weeks," I answered. "We're working hard on getting the interviews transcribed. That'll take eight to ten days. The engine is still stranded at Al Udeid, where it's been for almost five days. I've outlined two options for my opinion. I'm just waiting for the engine analysis from Rolls-Royce."

"I'll check with the boss tomorrow morning. There's a lot of pressure to get the accident report done. I have to reiterate; you may have to complete your report without the engine analysis. The families are very restless. Get this wrapped up soon."

"Yes, sir, I understand," I replied. "The Family Liaison Officers (FLOs) have been calling to see if we have a projected completion date. Currently … I don't. About the engine … we're waiting to compare data we received from the NST to the Rolls-Royce tear-down data. It's critical to our investigation. When you speak to the boss, would you please pass that along?"

"Sure … I'll call you in the morning." He hung up.

The Air Force, politicians, families and the media pressed the command for our report. A premature release with incomplete evidence might serve some without a fair accounting to the families or crews still flying the airplane. But questions lingering after publishing the report would fail to give the families proper closure or provide additional margins of safety for crews flying the Osprey.

We had far exceeded our original estimates of the time it would take to complete our investigation. During the evening staff meeting with the investigation team, I asked everyone to work full days on the next Saturday and Sunday. I planned to write the executive summary of my opinion and I wanted the board members to critique it.

"Sir," Dolan said. "What about the engine analysis? We can't finish our report without the information from Rolls Royce."

"Good question," I answered. "The commander may want a report without the engine findings. I referenced the NST report when I spoke with General Dobrinski asking him for more time to compare data. He'll call me in the morning with the commander's decision. In the meantime, we press on, and finish the report."

After a short night, I entered the office to the usual aroma of fresh coffee and moisture condensing on my sunglasses.

"Good morning, everyone," I said. "Anyone have a remedy for fogged specs?"

"Yes, sir," Adams said with her ever present smile. "We use the lens solution and tissues here on my desk."

"Thanks," I said. "Are you ready to start our morning meeting? I have some good news."

Harper and Dolan, true to their jocular custom, dawdled. Impatient with the pace of the team's compliance and anxious for good news, Winsett morphed into one of his many rolls … sergeant at arms.

"Everyone take your seats, please," said Winsett. "Sir, we're ready. What's the good news?"

"AFSOC consented to waiting for the engine analysis but wants our report immediately after we have reviewed the Rolls Royce analysis."

"Sir," Dolan said. "The engine is still stranded at Al Udeid."

"Better news … AFSOC pressed the Air Mobility Command for priority," I said. "It'll be loaded on the next C-17 to the U.S. The engine should arrive in Oakland on July 21st. I propose we designate a CV-22 engine expert to be in Oakland when it arrives. He'll watch the engine disassembly and write an independent report."

"I like your idea, sir," Dolan said. "MSgt True would be my first choice."

"I'll see if he's available," I answered.

I struggled with the format and content of my opinion for many hours. After our afternoon meetings, we continued working in the office until late at night. Before everyone departed, we would end the night by doing a dry run of my presentation. We projected the PowerPoint™ slides onto a bare office wall while I read my narrative. Afterward, we analyzed and made corrections to the briefing. Regardless of the details I planned to present, there would undoubtedly be pointed questions.

The engine finally arrived at Rolls-Royce in Oakland on July 22nd. The accident report was more than ninety-five percent complete and the only slides missing from my PowerPoint™ were my opinion and explanation of opinion.

When I got back to my billeting room that night, I scrolled through emails as I sat on my bed. An email from MSgt True caught my eye. He had flown to Oakland on July 20th to be at Rolls Royce when the engine arrived.

July 22, 2010 – 8:13 a.m.: Sir, The CV-22 engine arrived in Oakland this morning. Everything looks good. We moved the crate into a hangar to unpack and prepare for immediate disassembly. I will keep you informed as we proceed. Very Respectfully, MSgt True.

True had jumped at the chance to monitor the Rolls-Royce analysis and gladly volunteered to share his observations. I replied to his email and requested he estimate a projected completion date. We relied on the engine being intact enough to determine if it was operating close to 100% rpm when it hit the ground, or if it had suffered internal damage due to fire or failure of an essential component. If Rolls-Royce could estimate the engine's rpm on impact, I hoped to compare their findings to further validate the data from the NST.

I had already completed writing an opinion involving a single or dual engine power malfunction. The opinion included nine other contributing factors as causal for the accident. Not knowing what the Rolls-Royce report would reveal, I also wrote a second opinion that did not include one or two engines experiencing power loss. Absent an engine(s) problem, I attributed the accident to crew performance during a critical phase of the flight. I explained the crew could have been distracted and failed to monitor and arrest the rapid rate of descent. The crew was slow, or late, in applying power and failed to account for the sudden tailwind.

O'Leary and I tested the "pilot error" scenario in the simulator. We forced ourselves to hesitate before applying go-around power. A delay of three to four seconds allowed the descent rate to progress to a point where the airplane would impact the ground. Advancing power within one to two seconds allowed the airplane to fly safely away from the ground every time. Even in the simulator, it was uncomfortable to wait three to four seconds before advancing power. It definitely was not natural for a pilot to hesitate that long.

The next morning, as I walked into the office, I was immediately greeted by Winsett.

"Lots of news for our staff meeting this morning, sir," said Winsett. "As soon as you're ready, I'll assemble the team."

"I'm ready," I said as I removed my sunglasses and wiped the fog off the lenses. "Let's get started."

"Sir, with your permission, I need to travel to my home base in Clovis, New Mexico. My wing commander scheduled an Operational Readiness Exercise (ORE) beginning next Monday morning. The only other lawyer in our office had to unexpectedly deploy last week. The unit is in a bind. If you approve, I'll travel on Saturday night and return to Hurlburt Field by Thursday. I told my wing commander I'd let him know your answer by the end of the day."

"Okay," I said. "You won't have to wait until the end of the day. You'll know my answer in an hour."

"Sir, can I go next?" Adams asked.

"Sure, go ahead."

"Sir, we'll finish transcribing the last two interviews today. We're very happy to finally be done. The other court reporters have asked for your permission to return to their bases. I couldn't have done it without them."

"Absolutely," I said. "Tell them they're released. I'll make sure to personally thank them for their great work before they depart Hurlburt Field. Does this mean you'll be leaving us soon?"

"No, sir. I forget you've not done an accident investigation board before. I'll be the last person to leave. Part of my duty includes cleaning the office and making sure all equipment is returned to the proper offices. You are stuck with me until the very end."

"Very good," I said. "Kelly, did you have something for us?"

"Sir, with the last two interviews from Adams and your final written opinion, we're done with the report. We'll insert the Rolls-Royce analysis and the report from MSgt True into the report when we receive them. I can't believe we're this close to the end."

"There's life after this investigation report is turned in," I said. "You've been a phenomenal group of people. I can never thank you enough."

I could feel tears welling up in my eyes. I looked down and blinked to make them go away.

"O'Leary … do you have any news to share?"

"Sir, I completed my sections of the report and made changes to your PowerPoint™ presentation. If you have other updates, I'll finish them for you today. Oh yeah, one last thing; with your approval, I would like to attend the memorial at Arlington National Cemetery for Maj Voas on July 29th."

"Absolutely … approved," I said. "In a minute I'll cover a couple things you can add to the presentation. Scotty …?"

"Sir, it's a special day. To celebrate the end of this journey, how about I reserve a table at one of my favorite restaurants tonight? Is seafood okay with everyone?"

"Okay with me. Everyone else good with that?" I asked.

I suspected no one would object, and they didn't.

"We'll skip the evening staff meeting … presentation practice will start at 5:00 p.m. Dolan … Doc … you guys have anything for us?"

"Sir, nothing new to report."

"Okay everyone. I've written my opinion. This copy is for all of you to review and mark with comments. My opinion is unique in that I have written two possible scenarios as causal for the accident One scenario involves a power malfunction and the other scenario involves crew error. Neither scenario can be proven one hundred percent. I'm confident the pilot attempted to go-around or reset for an approach into the wind. Something happened that prevented the go-around. Without clear and convincing evidence proving a single or dual engine malfunction occurred, I elected to include a scenario where the pilot delayed or failed to advance power during an abnormal descent. Our simulator experience indicated it could happen, but the delay would have been unnatural to an experienced pilot. In my mind today, without the Rolls-Royce report, that's the way I see it. Once Winsett and Kelly approve of my opinion as written, I'll forward a copy to Colonel Youngner, the AFSOC Staff Judge Advocate General (JAG) for review. O'Leary, while the lawyers review my written opinion, we'll work on adding slides to my PowerPoint™. Any questions? If not, let's finish our work today so we can go out for a nice dinner together."

After Winsett and Kelly approved my opinion, I drove to the AFSOC Headquarters building to drop it off at the legal office. Col Youngner promised to review it and get back to me as soon as possible. After dropping off the opinion, the ton of wet sand I had been carrying on my shoulders for the last four months was lifted away.

We enjoyed a great meal together that evening. Over the past four months, we had worked six to seven days every week, staying focused on finding facts and information. The journey wasn't easy, but it was well worth the long days and short nights to complete an investigation with pride.

I gave the accident team members remaining at Hurlburt Field the first weekend off since the investigation started in April.

Prepared and confident, I continued to practice my presentation, thinking I would be asked to deliver it within the next few days. Early Monday morning, my euphoria instantly evaporated when I received a voicemail from Winsett who was working at his wing in New Mexico.

"Sir, Colonel Youngner just called me. The AFSOC commander is very upset. Please call me as soon as you get this message. It's extremely urgent. I will be flying back to Hurlburt Field sooner than planned."

CHAPTER THIRTY NINE

LEGALLY SUFFICIENT OPINION

Dread washed over my entire being. I had received numerous calls since the accident on April 9th; the call from General Dobrinski being the first, and very few of the calls were good news. I dialed Winsett's cell phone number.

"Thank you, sir, for the quick response," said Winsett. "I left messages at the accident board office and the public affairs office. Ignore those. Colonel Youngner called very early this morning to say he adamantly rejected your two-scenario opinion on the grounds it's *legally insufficient*.

He states a scenario that *could have* happened, equates to declaring a cause of the mishap. He cites Air Force Instruction 51-503, *Aerospace and Ground Accident Investigations* – a mishap *cause* can only be specified when *clear and convincing* evidence exists. Otherwise, your opinion must be limited to *substantially contributing* factors. Anticipate a pointed discussion with the AFSOC commander and his vice. Apparently, they are very upset."

"Thanks for the heads up. I confess, I'm surprised. I've seen other accident reports stating two scenarios in an opinion. What changed?"

"Sir, we asked for his legal opinion and that's what he provided. He's the commander's advisor, so prepare to defend, or abandon your two-scenario opinion. The analysis we've drafted fits the *substantially contributing factors* criteria. I'm off shift in seven hours. Run it by Kelly and I'll call you when I finish my work here. I wish I was there to help and advise you. I have a bad feeling about this, sir."

The truckload of wet sand returned to its four-month roost. The unwelcome news surprised both me and my most experienced lawyer, Winsett.

I walked to my car deciding on a destination. I checked my cell phone messages one last time before shifting my car into "drive." Nothing from the commander, or his vice … I drove to the accident investigation board office.

Adams must have seen me park and met me at the door.

The look on everyone's face said they knew.

"Bad news travels fast." I said.

"Sir," Kelly said. "We'll help you find a solution."

"Sir, I can cancel my Washington trip," O'Leary said. "I can't leave you in a crisis."

"No, go to D.C. Give our best to Mrs. Voas and her family. I've decided how to handle this. Let's meet at the conference table. Kelly, bring a notebook and a sharp pencil. We'll brain-storm the facts we've discovered over the past few months to support the opinion I plan to write."

The team settled into their usual seats.

"Label the top of one page *Engine Power Loss* and the top of another page *Crew Error*," I said. "Okay team … in no particular order, let's list the facts that support each header."

O'Leary responded, "The picture of the landing markings. It indicates the crew intended a roll-on landing. Despite the crosswind, the main gear tracked straight and the nose wheel marking was perfectly centered between the main landing gear tire marks. The pilot made perfect rudder inputs. There's no evidence suggesting the crew inadvertently rode the airplane into the ground. The markings would have been very different if the airplane had hit the sand violently."

"Good," I said. "How about excited conversation in the cockpit? The tail scanner testified he heard it. Put it under the *Engine Power Loss* header."

Dolan raised his hand.

"Sir, the engine data … the most recent power check on the right engine – on April 6th was 95.3%. Had it been accomplished in the hover mode; the value would probably have been a lower percentage. In the days between April 6th and 8th, after the last check, the aircraft made four low visibility dirt landings. Then, one more thing … the left engine air particle separator (EAPS) failed for a minute and a half while performing one of the dirt landings the morning of April 8th. We have no way to estimate how much sand was sucked into the engine and how it may have affected the engine power."

Kelly waved her pencil.

"We should put the NST data on that list ... they calculated the engines were operating at a lower than normal rpm inflight and after landing."

"Yes, for sure," I said. "Add the misty trail visible in the accident video ... could have been fuel being dumped or unburned."

"Sir," O'Leary said. "The spike in fuel flow in the final seconds of the fight coincides with the misty trail. It's possible the crew was dumping fuel to reduce the airplane weight."

"The simulator scenarios," Harper said. "We proved, under certain conditions, a power loss prevented the capability to conduct a successful go-around."

"Excellent," I said.

Adams leafed through her notes.

"Sir, in Claybaker's testimony, he said Major Luce told him and his wife the crew tried to save the airplane."

"Okay, let's add it to our list," I said.

O'Leary thumbed through his notes.

"Sir, the pilot had the situational awareness to adjust the glide path to clear the deep wadis. Then he executed a textbook roll-on landing ... not the actions of an unengaged pilot. If he'd had the power to go-around, I'm convinced he would have."

Kelly flipped her notes to the blank page listing crew factors.

"Sir, what should I record on the crew page? We haven't noted anything."

O'Leary closed his notebook and shrugged his shoulders.

"We discovered no indications of an aural warning, caution, or advisory. The contributing factors … tailwind, inadequate weather briefing, and pressing to complete the mission are all we need for the Crew Factors page."

"I think we have enough information to formulate my opinion. O'Leary, would you please delete the dual scenario from our PowerPoint™ presentation? I'll have my opinion done in a few hours."

I refreshed my coffee and walked to my desk. I spent the next two hours writing. When finished, I walked a copy over to Kelly's desk and laid down the four pages.

"My opinion of what caused the accident is based on ten substantially contributing factors," I said. We'll refine it and then email it to Winsett for his review. After you read it, have the rest of the team review it. Let's talk about it at today's 5:00 p.m. meeting. Meanwhile, AFSOC Headquarters has called and requests my presence. I'll see you later this afternoon."

"Yes, sir. Are you sure you don't need your legal counsel along … just in case?"

"I'll text if I need you. Besides, you need to supervise Harper and Dolan. Do they ever stop talking?"

She smiled, "No, sir. Pretty much like this the whole time they're in the office."

I drove to AFSOC and walked up the two flights of stairs to the command suite. I could feel the entire executive staff's eyes on me when I opened the door and walked into the office.

"Hi everyone. Is Captain Pierce in?" I asked.

"Yes, sir," one of the secretaries said. "She's at her desk."

I made my way back to her cubicle.

"Sir, how are you?" she asked as she flashed a smile that could brighten any dark gloom.

"Good, for the moment. What's going on with the commander today?"

"Not sure, sir. He's definitely not happy. Every lawyer at AFSOC has been up here most of the morning. Has something to do with your accident report."

"I guess I may as well get it over with. Wish me luck."

I walked out of her office straight to Dobrinski's executive assistant.

"Please tell General Dobrinski I'm here to see him. I'll be in my office until he's ready."

"Sir, he knows you're here. Go right in. He requested you close the door behind you."

I gently knocked on the door and stepped in.

"Sir, did you need to see me? Have I done something wrong?"

"That's an interesting opinion you wrote … two scenarios … where'd that come from?" he asked while staring at me intensely and impatiently rocking back and forth in his chair.

"I didn't make it up, sir. It's been done before. Given the circumstances of our investigation, it made sense to me. I hear AFSOC legal advisors disagree with my opinion."

"Justifiably so," said Dobrinski. "I also do not approve of your opinion."

"Sir, if the two-scenario opinion is not acceptable, I'll write a new single-scenario opinion. I assure you the lawyers will find it *legally sufficient.*"

"Then do it. Run it by Colonel Youngner before you send it up here. We're ready to wrap this up by the end of the week. The engine analysis is complete at Rolls-Royce. I don't know what they discovered. You should have the report today. The boss wants to brief the families this weekend. Make sure you're ready. That's all."

He turned his chair to face his computer screen, obviously irritated with me.

"Yes, sir," I said as I stood up and walked to the door without looking back at him.

I didn't know what the command had expected from me … anger, disappointment, or frustration? I had little empathy for their disappointment. I smiled at the receptionist closest to the exit and checked the wall clock across the room. I'd been there less than five minutes. It had seemed like two hours.

When I arrived back at the accident board office, the beehive of activity ceased when I walked through the door.

"What is it? My glasses are fogged. I'm not in the wrong office, am I?" I said kiddingly.

"How'd it go, sir?" Kelly asked. "We thought you'd be gone for at least an hour."

"I don't think I could've cut the air in the command suite with a machete. I was told to rewrite my opinion immediately. AFSOC would like the accident report completed within the next few days so I can start briefing the families of the deceased this weekend. Did you have time to review my new opinion?"

"Yes, sir, but first … we're glad to see you."

"Thank you. It's much more fun to be amongst friends."

"I understand, sir. We were very worried about you. Anyway, I reviewed your opinion and sent it to Colonel Winsett. We made a few minor changes, but overall, it's excellent. We're seating a murder board to go over it together. Let us know when you are ready."

"Sure, let me get a bottle of water … mouth's a little dry. I'll be right there. Dolan, before I forget, the Rolls-Royce analysis of the left engine is complete. Be on the lookout for the report."

"Will do, sir."

We spent the remainder of the afternoon reviewing every word of my opinion. After reviewing it a half dozen times, it was finally complete.

> *After a thorough, careful and complete investigation,*
> *I ruled out multiple causes including: enemy action,*
> *brownout, vortex ring state, mid-air collision, loss of*

hydraulic system, electrical failure, drive shaft failure, swashplate actuator mount failure, flight control failure, thrust control lever (TCL) rigging, avionics failure, and crew physiological events. I analyzed the testimony from over a hundred interviews, conducted an aerial analysis of the crash site, visited the main and forward operating bases, consulted with subject matter experts, thoroughly examined the mishap crew's training records and all applicable publications, viewed and analyzed photographs and videos of the mishap, analyzed the data transfer module contents, and flew the exact mission profile for over eighteen hours in the CV-22 simulator (with and without aircraft malfunctions).

I was unable to determine, by clear and convincing evidence, the cause of this mishap. Clear and convincing evidence is a determination, without serious or substantial doubt, where the evidence shows that it is highly probable that the conclusion is correct. I determined by a preponderance of the evidence, that ten factors substantially contributed to this mishap. Preponderance of the evidence is the greater weight of credible evidence, which when fairly considered, produces the stronger impression. This evidence is more convincing as to its truth when weighed against the opposing evidence. These ten substantially contributing factors fall into one of four categories: mission execution, environmental conditions, human factors and aircraft performance.

Substantially Contributing Factors

Mission Execution

Inadequate weather planning: During mission planning, the crew did not seek out easily obtainable and specific weather data for the landing zone and surrounding forward operating bases. As a result, the mission was planned for an east to west run-in to the landing zone. More specific weather data would have led the mission planners to choose a run-in heading that accounted for the forecasted easterly winds of ten to twenty knots.

Poorly executed low visibility approach (LVA): The data transfer module (DTM) data provided irrefutable evidence that the mishap pilot managed the time over target poorly and flew a non-standard approach profile. The mishap pilot responded to this situation by performing a rapid conversion for landing.

Environmental Conditions

Tailwind: Near the descent point, the right quartering wind, which translated to an approximately seventeen-knot tailwind, impeded the slowdown of the mishap aircraft. It added to the mishap crew's task saturation and reduced available time for critical decision making.

Challenging visual environment: The low illumination, described by pilots as a "varsity night," decreased normal peripheral vision, depth perception, and visual acuity. The visual conditions required the mishap pilot and copilot to rely on instrument flying more extensively.

Human Factors

Task Saturation: During the final phase of the approach, the mishap crew needed to accomplish the following immediate tasks: 1) reduce excessive ground speed and correct heading to land at the landing zone, 2) maintain level altitude, 3) assess mishap aircraft configuration and performance, 4) decide whether to go-around or continue the approach based on speed and distance from the landing zone, and 5) communicate within the aircraft to the mishap crew and passengers. If the mishap crew made the decision to go-around, they would be very busy with 1) go-around route and altitude, 2) a new run-in heading into the wind, 3) enemy threats, 4) terrain considerations, 5) new time over target, and 6) radio calls to other aircraft in the formation, as well as mission support aircraft.

At .4 nautical miles to the landing zone, the mishap aircraft began a rapid descent prior to reaching the normal glide path descent point at .15 nautical miles to the landing zone. Photographs of the ground markings prove that the landing gear was down. There was no evidence the mishap crew made a radio call. The absence of a radio call can be explained by the intermittent radio problems experienced multiple times that evening. However, there was an excited discussion within the cockpit during the last few seconds prior to impact. It is more likely than not, that this discussion included attempting to go-around. The greater weight of credible evidence shows the mishap crew was task saturated. The priority would have been to fly the aircraft first, then talk on the radio. The complexity required to simultaneously slow down and maintain altitude during this aggressive approach further increased the mishap pilot's task saturation.

Distraction: The mishap copilot stated he was confused by the landing zone illumination. The copilot's confusion distracted the copilot from accomplishing normal copilot duties. These duties included monitoring the altitude, speed, and aircraft performance parameters.

Negative Transfer: Negative transfer occurs when an individual reverts to a highly learned behavior from a previous system, causing mission performance to be degraded. The copilot admitted that his attention to monitoring instruments during the approach was disrupted due to his crosschecking references outside of the airplane.

Pressing: Pressing is when an individual knowingly commits to a course of action that pushes them and/or their equipment beyond reasonable limits. The 8th SOS had a high standard for mission execution and a strong desire to impress their supported unit. The mishap crew also wanted to excel during the first combat mission of their deployment.

Aircraft Performance

Unanticipated high rate of descent: Video analysis indicated the mishap aircraft maintained a relatively steady, but high rate of descent, beginning at .4 nautical miles from the landing zone until the main landing gear impacted the ground. At one point during the final seven seconds, the descent rate exceeded 1,800 feet per minute. The normal rate of descent during this phase of flight should have been 200 feet per minute. Simulator flight confirmed that a go-around would have been possible if the descent rate was caught early enough and the pilot made appropriate control inputs, and the engines were performing normally.

Engine Power Loss: A critical question in this investigation was whether an engine power loss played an important role in the sequence of events. I determined by a preponderance of the evidence the following facts indicate that the mishap aircraft experienced engine power loss after the one minute call: 1) location and characteristics of landing gear ground markings, 2) video analysis of the proprotor revolutions per minute (RPM), 3) analysis of the proprotor ground strikes, 4) mishap aircraft smoke, heat, and/or mist emissions captured on video, 5) engine performance degradation, 6) aircraft computer generated voice warnings (after airplane touched down), and 7) excited cockpit conversation and rapid countdown.

Although fast and descending quickly, the mishap pilot had sufficient time to evaluate and select a landing location just past three deep wadis (ditches). Close review of the A-10 video shows that the pilot adjusted the airplane pitch attitude and glide path to land beyond the last wadi. Without the flight path adjustments by the pilot, the airplane's initial impact would have been catastrophic.

The ground markings would have looked different if flight path corrections had not been made by the pilot. The nose gear impact would have been approximately three feet to the right of center. The touchdown was smooth enough to leave the ramp, main landing gear tires and doors, and the underside of the airplane intact. The absence of large impressions in the sand, at the initial impact point, indicated an intentional, perfectly executed, and straight, roll-on landing. The greater weight of credible evidence shows the pilot would have only executed a roll-on landing if he believed the mishap aircraft did not have sufficient power to execute a go-around.

Analysis of proprotor speed (Nr) during the last seconds of flight showed that the Nr was abnormally low. Also, analysis of the proprotor blade strike markings on the ground corroborated that the Nr was abnormally low when the mishap aircraft flipped. I considered the margin of error while evaluating the validity of the Nr percentages. Reduced Nr produces less lift and is an indication that the mishap aircraft's engines were not operating normally.

Close analysis of the accident video indicates there was an unidentified contrail type emission from the mishap aircraft during the last seventeen seconds of flight. The abnormal and intermittent emission could have been fuel mist (fuel being dumped), an attempted engine auto-relight, or faint smoke.

I considered engine percent performance, which was last measured on April 6, 2010 (99.5% for the left engine and 95.3% for the right engine). After the engine percent performance data was recorded, the mishap aircraft performed four austere landings, including one with the left engine air particle separator failure. Degraded engines could have led to engine failure, surge/stall or insufficient power when a high-power demand was required.

The mission tail scanner indicated that he heard aircraft computer generated voice warnings after the mishap aircraft impacted the ground. After considering all the possible warnings, the following malfunctions could have triggered the voice warnings: rotor RPM (Nr) low and engine failure.

The pilot and flight engineer both had reputations for remaining calm under pressure. The tail scanner heard an excited cockpit discussion during the approach. A passenger who was monitoring the intercom on the mishap aircraft indicated that he heard a rapid countdown prior to impact. The excited conversation and countdown show they were aware of their descent rate, attempting to correct it, but unable to do so, because of abnormal engine response. [8]

After I finished reading the opinion aloud, I took a deep breath and looked around the room.

"Does anyone have any changes or questions?" I asked.

"Outstanding, sir," said O'Leary.

"I agree," said Winsett.

"Okay, that's it then," I said. "The ten *substantially contributing* factors should pass the *legally sufficient* test. Let's send this to the AFSOC legal office."

"This is excellent, sir." Kelly said. "There are no legal issues, but the *power loss* contributing factor is going to raise a lot of eyebrows. Have you started to write the discussion of your opinion?"

"Not yet. I'm waiting on the engine reports from MSgt True and Rolls-Royce. Their analysis will either support my engine power loss opinion or void it. I need to know what they found after tearing the engine apart."

Dolan, please check your email again," I said.

He stood up from our conference table and walked over to his desk.

"Adams, we'll need a total of fourteen copies of the final accident investigation report. How long will it take to make thirteen copies of our original report?"

"At least three days, sir."

I could hear Dolan tapping on his computer keyboard. He pushed his chair away from his desk and stood up.

"General Harvel, email from MSgt True. He sent us the Roll-Royce analysis, and his report. Also some interesting pictures of the engine as they took it apart. You're not going to believe what they found."

CHAPTER FORTY

ENGINE ANALYSIS REPORT

Dolan printed copies of the report and handed them out to each board member.

"Sir, the report's addressed to you and the AFSOC senior staff," Dolan explained. "It's a five-page report with three pages of photographs."

With only the sound of rustling paper, we clustered around the conference table and studied each page looking for any bit of information to substantiate the Rolls-Royce findings.

MEMORANDUM FOR CV-22 Accident Investigation Board
SUBJECT: Teardown Analysis of CV-22 Mishap Engine
FROM: MSgt Coby True
1) On 23 June 2010, engine number CAE130322 was recovered from CV-22 wreckage located at a forward deployed location. The engine was connected to the nacelle and proprotor gearbox and all associated mounting points were intact. The engine was removed using conventional tools to disconnect mounting hardware and required minor cutting (power saw) to separate the engine. Upon removal, the engine was sprayed with liquid wax to mitigate composite fibers and then wrapped in plastic. A wooden pallet was then constructed, and the engine was secured using cargo straps.
2) On 22 July 2010, the engine was received at Rolls-Royce Engine Services Oakland (RRESO). Upon arrival, the engine was uncrated and prepped for disassembly. Initial disassembly of the engine was accomplished using normal teardown procedures and performed by RRESO maintenance technicians. Due to extensive compressor air inlet housing damage, the housing was removed prior to placement of the engine in the maintenance stand. Disassembly of the modules was performed using standard tooling. Due to post-crash demolition, some prying of composites was necessary to disengage stuck mating surfaces.

3) On 23 July 2010, the modules were ready for inspection by the safety investigation team. The team was comprised of Air Force Special Operations Command /A4MSP (MSgt Coby True), Rolls-Royce Senior Air Safety Investigator (Mr. Mike Weber) and NAVAIR Field Support Team Lead Engineer (Mr. Roger Counts). The team used a Rolls-Royce checklist to accomplish inspection and analysis of the engine modules and available components.

a. Compressor Section - Analysis indicated the compressor was rotating under power at the time of impact. Compressor blades stages 1 and 5 had minimal damage. Compressor stator blades had minor to moderate damage at most stages. The variable guide vanes position at impact could not be determined due to post crash fire. Compressor blade tracks were heat distressed and the track coating melted. As a result, there were no visible imprints of blade strikes on the compressor case. The compressor did have ingestion of sand and composite material throughout all 14 stages, consistent with engine operation.

b. Diffuser Case – The diffuser had external damage and was punctured through the combustion liner. Debris was found inside liners and around the fuel nozzle areas. No significant findings were observed related to impact and damage was consistent with post-crash demolition.

c. Gas Generator (GG) Case and Rotor – Analysis indicated the GG rotor was rotating under power at the time of impact. The GG case was substantially dented at the 2 o'clock position. During disassembly, it was noted that the blade tracks around the dented zone were noticeably damaged. The GG rotor blades had one-half of the Z-shroud missing on the entire second stage wheel. The remaining blades were nicked and damaged from debris. The second stage blade tracks had significant rub due to contact with the Z-shroud portion of the blades. Damage is evidence of impact between the rotating blades and the stationary blade tracks resultant of the substantial dent in the GG case.

d. Power Turbine (PT) – Analysis indicated the PT rotor was rotating under power at the time of impact. The PT displayed both rotational damage and stationary damage. The blade tip and blade track damage was consistent with rotational impact. The PT also had numerous *broken blades, and a side entry hole. The side entry damage indicated the case, blades, and vanes were aligned at the time of occurrence. This damage is consistent with post-crash demolition.*

e. Accessories – The accessory gearbox was not recovered and only the accessory drive gear remained attached to the engine. The only engine accessories recovered were the anti-ice and coanda valves.

> *i. The anti-ice valve is a fail-safe open valve and was in the open position.*
>
> *ii. The coanda valve was closed. The valve did operate manually without obstruction or binding. Note: No specific determination could be made as to valve position(s) at the time of impact. However, based on observations, there does not appear to be any evidence to indicate the valves were malfunctioning.*

Team Conclusion: Engine module damage was consistent with engine rotation at and through the time of impact. The rotational damage and denting of GG case is consistent with a hard impact while the rotor rotation was at a high rate of speed. The compressor did not exhibit the same type of damage as the GG, but both modules are splined and rotate together. Analysis of the variable guide vane actuator rings and engine accessories was not possible due to the post-crash fire. As such, this prevented an accurate assessment of the engine's power setting other than the determination the engine was operating at the time of impact. [9]

Dolan folded his copy across the short edge of the report and flipped it on the table.

"This is no surprise, sir," he said. "Analyzing metal pieces and parts of an engine involved in an accident often reveals significant findings. In this case, not so much. If we had recovered the flight information recorder, the teardown would have been routine and perhaps pointless. The engine turning at a high rate of speed adds nothing to what we already know. NST calculated the rpm at 317, a rate indicating the engine was running, but at an abnormally low rate for the stage of flight. The nine words at the end of paragraph three summed up their analysis ... 'the engine was operating at the time of impact.' Shoot, we knew that on the first day we watched the video of the accident."

"Disappointing," I said. "I expected much more detail. Kelly, please file this in TAB HH of our report. We'll preserve this evidence, but, unfortunately, it changes nothing."

"Yes, sir. Shall we wait for the Rolls-Royce report?"

"I doubt it'll differ from MSgt True's account. The AFSOC commander will decide whether he wants me to wait another day. I can't justify delaying the final report any longer. The teardown analysis doesn't change my opinion. I'll write my *discussion of the opinion* this evening, and we'll critique it in the morning. When we're done, I'll fax a copy to Winsett for his review before I take it to the AFSOC legal office."

Before we broke for the day, I asked the team to sit through one last practice briefing. We added updates every day, making minor modifications to the text but not the argument. The twenty-minute narrative flowed well and allowed ample time for questions. When we had finished, I released the team for the evening.

Alone in the office, I sat at the conference table and penciled a narrative explaining how I arrived at my opinion:

Discussion of Opinion:

There is a preponderance of evidence that indicates mission execution, environmental conditions, and human factors degraded the crew's performance and played a direct role in the sequence of events. However, they do not provide a complete explanation or account for all evidence uncovered during this investigation. I determined that an aircraft performance issue could completely account for the pilot's decision to execute a roll-on landing. During a rapid descent, it is unlikely that this very experienced and competent pilot would have chosen to execute a roll-on landing on rough terrain if he had power available to go-around and set up for another approach. The pilot had the time to make a near perfect roll-on landing; therefore, it seems logical that the pilot also had enough time to apply full power with the thrust control lever (TCL) and go-around. It is unlikely that the pilot would apply less than full TCL power when attempting to arrest a rapid descent rate. If the pilot applied full TCL power, but applied it too late to prevent impact, then the ground markings and subsequent crash sequence would have been noticeably different. The roll-on landing made by the pilot was remarkable by any measure.

Although not a factor in causing the mishap, the presence of the drainage ditch and the collapse of the nose landing gear increased the severity of damage and injuries during the crash sequence. If the nose gear had not collapsed and/or the aircraft had not impacted the drainage ditch, the aircraft likely would have remained upright, and the injuries and damage would have been less severe.

The absence of the Flight Incident Recorder, the Vibration Structural Life and Engine Diagnostics control unit, and the right engine prevented the board from obtaining clear and convincing evidence of the cause of the mishap. [10]

I left a copy on the conference table with a note for whoever arrived before me in the morning:

This is my "Discussion of the Opinion." Please review and make comments. Thank you.

I turned off the lights and locked the office door behind me. I drove back to my room and changed into gym clothes, then took a long walk pondering possible reactions once my opinion was submitted the next day. The accident investigation process could be concluded. I would give my well-rehearsed briefing to the AFSOC commander and his staff by the end of the week and possibly begin briefing family members during the weekend.

I expected significant pushback regarding my opinion but remained optimistic. I had a strong and valid argument for how I arrived at my opinion of the accident. I had drawn on over thirty-five years of flying experience and more than 20,000 hours of military and civilian flight time. I could not have selected a more capable and experienced team to plow through a grueling, and extremely challenging, four-month investigation. We had conducted over a hundred interviews, and spent countless hours discussing the pros and cons of every word and piece of evidence. The facts, and nothing else, brought me to the only conclusion I thought possible. I knew my opinion of what caused the accident would be controversial.

My opinion arrived at AFSOC Headquarters, and my worst nightmare was realized. My world was forever changed by what happened next.

CHAPTER FORTY ONE

SUBSTANTIALLY CONTRIBUTING FACTORS

Winsett returned to Hurlburt Field late Wednesday night and by noon on Thursday, he and Kelly had reviewed my newly revised op*inion* and d*iscussion of the opinion* documents.

"There's no question they're *legally sufficient,*" Winsett said. "Want me to drop them off at the AFSOC legal office?"

"No, thanks. I'll deliver them myself," I said.

O'Leary called during a layover as he traveled back to Hurlburt Field from the memorial service he attended in Washington, D.C. He was apologetic about leaving me and the board in a bind. We updated him on everything that had transpired during his two-day absence.

Upon arrival at the legal office, I was greeted by the receptionist.

"Sir, Col Youngner is at lunch. I'll make sure he gets these documents as soon as he returns."

I thanked her and returned to the accident investigation board office. Later in the day, I practiced my presentation one last time. I felt very comfortable with the slides and the narrative. We closed the office 'early' at 6:00 p.m. and called it a night.

Friday morning, we conducted our 8:00 a.m. staff meeting without having heard anything from the AFSOC legal office. The accident board members continued to read and make minor corrections to the accident report as we waited for approval of the opinion. The report filled four thick binders and consisted of more than two thousand pages. Without approval of my *opinion* and the supporting *discussion of the opinion*, there was no reason to start making copies of the report.

By late Sunday night, there was still no phone call or email from the AFSOC legal office.

During the 8:00 a.m. Monday staff meeting, O'Leary shared his experience at Arlington cemetery with the other team members. Afterward, I met with an AFSOC public affairs officer for nearly an hour and a half as I prepared to brief the families of the critically injured and deceased.

After returning from lunch, Winsett checked his computer and scanned his emails.

"Sir, we have an email from Colonel Youngner," said Winsett. "The subject line reads: *Major General Dobrinski, the attached memorandum answers the questions about Brigadier General Harvel's opinion.*"

"Print out copies of the memorandum so we can review it together," I said.

I sat at the conference table with the other accident board members and read the memorandum. Col Youngner's memorandum started out with a summary of my opinion. He explained that I was not able to find a cause of the accident using the Air Force guidance of "clear and convincing" evidence. If the copilot had been able to remember what happened and shared the information with the accident investigation board, I would have had "clear and convincing" evidence. If the flight information recorder (FIR) or the vibration/structural life and engine diagnostics (VSLED) had been recovered from the accident site, I would have had "clear and convincing" evidence. Absent those items and the copilot not remembering the last thirty seconds of the flight, I had to use *substantially contributing factors* as causal for the accident.

The memorandum included all ten of the substantially contributing factors contained in my opinion. It discussed the accident location and the subsequent decision to bomb the Osprey accident site once the survivors and classified equipment were removed. I thought it was interesting that Youngner also mentioned the main landing gear marks on the sand being indicative of a perfect roll-on landing. I highlighted the sentence and thought, how could AFSOC be so adamant about the accident being "pilot error," yet agree the pilot made an exceptional roll-on landing? In the final paragraph, he discussed legal issues and errors. Youngner stated the tenth substantially contributing factor, engine power loss, in his mind, posed controversy as a substantially contributing factor. I had to pause for a moment and think about how he could possibly come to such a conclusion. I wondered if he had read my discussion of the opinion. Maybe he was told to make the tenth contributing factor disappear … don't care how, just make it go away.

The memorandum concluded with four options for Dobrinski to consider. Option One: approve the accident investigation report with the understanding his approval did not suggest or denote agreement with the statement of opinion. Option Two: approve the report and add comments. Option Three: find the accident investigation report "insufficient" and return it to the board President for further action. Option Four: remove the accident investigation board President and appoint a successor. I thought about the media storm the fourth option would create, but I reasoned AFSOC might not care. Col Youngner suggested Dobrinski select Option Two. He recommended the accident board findings be approved with additional comments from the convening authority (Dobrinski) about engine power loss not being a substantially contributing factor. His suggested wording; "I find the preponderance of the evidence in this report does not support a finding of engine power loss as a substantially contributing factor."

I put down my copy of the memorandum and sighed loudly.

"Sir, Col Youngner has accepted your opinion as legally sufficient," Winsett said. "But he's concerned about your tenth contributing factor, engine power loss. He provided Dobrinski with options. We have to wait to see which option he chooses before we can proceed."

"One of which, I see, is to appoint a new board president," I answered. "Does that mean the investigation reopens from the beginning?"

"I've never heard of that being done, sir," said Winsett. "It would be a first for me, so I don't know."

I re-read Youngner's assertion that my opinion failed to meet *substantially contributing factors* criteria for engine power loss. In the end, AFSOC could agree with nine of the factors and write a statement disagreeing engine power loss contributed to the accident. The investigation would be concluded, and I would immediately move to the next phase - briefing the families of the deceased and injured.

From the first day of my assignment, I had conducted the investigation under the cloud of *pilot error.* It dominated rumors, the news, and printed articles. After an intense four-month investigation, I wrote my opinion stating ten substantially contributing factors caused the accident. The command refused to accept the fact that power loss, in some way, contributed. They could refute my opinion with one of their own when the accident investigation report was officially accepted. The AFSOC legal advisor made it clear with his suggestion to "accept the report with comments." Col Youngner's email clearly gave the command a side door avenue to get the result they desired. All they had to do was copy the sentence Youngner gave them as a recommendation.

I was perplexed as to why I was not given the opportunity to explain how I arrived at engine power loss as a significantly contributing factor. I was getting a strong feeling all the legal maneuvering had absolutely nothing to do with the actual accident, and everything to do with calling it "pilot error" and getting the accident buried and forgotten as quickly as possible. I needed to plead my case, or at least get an explanation as to why the command refused to listen. I wanted to hear answers to my questions directly from the AFSOC leaders. Four months of extremely hard work was essentially being ignored, because it was not the answer they desired.

"I've had enough," I said, as I stood to my feet. "I'm heading to AFSOC Headquarters. I may need witnesses ... any volunteers?"

CHAPTER FORTY TWO

SUBJECT MATTER EXPERTS

Three volunteers accompanied me to AFSOC Headquarters … Winsett, O'Leary, and Kelly. No one spoke during the short ride. I backed into my designated parking spot, but before I could open the door, Winsett tapped me on the shoulder.

"Sir, Colonel Youngner's email is thirty minutes old … to us … but you can bet the commander and vice commander were briefed Sunday, if not Saturday. They've had the weekend to consider their response. They are going to be much better prepared than we are."

"If you're trying to make me feel better, it's not working," I said. "Let's get this over with. Since you haven't been in the command area for a while, pay attention to the frosty reception I receive these days. The plan is to walk through the main entrance and go straight to my office."

As we opened the door to the command suite, a few of the executive assistants and secretaries looked up from their computers and immediately put their heads back down and continued working. The four of us bee-lined to my office. We closed the door and pushed three chairs to the front of my desk so we could talk.

"Don't get too comfortable," I said. "I bet someone will knock on the door within a minute, two at most."

Before I said another word, Dobrinski's secretary rapped at the door.

"Sir, he would like to see you."

"Thank you, Donna, we're on the way," I answered as I directed my posse out the door.

Winsett asked, "sir, do you want us to go into his office with you?"

"Trust me, if he doesn't want you in his office, he'll say so immediately. If he allows you to stay with me, listen to what he says. I want to make sure we fully understand his instructions."

We filed out of my office directly to Dobrinski's door. I knocked and then looked in.

"Sir, I have three accident board members with me. May they come in?" I asked.

"Sure. Close the door behind you," he said. "Did you read Colonel Youngner's email?"

"Yes, sir. All of us read it."

"I have serious reservations about your tenth substantially contributing factor. Your report is insufficient due to lack of evidence of an engine power loss. Engage outside experts on the subject and revisit the data that led to your conclusion. Then, after closely considering their opinions and recommendations, revise your opinion and send it back to the AFSOC legal office. Time is of the essence. Get this done immediately. Questions?"

I looked at my team. Appearing surprised by Dobrinski's statement, but without questions, they shook their heads indicating they had no questions.

"Sir, I'll notify you later today with a plan to comply with your request," I said. "Have a nice afternoon."

We walked to the command suite exit door, jogged down the stairs and exited through the front door of the Headquarters building. Once away from all the people coming and going from the building, I stopped and faced the group.

"I didn't expect Option Three. Our investigation is *insufficient*? Anyone else surprised?"

"Yes, sir. To be honest though, I expected worse," Winsett said. "I suggest we brief the rest of the team before you decide how to move forward and comply with Dobrinski's request."

"I have a couple ideas, sir," O'Leary said. "I'll share them with you after we get back to the office."

Once we returned to the accident board office we immediately assembled the team. I explained what had happened at Headquarters.

O'Leary immediately spoke up. "Sir, the only contributing factor being questioned is the engine power loss. I don't know what experts General Dobrinski had in mind, but my recommendation is to bring in an experienced and respected test pilot from the CV-22 community. We can have him study the NST calculations, review key interviews and read your opinion. I have someone in mind. Give me the word, and I'll get in touch with him."

"Great idea," I said. "Any other discussion?"

Winsett scanned the room in an apparent search for consensus.

"Yes, sir, it's a start. Rather than limit our outside help to a rated officer (a pilot), I recommend we also enlist the advice of an engine expert to evaluate sections of the report dealing with technical engine data … the engine teardown reports and other facts Sergeant Dolan has gathered."

"Sir," Doc Harper said, "I think we should invite a human factors expert to validate sections I've written. He, or she, can also assess all ten substantially contributing factors."

"All are excellent ideas," I said. "Let's proceed with your suggestions. O'Leary, schedule another simulator period. Let's check with the 8th SOS and ask if they can provide a current and qualified crew. We'll observe and record their response to the most likely accident scenarios. Once we have opinions from the invited experts, I'll re-evaluate my opinion. Adams, Kelly, Scott … you have anything to add?"

"No, sir," they said in unison.

"Okay, let's get back to work. My goal is to complete this in seven … no more than ten days. I'll advise General Dobrinski about how we plan to address his concerns."

O'Leary secured the services of Lieutenant Colonel Sean Londrigan. He and O'Leary had met while they performed operational testing of the CV-22 at Edwards AFB in California. His permanent duty assignment was currently the Deputy to the Head of the Department of Engineering Mechanics, United States Air Force Academy. The cadets were still conducting summer training. The academic year was still a few weeks away so the timing was perfect to allow Lt Col Londrigan to spend four to five days at Hurlburt Field. When O'Leary spoke with him, he was excited about the opportunity to assist with the accident investigation.

Londrigan's experience included flying the HH-60 Pave Hawk[17], instructing in the helicopter test pilot school, and duty as an acceptance pilot in the CV-22 integrated test program. He was intimately qualified to provide expert analysis and support. He possessed the security clearance, as well as the command and line pilot experience required to assess the technical elements of CV-22 combat operations.

Having Londrigan aboard was like having two O'Leary's in the room. Both possessed similar technical expertise, intelligence, and confident demeanor. They spent their days discussing sections of the report while making notes, checking calculations and drawing illustrations on the office white boards. They combed through every piece of evidence with such microscopic precision that the rest of us would stop work, mesmerized by the science and logic of their discussions. Londrigan's academy assignment fit his intellect, mission orientation, and communication skills. O'Leary would have made an excellent Academy instructor, too.

At the end of the week, we received the engine teardown analysis from the Naval Air Systems Command (NAVAIR). Their report mirrored the detail we had already received from MSgt True … saying the left engine was running at the time of impact … at what rpm, they were unable to determine.

Dolan solicited other engine experts to evaluate our data, and they concurred with the reports and information as written in the accident report.

We worked long hours over the weekend and into the following week. I had given up practicing my PowerPoint™ presentation pending the results of the experts' analysis.

17Pave Hawk -The HH-60 Pave Hawk is an all-weather day/night Air Force transport helicopter. It is a special version of the UH-60 Black Hawk helicopter. The HH-60 missions include the rescue of downed airmen and the insertion of Special Forces units behind enemy lines.

Our accident report information had been under review for five days. The simulator data, human factors data and engine data had been reviewed, and the reports submitted validated the information presented in the accident report. We patiently waited for Lt Col Londrigan to write his evaluation. I knew the experts' opinions would either contradict or validate our findings. So far, our interpretation of data was correct. Late Wednesday evening, O'Leary came over to my desk.

"Sir, are you busy?" asked O'Leary.

I looked up from reading emails on my computer and replied, "No, what's up?"

"Londrigan is finished with his review. He told me he will give us his report in the morning. We can get the investigation back on track tomorrow. Just thought you'd like to know before you head back to your billeting room tonight."

"Thanks. I look forward to reading his analysis. I appreciate the hard work both of you put into getting this done. I'll be here another hour. You should go get some rest. Have a good night."

As O'Leary departed the office, Winsett and I organized documents and notes on the conference table and reviewed the briefing slides prepared ten days earlier.

"I wonder how much of this will have to be changed," I said.

"We'll know tomorrow, sir. We could have another long day. I think I'll call it a night."

"I'm right behind you."

"Have a good night," I said. "I don't know if I've ever told you this, but you're a great lawyer. I'm lucky you drew this assignment."

"I'm the lucky one, sir. Good night."

The next morning, I arrived in the office before 8:00 a.m. with the room already buzzing with activity.

"Good morning, sir," O'Leary said. "We have Londrigan's report. We're ready to brief findings from all the reports we've compiled over the last week."

I sat at the end of the conference table. A knot rose in the pit of my stomach. If any of the reports challenged my opinion of what caused the accident, I would have to honor the credibility of the subject matter experts and revise my opinion accordingly. I was confident in the investigation and my opinion, but I was not overconfident. We were about to find out if I was right, or if I had missed something, resulting in an irrational conclusion. Dolan, O'Leary, and Harper held the reports submitted to them and awaited my instructions.

"Okay," I said. "Who has information in their 'expert's' report that differs from our accident report? In other words, which one of you has bad news for me?"

CHAPTER FORTY THREE

EMOTIONAL BRIEFING

I tossed a blank legal pad and pen on top of the three neat stacks of paper without reading or scanning the documents. Dolan squirmed in his seat and raised a hand.

"With your permission, sir, I'll go first. I don't have bad news .. but I do have great news."

"Press on," I said.

"Thank you, sir. The Rolls-Royce report noted details we didn't see in MSgt True's report. They reported no failed or failing components prior to impact. The engine exhibited internal signatures indicating it was providing some level of power. The turbine was rotating under its own power. Photographs of the turbine assembly showed both rotation and stationary (impact) damage. They concluded the engine was operating when the airplane hit the ground. I consulted MSgt Frank Stookey, an engine shop supervisor from Kirtland AFB, New Mexico. He reviewed the Rolls-Royce engine teardown and agreed they did an excellent job. In his experience, mean time between engine changes on the Osprey averaged eighty hours. For comparison, the mean time for changing MH-53 helicopter engines averaged two hundred and ten hours. Time between engine changes on a CV-22 operating in a dust/dirt rich environment might degrade performance from 100% to 95% (mandatory engine change) within a week. I have personally seen a 100% engine degraded to a level requiring an engine change after thirty-four hours of operation. After hours of consultations with other CV-22 engine experts, I won't change a single word in my section of the accident report, sir."

"All right thanks, great work."

I looked over to Doctor Harper. I knew the most contentious report would be the one O'Leary was holding. I wanted to save it for last.

"Doc Harper, do you have an update on the human factors section?"

"Sir, after a full day's search I found the expert we needed. His name is Major James Young. He is a member of the 720th Special Tactics Group (STG) based here at Hurlburt Field. He has a PhD in human factors. I spent over two hours talking with him about portions of our investigation. I wrote a summary of our conversation as a memorandum for record (MFR). It will be added to my section of the accident report. He agrees with our findings, and the information in the human factors section of our report. I'm making no changes, just adding his discussion as further evidence. Questions for me, sir?"

"I'll reference your MFR in the email to Maj Gen Dobrinski. Nice job."

"Thank you, sir," Harper said.

"Perhaps it's fitting Lt Col O'Leary is last. You've had a busy week. Do you ever sleep?" I asked.

O'Leary's face lit up with his ear-to-ear smile.

"Yes, sir, but not a lot this week. Lt Col Londrigan and I first discussed reasons Maj Voas would make a roll-on landing. Absent a detailed survey of the landing zone, there'd be no reason for an accomplished Osprey pilot to infiltrate making an unplanned and unbriefed roll-on landing. We discounted to zero the probability that the pilot elected to execute anything but a vertical approach and landing. No sane pilot ... at night ... onto an un-surveyed desert location ... except in a dire emergency, would attempt a roll-on landing. With power to fly out of a bad situation, he would have done it. For reasons of their own, it was suggested, by unnamed sources, the pilot believed a roll-on landing was the best way to conduct the mission. Every pilot we interviewed suggested such a decision to be suicide. There is no way an experienced pilot would have attempted a dangerous roll-on landing unless it was the last, and only, available option. Maj Voas had no other option ... that's why he attempted the roll-on landing."

"You and I have had this discussion before," I said. "I'm glad to hear another expert Osprey pilot agrees with us."

O'Leary acknowledged and continued, "we spent a day debating NST information. Londrigan requested the NST provide a margin of error for their calculations. They offered a 90% confidence (10% margin of error) for calculations of rpm using the proprotor markings in the sand and 80% using photogrammetry techniques. Assuming engine power at the high end of their margins, the values using either method remained well below the rpm expected during that phase of flight.

"We also had a combat-qualified crew fly ten different scenarios in the simulator. The crew's observed reactions mirrored the results we experienced during our previous tests. We recorded no new observations as a result of the additional simulator flying. But, I am noting that during the debriefing following the simulator flights, the flight engineer observed an unknown malfunction must've reduced the power available to the crew or they definitely would've aborted the approach.

"To sum up the week, I found no new evidence. The re-evaluation of the engine, proprotor rpm, and human factors evidence confirms the conclusion that a solid chain of events, as you described in your opinion with the substantially contributing factors, was causal for the accident. Any questions for me, sir?"

I took a deep breath. I did not expect for the evaluation of all the sections of our report to go so well.

"Yes. As I understand it, the only change you'll make to the accident report is adding the summary of events from the additional three hours of simulator time, and the margin of error for the NST calculation?"

"Yes, sir."

"Thank you," I said. "The next question is for our two lawyers. What do you recommend?"

Winsett and Kelly conferred for a few seconds.

"Sir," Winsett said. "You're required to advise General Dobrinski of your decision. We recommend you outline what we've done this week. Make sure the last paragraph indicates you are either changing your opinion or your opinion remains unchanged. Please let Capt Kelly and I review the letter prior to delivering it to AFSOC legal."

"I'll have it ready for review in an hour or two. I appreciate the hard work this week, thank you. We'll have a staff meeting later tonight where I want to go through one last practice briefing."

I poured a cup of coffee and walked back to my desk in the corner of the accident investigation office. I took a deep breath and composed the following letter to Maj Gen Dobrinski:

MEMORANDUM FOR CONVENING AUTHORITY
FROM: BRIGADIER GENERAL DONALD HARVEL
PRESIDENT, ACCIDENT INVESTIGATION BOARD
SUBJECT: Action of Convening Authority – August 17, 2010
CV-22 Accident Investigation Board (AIB), April 9, 2010, Tail Number 06-0031

1. On August 17, 2010, you returned the AIB's August 13, 2010 report with concerns of whether the report was sufficient. You requested that I review all identified substantially contributing factors for internal and external consistency. During the last week, I carefully reviewed all the evidence and took further investigative steps as summarized below. I conducted another thorough review of the preponderance of evidence standard and evaluated whether each substantially contributing factor met the greater weight of credible evidence. My opinion remains unchanged that the preponderance of evidence supports that ten substantially contributing factors each played an important role, either directly or indirectly, in the mishap sequence of events. During the review process, I decided to modify the statement of opinion to limit all discussion of engine power loss to the tenth substantial contributing factor. I still do not know, without serious or substantial doubt, the actual cause of the mishap.

2. The AIB investigated the following areas between August 17 to 24, 2010:

a. Engine Analysis Report: The AIB received the Rolls-Royce report of the left engine teardown. The report is consistent with earlier reports by NAVAIR and AFSOC/A-4 that the left engine was operating under its own power at an undetermined power setting at impact. The only modification to the AIB report is to add the Rolls-Royce report to Tab HH-39.

b. Engine Expert Interviews: The AIB conducted supplemental interviews with MSgt Coby True, AFSOC/A-4, MSgt Frank Stookey, 58th Aircraft Maintenance Squadron (AMXS), and Mr. John Tsaio, Air Logistics Center, Oklahoma. After numerous hours of telephone and personal interviews, the only change to the AIB report is removing the reference to the engine anti-ice valve from the statement of opinion under the engine degradation section.

c. Human Factors Expert Consultation: Members of the AIB interviewed Maj James Young from the 720th Special Tactics Group (STG) based at Hurlburt Field. He completed a one-year post-doctorate program studying human factors with NASA. Maj Young stated that a 'high-pitched' voice indicates an acute stress reaction by the mishap pilot. I considered whether under acute stress the mishap pilot forgot or delayed a highly practiced task, like advancing the TCL at the appropriate time during the deceleration. While possible, I found this less likely, especially considering the mishap pilot's ability to execute to near perfection, seconds later, a less practiced task, such as a CV-22 roll-on landing. A memorandum for record was added to the post-investigation memorandum summarizing the entire interview.

d. Proprotor RPM Analysis: The AIB requested a confidence rating and margin of error from the NST. Mr. John Vulgamore had a 90% confidence rating in the proprotor strike analysis with a margin of error of plus or minus 10%. He had an 80% confidence in the in-flight proprotor RPM analysis, with a margin of error of plus or minus 20%. In order to further assess the accuracy of the in-flight proprotor RPM analysis, Mr. Vulgamore has reviewed two additional CV-22 in-flight videos. His calculation of proprotor RPMs for the videos were within plus 2% and minus 6% of the known RPM - well within his expected margin of error. Even *with the margin of error, the proprotor RPM NST arrived at is below the normal RPM. The AIB statement of opinion was modified to include reference to a margin of error and a conclusion that the proprotor analysis was abnormal instead of at a particular percentage.*

e. Simulator Flights: The AIB observed and recorded a combat-qualified aircrew fly ten simulator flight scenarios. The scenarios included six delays in TCL input and four engine malfunctions. We asked the pilot to delay advancing TCL power by audibly counting out three seconds in order to allow the rate of descent to increase to 1,800 feet per minute. After the three seconds, he was advised to arrest the rate of descent and continue the approach to land the airplane. Both times, he arrested the rate of descent and flew past the landing zone. When asked to delay for four seconds, the airplane crashed short of the landing zone. Delaying four seconds before advancing TCL power allowed the airplane to develop a rate of descent greater than 3,000 feet per minute. That rate of descent proved to be unrecoverable. During one of the scenarios, a dual-engine compressor stall, the pilot recovered the seven-second, 1,600 feet per minute rate of descent at sixteen feet above the ground and one-fourth of a mile from the landing zone. The only change made to the AIB report is the additional three hours of simulator time and the results of the scenarios flown.

3. did play a role in the sequence of events. I fully recognize that others may disagree that an engine power loss played a role in the mishap. Similar debates took place daily during the AIB's internal assessments of the evidence. While I remain open to considering new evidence if it becomes available, I see little benefit in further consideration of the existing evidence. I respectfully request approval of the AIB report, with or without comments. [11]

I signed the letter and handed it to Winsett and Kelly for review. After reading and studying my comments, they conferred about each paragraph.

Winsett stood up. "Sir, this is perfect. Don't change a thing. Capt Kelly and I have to go to the legal office to sign documents. We would be happy to deliver this letter for you."

"Sure, that would be fine," I said. "I'll see you later this evening for our 6:00 p.m. meeting."

I walked into the hot, humid Florida sun and drove to a restaurant just off the base and ate alone. My thoughts were about briefing the families of the deceased and severely injured soon after meeting with the command staff to conduct my accident report briefing. I had maintained a file of personal information for each of the families. I looked forward to meeting them and sharing the results of the investigation.

I drove back onto the base and directly to the accident investigation office.

"TSgt Scott, please cue up my PowerPoint™ presentation," I said.

"Yes, sir. I'll gather up the team so you can practice."

The team took their seats and we went through the briefing … slide-by-slide. When finished, I looked around the room.

4. The statement of opinion is my best assessment of all the evidence and expert analysis. I believe all ten substantially contributing factors can, and "Well, what do you think?" I asked.

No one spoke a word. The presentation went very well. I had done it enough times to memorize most of the narrative of each slide. It was a very well organized and thought out presentation. I scanned the room one last time. I was choked up to see Kelly and Adams had tears slowly rolling off their cheeks.

CHAPTER FORTY FOUR

SUDDEN RETIREMENT

The next morning I followed my usual routine, checking voice and email messages before heading to the office. Emails had slowed to a trickle and I saw nothing from the command regarding our report.

By 7:45 a.m. I assumed AFSOC legal had spent most of the previous afternoon and evening answering questions and conferring with the leadership. At some point during the day I would visit the command, but felt confident I could answer any conceivable questions.

Adams greeted me entering the office. While the rest of the team busied themselves with their computers and mobile devices, Adams and I sat at the conference table and discussed making copies of the accident report. She had discovered an office on base that could handle the volume and number we would need.

"Sir, regulations allow an accident report binder to be no more than one and a half inches thick. Our report will fill four binders. It's the largest I've seen," she said. "As soon as there're no more changes, I'll drop it off to be copied. We need fourteen total reports, right?"

"Yes, fourteen … perfect."

Winsett interrupted. "Good morning, sir. I just spoke with Colonel Youngner. AFSOC is still considering options. They'll let us know their decision soon."

We sat around the conference table engaging in small talk.

"Sir, my boss called this morning," Kelly said. "They're short staffed in my office back home. They want to know if I have a return date yet. I told him we're close to wrapping up our report. Do you think I can give my office an estimated date for me to return?"

"I hope you can tell them by the end of the day. I will conduct my accident investigation presentation in the next day or two. Once that's done, you can return home to Bolling AFB. I appreciate your tremendous support and guidance. Thank you. I won't keep you … or anyone else assigned to the accident investigation board longer than necessary."

The office phone, my cell phone, and Winsett's cell phone rang in unison. The screen on my cell indicated a call from Capt Pierce. I answered immediately.

"Good morning, sir. General Dobrinski would like to see you and the accident investigation lawyers immediately. Can you head to the Headquarters building?"

"Tell him we'll be there in five minutes."

"Will do, sir."

"Sir, Colonel Youngner said we should meet him at AFSOC Headquarters immediately," Winsett said.

"Let's go," I said. "We'll take my car."

No one spoke during the drive to Headquarters. We piled out of the car and flashed our IDs to security guards at the door. We jogged up the stairs and stopped for a few seconds to catch our breath and compose our emotions before entering the command suite.

I looked at the expectant faces behind me. This was our moment of truth. "Ready?"

"Sir, we're ready," Winsett said. "Are *you* ready?"

I nodded and opened the door. The secretaries and administrative staff in the command suite glared and stared while we headed straight to Dobrinski's office.

"Sir, go on in, he's expecting you," his executive assistant said.

I knocked on his door and peeked inside.

"Come in."

"Sir, I have the two accident team lawyers with me."

"Fine. Colonel Youngner is on the way. He'll be here in a minute."

Obviously irritated, his words were clipped, and he looked straight at me, bobbing his head, pointing toward me with his forehead as he spoke.

"You write in your opinion that not one, but two, engines had a power loss. Do you realize the odds are astronomical?" he asked.

"Yes, sir, but the probability is clearly outlined in the discussion of my opinion. Comparable events have happened, most resulting in dire consequences and loss of life. In July of 1989, Captain Al Haynes landed a United Air Lines DC-10 after a tail engine failure destroyed all hydraulic systems powering the flight controls. No emergency procedure existed for what the design engineers call an *unacceptable mode of failure*. No emergency checklists existed for such an event, but when the improbable happens, the crew draws on experience and common sense to deal with the situation. I didn't consider odds when I investigated this mishap or wrote my opinion. Facts and findings determined my opinion, sir."

He expressed no interest in what I said. He dismissed my comment by turning away and shaking his head. Now he was thoroughly pissed off.

Youngner knocked on the door and stepped into the office. Perfect timing, I thought. His entrance might have saved me from potential physical abuse.

"I got here as quickly as I could, sir," said Youngner as he looked around the room. I'm sure he was thinking he might have missed something, judging by the looks on our faces.

"Do you have a copy of my letter for Brigadier General Harvel?" Dobrinski asked sternly.

"Yes, sir."

Dobrinski flipped his hand and pointed in my direction.

Youngner handed me the letter and said, "here you go, sir."

ACTION OF THE CONVENING AUTHORITY

I reviewed the report of the Accident Investigation Board, conducted under the provisions of Air Force Instruction

510503, that investigated the April 9, 2010 mishap in Afghanistan involving a CV-22, Tail Number 06-0031, assigned to the 8th Special Operations Squadron, Hurlburt Field, FL on August 26, 2010. The investigation and report are sufficient and in compliance with applicable laws and regulations. I find the preponderance of the evidence in this report does not support a finding of engine power loss as a substantially contributing factor.

Kent Dobrinski, Major General, USAF, Vice Commander, AFSOC [12]

I scanned the letter and handed it to Winsett. I took a breath to calm myself. I wanted to ask him if he had read any of the report or the discussion of my opinion. I then reconsidered and decided it might be best to not ask the question and just move on.

"What's the next step, sir?" I asked.

"You submit your report by delivering the appropriate number of copies to the legal office as soon as possible."

"Yes, sir. We're producing fourteen copies of the report."

"Your investigation is complete," he said. "You, and your team, are dismissed from accident investigation duties and cleared to return to your assigned bases."

"And the briefing for you and the commander, sir?" I asked.

"That won't be necessary."

I stifled an involuntary gasp and looked at my two lawyers. Both seemed no less shocked.

"No briefing at all?" I asked with confusion.

"No, general, that won't be necessary. The boss has no interest."

"How about the briefing I plan to give to the families of critically and fatally injured personnel?" I asked.

"No. You won't brief the staff, the commander, or the families … no one. We'll assign another general officer to conduct the family briefings."

His words drew all the oxygen from my lungs. Unable to speak, I had no further questions or comments. We stood up and silently left his office. I headed directly to the parking lot … not looking at anyone or anything as I hurried to the car before my jelly-feeling legs collapsed. I put my hands on the steering wheel and replayed what had just happened over and over again in my mind.

"Sir," said Winsett.

I looked to my right to see him sitting, staring, and looking as stunned as I felt.

"I didn't see that coming. What do you think?" I asked.

"Sir, we're dumbfounded. I'm not sure their actions comply with regulations. I mean, sure they can accept the report with comments. No issue with that, in fact we expected it. But refusing to hear your briefing and the justification for your opinion is beyond disrespectful to you, the board, the process, the families, and the Osprey community."

"Sir, you delivered the honest truth concerning the accident," Kelly said. "You've maintained your honor and preserved the integrity of Air Force accident investigations. Treating you and the facts in such a manner is disgusting and shameful."

When we arrived at the office, I recounted to the rest of the team what had happened. We all sat at the conference table in shocked silence as we processed the reality of the situation. So much work, so many interviews, so many miles travelled, for what now seemed like nothing.

I broke the silence by saying, "four months ago, we sought the truth investigating this aircraft accident. You've labored long days with little rest, or time to yourselves, gathering evidence and producing a report for which you can be proud. Don't surrender to disappointment, or feel sorry for me. It'll pass. One day we'll be vindicated. The truth will prevail. Celebrate the accurate representation of what happened. I'm not angry. I'm disappointed. I'd have preferred to present and explain our accomplishments and the logic of my opinion. But it won't happen. The families of Major Voas and Senior Master Sergeant Lackey deserve to know the respect, honor, and gratitude their fellow warriors have for them. They're entitled to the honest truth, not the political or expedient version of the accident events. Sixteen lives owe their existence to the professional skill and courage of Voas and Lackey. The outcome notwithstanding, we're done. Return to your homes and families with my blessing and eternal gratitude. With Sergeant Scott's and Sergeant Adams' assistance, I'll ensure the report is copied and delivered to the appropriate agencies. Once we finish delivering copies, Adams ... you're released to return home. Scott and I will clean this office and return all borrowed equipment. Thank you from the bottom of my heart for your exemplary work, support, and friendship. Please allow me to personally say good-bye to each of you individually before you depart Hurlburt Field."

A great weight had been lifted from our individual and collective shoulders, yet no one seemed jubilant. We shed tears, offered hugs, and exchanged a few words. One by one, over the next two days team members departed Hurlburt Field.

At the end of the week, TSgt Scott and I delivered fifty-six, one and a half inch thick binders to the AFSOC legal office. The Osprey accident investigation was officially complete.

On September 15, 2010, I retired from the Air Force and returned to the support of my loving family. My thirty-four year career in the Air Force and Air National Guard ended with little fanfare ... just as I desired.

I quietly settled into my life as a commercial airline pilot, enjoying the extra time with my family.

On November 16, 2010, I received a late night phone call. Despite the unrecognizable number showing on my cell phone screen, I answered.

"Is this Brigadier General Don Harvel?"

"Yes, it is."

"This is General Norty Schwartz, Chief of Staff of the U.S. Air Force. Do you have a few minutes?"

CHAPTER FORTY FIVE

CHIEF OF STAFF U.S. AIR FORCE

I had no idea what to expect from the Chief of Staff of the Air Force. After more than two months, he'd had time to digest the accident report and form an opinion. Or, he could join the chorus of senior officers at AFSOC and attempt to dissuade me from my considered opinion. I'm retired, why should I care what he wants?

"Yes, sir, I have time," I responded.

"I won't keep you long. You were the Accident Investigation Board President for the CV-22 accident on the morning of April 9, 2010, in Afghanistan. Is that correct?"

"Yes, sir."

"My staff will mail you a letter with this information, so don't worry about writing it down. I am reopening your investigation for you to consider evidence, which could affect your statement of opinion. The additional evidence consists of three reports, two from NAVAIR and an analysis of video prepared by the Convening Authority (CA) Maj Gen Dobrinski. You have discretion as to which board members you need to assist you and the way you conduct your meetings. Upon completion of your evaluation of the new evidence, prepare an addendum to your report to include a summary of facts and statement of opinion addressing your consideration of this new evidence and its effect, if any, on your opinion. All directives and guidance in the convening authority's appointment letter dated April 16, 2010, remain in effect. Do you have questions?"

"Yes, sir, a couple of questions. First, I'm retired … a civilian. In what status do I perform this duty?"

"Work that out with AFSOC. They'll assign an action officer to handle all details."

"Second question, sir. I mean no disrespect, but what if I fail to see the need to consider the additional evidence? We conducted a thorough investigation and determined ten substantially contributing factors. I understand AFSOC has a problem with power loss being a substantially contributing factor ... but I don't. Within days of the accident, and absent a report from any investigating authority, AFSOC determined the cause to be pilot error. After four months of interviewing more than a hundred witnesses and amassing volumes of evidence, I couldn't disagree more. A point of fact, sir, were it not for the skill and airmanship of Maj Voas and SMSgt Lackey, twenty lives would have been lost on the morning of April 9th in Afghanistan. I reviewed evidence numerous times and in excruciating detail. At this point sir, I'm inclined to tell the Convening Authority to take their addendum and ... well ... what if I refuse?"

"Set your emotions aside and think of the families of the casualties. They're still waiting to be briefed about the accident and to see your final report. AFSOC is concerned the families have had to wait a long time."

"Sir, the families haven't been briefed yet?"

"No."

"That's the command's decision, sir. I would've been happy to brief the families months ago and would do it today. I can't believe the families have waited this long."

"General ..."

"All right, sir. Out of respect for the families, I'll do it," I said.

"Your action officer will be in touch soon. Good evening."

I hung up, wondering about the "new evidence." And emotional? To this point, I had kept my personal feelings subordinated to the tasks at hand. Like a good soldier, I would give it a fair chance.

I'd had no previous professional contact with Gen Schwartz, but he and his Air Force Academy classmate, Lt Gen Becker shared a longtime relationship. I could only imagine how Becker had characterized me and the opinion I wrote concerning the accident. This made the third attempt by the AFSOC commanders to push facts and findings in a direction to their liking, rather than supporting facts and the truth.

A few minutes later, my phone rang again. This time, it was a Florida number.

"Hello, sir. This is Major Warren Bildstein, with the AFSOC commander's action group (CAG). I've been assigned as the liaison between your accident investigation board and the command."

"I don't think I've met you. Are you new to the CAG?" I asked.

"Yes, sir. I've been working in the CAG for three weeks."

I shook my head ... the newbie got assigned the short straw to coordinate with me.

"Then, we've not met?"

"No, sir. But I feel as if I know you. Officers in the CAG speak highly of you."

"If you have detailed instructions from the commander or his vice, please tell me what they expect from me and the board," I said.

"Yes, sir. I'm to assist you and your selected members of the accident investigation board who will assemble and examine the AFSOC addendum to your report. After studying the new evidence, you're to alter your opinion, if necessary, and the investigation report in accordance with applicable regulations, instructions, and the letter provided by the Chief of Staff." [13]

"Maj Bildstein, what's the timeline to conclude this?"

"Sir, the commander asked that it be completed within a week."

"Really? A week? I asked. "That may be an issue."

"Sir, his goal is to brief the families prior to Thanksgiving Day. He's concerned about families going through the beginning of the holiday season waiting and wondering about the cause of the accident."

Clever. Guilt. The Air Force Chief of Staff himself, and through Maj Bildstein, insinuated I had prolonged the suffering of the victims' families, but had the command accepted my findings and report, I would have briefed them months ago. I hadn't prolonged the anguish. That ball languished on the desks of commanders who were now pressing, for the third time, for me to abandon my honest and considered opinion.

"Yes ... closure ... for sure," I said. "I'll do my best to make the timeline. Do you have a list of the accident investigation board members?"

"Yes, sir."

We discussed details of the board members traveling to Atlanta. We would work from November 18th to 22nd to review the new evidence and write an addendum to the AFSOC addendum.

Two days later, a package arrived at my home. The package had the official letter from General Schwartz reconvening the accident investigation board and a report from the Aeromechanics Safety Investigation Support Team (ASIST) at NAVAIR. The thirty-page report was written by four NAVAIR engineers – Gary Wilshire (mishap lead engineer), with Bill Sawtelle, Jack Miller and Eric Jason (supporting engineers). The package also included an eighteen-page discourse on *Structural Evaluation of CV-22 Mishap Post-Impact Events* written by a rotary wing load and dynamics technical specialist from NAVAIR. Maj Gen Dobrinski had added a two-page speed calculation detailing how the accident investigation board made an error when calculating the airplane's touchdown speed. He concluded the Osprey touched down at 90 knots and maintained the speed while rolling across the sand for over 240 feet, flipping over and sliding to a stop. Using 90 knots as the speed when the proprotor marks were gouged into the sand, the engine rpm, he concluded, would be close to normal engine rpm values.

I read the documents and jotted notes in the margins. It required quite a bit of imagination to draft the paragraphs. It made little sense to me. I looked forward to watching O'Leary's expression as he commented on these bizarre reports.

CHAPTER FORTY SIX

AEROMECHANICS SAFETY INVESTIGATION SUPPORT TEAM (ASIST)

On Thursday, November 18th, TSgt Scott and Lt Col O'Leary greeted me as I walked into the lobby of the Renaissance Hotel at the Atlanta International airport.

"General Harvel, how are you, sir?" Scott asked as he greeted me with a handshake and a hug.

"It's great to see you," I said. "How was your trip from Florida, Scotty? O'Leary, great to see you. Are you glad to get a break from Washington, D.C.?"

"Good," O'Leary said. "Thanks for the few days respite from the Pentagon. It's always nice to get away from that crazy place. I've missed you guys."

Scott grabbed my lone carry-on bag and walked to the check-in area of the hotel.

"Sir, after you check in, I'll show you the conference room I've reserved. I brought a vanload of equipment and supplies. Lt Col Winsett, Lt Col Harper, and MSgt Dolan are already there dealing with emails."

"Have you seen Kelly or Adams?" I asked.

"Yes, sir," O'Leary said. "Adams went for food. Said she'd be back in thirty minutes. Capt Kelly lands at 6:35 p.m. this evening. She'll meet us in the conference room later."

I checked in, stowed my suitcase, and hurried to the conference room with O'Leary and Scott. We walked down a flight of stairs to a cluster of conference rooms on the lower level of the hotel. Scott opened a door and announced our arrival.

"Look who we found," he said with his giant grin.

Winsett, Harper, and Dolan stood and shook my hand. We exchanged small talk to catch up on each other's lives.

"Sir, we're ready to interview NAVAIR's engineers tomorrow morning," Winsett said. "Maj Bildstein coordinated times and contact information. The schedule is tight, and we'll have a full day of activity tomorrow. Have you read the AFSOC addendum?"

"Yes, I've read it, but I'm more interested in your opinions."

"Have a seat, sir," O'Leary said.

I helped rearrange chairs into a close circle.

"How many times did we call NAVAIR for assistance during the four months we worked on the accident report?" I asked.

"Sir," O'Leary said. "Thirty, maybe forty times and they totally ignored us. They seldom, if ever, returned our calls and we ended up with absolutely no help from them. No doubt the NAVAIR ASIST engineers are a talented group. They had their chance to participate when we begged them for information. Their flight simulator tests, as far as they go, are nearly identical to ours. Their data might be interesting casual reading, but at this point it's totally irrelevant."

"I agree." I said. "The command provided them very limited information. Definitely not enough to formulate an educated and detailed evaluation."

"Yes, sir. This is what they were given as their primary task," O'Leary said.

The ASIST engineers were tasked to look at both dual and single engine wave-offs (go-arounds) after the last recorded data point from the Data Transfer Module (a device that records position, altitude, and true airspeed every ten seconds and transmits the information via satellite). They were to provide an assessment of the available performance using the mishap flight conditions. [14]

"And … they used the wrong winds for calculations?" O'Leary said while shaking his head in disbelief.

"Yes," I said. "I noticed their mistake too."

"This is my favorite part," O'Leary said.

> … *Two seconds prior to impact, at approximately 80 knots calibrated airspeed, adequate wave off performance did not exist with one engine inoperative. However, the probability of an engine failure less than two seconds prior to impact is considered highly remote. All these facts, when examined together, lead us to conclude this mishap was related to a loss of situational awareness and not a failure of one of the aircraft's engines.* [15]

"Notice they used the word 'probability' in the discussion?" said O'Leary. "I wonder why? You and Dobrinski discussed 'probability' more than once, didn't you, sir?"

I smiled and nodded in the affirmative.

Doc Harper likened the process to the TV game show, *Jeopardy*.

"The engineers took the answer, *pilot error*," said Harper. "From there, they manipulated the few pages of guidance and information they'd been fed to support the answer given to them. I definitely don't get their investigative process."

The next morning, we ate a quick breakfast, and hurried to the conference room reserved for us. First task was a conference call with Nan Morton, a rotary wing loads and dynamics technical specialist from NAVAIR.

"Has everyone read her report?" I asked. "Questions, comments, before we start?"

"Sir, I concede she's a very accomplished engineer," said O'Leary. "But her report states the engines/proprotors were turning when the Osprey touched down. In all honesty, sir, we knew that on the second day of our investigation. I see nothing to consider in this report. It says nothing."

"Sir, I agree," Dolan said. "She cites an excess of accurate, but worthless, calculations to support a fact obvious from the start. What's the point?"

"Sir, it's time to call," Winsett said. "Unless she has something else to offer, this'll be a very short discussion."

Capt Kelly dialed the number and slid the speaker phone to the center of the conference table.

"Hello, this is Heidi."

"Ms. Morton, this is Captain Christie Kelly. I am here with the CV-22 accident investigation board. Is this a good time for you to talk?"

"Yes. I expected your call," she said.

We introduced ourselves. I read the legalese and started the interview.

"What information were you given to use as background to write your report?" I asked.

"AFSOC provided a video depicting the mishap aircraft approaching the landing zone. I was also given photographs of ground markings indicating the aircraft touched down and traveled over the sand. I also had a photo of the gouges made in the sand by the proprotor after the airplane flipped onto its back. I was given a copy of the accident investigation board President's opinion and the AFSOC addendum to the accident report."

"Were you given instructions by AFSOC?"

"Yes. I was asked to provide supporting evidence regarding the operational state of the mishap aircraft's engines at the time of impact. Specifically, they wanted me to look from a structural viewpoint to determine if the post-impact breakup of the aircraft was a reasonable structural response. They also wanted to know if there was sufficient evidence from the post-impact events to confirm the state of the mishap aircraft's engines just prior to impact."

"What did you find?" I asked.

"I concluded the post-impact breakup sequence was consistent with the CV-22's design characteristics and the dissipated energy. I considered it logical the fuselage would flip end-for-end when the nose plowed deeper into the sand. For that section of the report, I concluded the post-impact sequence is not reliant upon the condition of the mishap aircraft's engines prior to ground impact. The other section of my report addressed the state of the mishap aircraft's engines just prior to impact. I concluded engine power was required to cause the fuselage to breakup and flip over the cockpit, as it did in this mishap. I believe the proprotors were powered when the Osprey contacted the ground due to the anecdotal reports of *broom straw* failure of the proprotor blades."

"I want to make sure I understand correctly ... the proprotors were turning when the airplane impacted the ground. That's what you just said, right?" I asked.

"Yes," she answered. "From a structural standpoint, the post-crash breakup of the airplane is consistent with the design of the aircraft, the terrain, and speed upon impact."

"You provided no data to support either engine's specific rpm or information confirming one or both engines operated under power," I said. "You are only confirming the engines were operating. Correct?"

"In simplified form, yes."

"I'm done," I stated as I pushed her report away from me. "Anyone else have a question?"

"Yes, sir, I have a question," said O'Leary. "You stated the airplane came to rest 291 feet from the location of the nose landing gear collapse. On page five of your report, you state when the airplane flipped over on its back, the speed at that time would have been between 10% to 50% lower than the touchdown speed. Is that correct?"

"Yes, that is correct due to the drag when the airplane moved across the sand and the nose plowed into the ground. The 10% to 50% is the correct range."

"Just to make sure the other accident board members understand what we are talking about. For example, if the airplane touched down at 80 knots. From a structural engineering standpoint, the maximum speed when the airplane flipped would have been 72 knots, and the minimum speed would have been 40 knots. Correct?"

"Yes, 40 knots minimum and 72 knots maximum due to drag degradation. The distance the airplane skidded on its back indicates the speed was closer to 55 knots."

"Any more questions?" I asked.

I looked around the table. Everyone shook their head no.

I read the post interview legal statement and hung up.

"Wow, they sure wasted her time," Adams said. "Eighteen pages of engineer's techno-babble to state something validated by the most casual observer in the video and a couple photographs."

"Thanks for asking the question about how much the airplane slowed as it rolled across the sand and flipped over," I said. "We've been conservative using our touchdown speed to calculate the engine rpm. If we use 50% of the speed, it would make the rpm lower than the number we stated in the accident report."

"Let's call the next engineer. See if he'll consent to starting the interview early," I asked. "We may have to conduct only one interview to see if their thirty-page report has any relevance."

"Sir, I have Gary Wilshire on the phone," said Kelly. "He'll be ready in a minute."

After a short pause, Mr. Wilshire came on the line.

"I'm ready. Thanks for calling early, this helps with my morning meetings."

The accident board members introduced themselves. I read the legal information, then asked the first question.

"Can you tell us what AFSOC requested of you and the members of your ASIST?"

"Yes, sir, General. We were asked to provide engineering assistance to the NAVAIR program office to look at both dual and single engine go-arounds after the last recorded data point by the airplane's data transfer module. They wanted our assessment of the available performance using the mishap aircraft's flight conditions."

"What did AFSOC provide for you to conduct your analysis?"

"Sir, we had the information transmitted by the data transfer module for every ten seconds of the flight. We had a video of the mishap. We also had multiple photographs of the ground markings at the crash site. We had copies of the interview transcripts of the surviving crewmembers, and a copy of your written opinion with the ten substantially contributing factors. The last document we were given was a two-page report written by the convening authority that negated any possibility of engine power loss as a substantially contributing factor."

"So, you did **not** receive accident investigation board memorandums for record, testimony of passengers aboard the mishap aircraft, or the engineering analysis provided by the National Geospatial-Intelligence Agency Support Team (NST). Is that correct?"

"Sir, that is correct."

"In your report you use winds of 050 degrees at 11 knots for all simulations. Where did you get that wind information?" I asked.

"Sir, it was provided to us by AFSOC."

"How did you accomplish the go-around simulations?" I asked.

"Sir, we used the Manned Flight Simulator (MFS) V-22. It is a 6 degree-of-freedom, non-linear engineering model of the air vehicle."

"So, it's a flight simulator."

"Yes, sir."

"And the results of your simulations?"

"Sir, we ran our tests using four calibrated air speeds, 100, 80, 70, and 60 knots. We evaluated two recovery methods. The first method had the pilot immediately apply full thrust control lever (TCL) power and hold the pitch attitude. The second method had the pilot attempt to gain airspeed. With both engines operating normally, we concluded that the pilot would have been able to accomplish a successful go-around at any point during the approach.

"Our test results also showed that up to the last two to three seconds of flight, the aircraft had go-around performance with one engine inoperative, provided the crew recognized their situation and applied swift corrective measures. At two seconds prior to impact and 80 knots or less airspeed, go-around performance did not exist with one engine inoperative. Our reports concluded the probability of an engine failure less than two seconds from impact to be highly unlikely. Sir, all these facts when examined together, led us to conclude this mishap was related to a loss of situational awareness and not a failure of one of the aircraft's engines."

"Sir, if I may?" O'Leary asked.

"Sure, go ahead."

"Gary, did you get a copy of the simulations we performed in the flight simulator at Hurlburt Field?"

"No, sir, we didn't have that data."

"I compared our data to the data you have in your report. We agree 100% with your dual engine and single engine performance numbers. The thing is our board president never thought or wrote anything about a single engine failure as a substantially contributing factor. Information you were not given included testimony from two people who were on headset the night of the accident. Both remember everything said during the approach. If an engine had failed, there would've been visual and aural (voice) warnings. No one heard a voice warning because a single engine did not fail. The information in your report, while impressive as far as it goes, is extremely flawed."

"Sir, I read the board president's opinion. One of the substantially contributing factors was engine power loss. Did I read that wrong?"

"Yes. Engine power loss on both engines due to compressor stalls. Run simulations in the MFS and test a power loss scenario occurring in the last eighteen seconds of flight. Compare your results to ours. You'll find the crew did not have go-around capability. Also, I disagree with your conclusion of lost situational awareness. If that had happened, there would have been a charred and smoking deep hole at the impact point with no survivors. Instead, as you can see from your picture of the landing gear markings in the sand, the crew was aware of their dire situation and made a remarkable landing saving sixteen lives."

"Sir, I think we're done with questions," Winsett said. "Please read him the legalese so he can get back to work."

I read the narrative and Kelly hung up the phone.

"Does anyone see any reason why we should interview the other engineers?" I asked.

"No, sir," O'Leary said. "They wasted a lot of time getting data we already had. I can't believe they concluded pilot error. It absolutely defies sensible logic."

"Kelly, will you please call the other engineers and cancel our interviews?" I asked.

"Yes, sir."

"It's like Doc remarked yesterday," I said. "They were provided with the pilot error narrative and asked to generate justification for it. We can ignore both reports. We only have one more to assess before writing an updated addendum. Let's look at Dobrinski's two-page report. TSgt Scott, can you get us a white board or some large pieces of white butcher paper we can tape on the walls. We'll go over Dobrinski's calculations together."

"Sir, there's strong language in this report." Dolan said. "He contends the NST's calculation of proprotor rpm provided to us is in gross error. He says, 'The analysis is faulty, and any conclusions drawn should be treated as suspect, if not discarded.' We definitely need to check the calculations again."

Winsett flipped to the second page of the report.

"It looks like he argues about the touchdown speed being wrong, therefore the rpm calculations are wrong."

"Yeah, you're right." I said. "It all comes down to who has correctly calculated the correct landing speed. We may have to revisit the A-10 video to reassess the points we used for our calculation. This may take a while. Anyone need a water or tea to drink?"

O'Leary's face lit up like a Cheshire cat. We could hear him clicking through a document on his laptop computer. I wondered what he was doing.

"Sir, this will only take a couple minutes. TSgt Scott, we won't need anything on the walls. Wait until you see this," he exclaimed.

CHAPTER FORTY SEVEN

ACCIDENT REPORT RELEASED TO MEDIA

O'Leary had sent Dobrinski's worksheet to the national support team (NST) explaining the investigation had been reopened to evaluate additional evidence provided by AFSOC. He told the NST engineers their calculations of rpms using proprotor markings in the sand were determined to be wrong. The NST engineers had a few days to reevaluate the data and cross check their formulas and calculations. O'Leary handed me a copy of an email from John Vulgamore (NST engineer).

"This is Mr. Vulgamore's answer to AFSOC's acquisition of calculations being incorrect." he said.

> *Lt Col O'Leary … during my initial analysis of the poor-quality A-10 video, I decided the CV-22 touched down at 75 knots. When I conducted the analysis, I had no National Technical Means (NTM) resources. Since that time, NTM resources have been made available. I cannot go into detail due to the security classification. If necessary, we can use secure phones or secure email to discuss further for your investigation. Using NTM resources, I determined the CV-22 touched down at 80 knots. I am confident that 80 knots is accurate. The airplane rolled across the ground for exactly 240 feet, from the point of touchdown to the first proprotor mark in the sand. The airplane would have slowed substantially due to the drag through the soft sand. If, for example, we error on the very high side, and use 75 knots as the speed when the first blade hit the sand. The distance to the next blade strike was 7.5 feet. The engine rpm would be 336. If the forward speed was even slower (which it probably was) the rpm would be even lower. The 336 rpm, or less,*

calculation indicates the engines were operating much less than the 100% [normal power]. You have my number. Please call if you have any more questions. [16]

"You're right," I said. "We don't need to waste time with Dobrinski's report.

It's irrelevant. In fact, all of the AFSOC addendum is irrelevant. Let's break for lunch and start writing our addendum when we return. This could not have gone any better or been any easier."

During lunch, we discussed the AFSOC addendum and our required response. O'Leary and I wanted to send back an insulting addendum stating AFSOC has once again wasted precious time and money on submitting faulty additional information for the accident board to review. Winsett and Kelly convinced us to follow protocol and draft a proper response.

Winsett explained, "Sir, you'll have to write another *executive summary* responding to what they call 'new evidence.' We'll summarize the facts and state their relative significance in relation to what we already know."

"What about the testimony from the structures and loads engineer's observation that the airplane's speed after flipping over would be 10% to 50% slower than the touchdown speed?" asked O'Leary. "Can we include that assertion in our report?"

"Yes, with General Harvel's approval," said Kelly.

We returned to the conference room and worked into the night. By the next morning, I'd finished my not-so amended *statement of opinion* and updated *executive summary*.

OPINION SUMMARY

The ASIST engineers did not have all the evidence or resources that were utilized by the accident investigation board to properly evaluate the mishap. Specifically, they had no pilot, maintenance, medical or human factors expertise. They did not have the benefit of imagery analysis or accident investigation board witness interviews. Additionally, ASIST used an erroneous weather source that listed an 11-knot quartering tailwind. The actual wind was a 17-knot tailwind. Finally, during their simulations, they used a constant 504 feet per minute rate of descent instead of the more accurate 1,800 feet per minute rate of descent. I also weighed the ASIST report's assertion that the probability of a single engine failure within the last two to three seconds was highly remote. While engine failures are rare, they are more likely to occur during a high-power demand situation such as landing with a limited power margin.

The ASIST report also concluded that since there was no evidence of a change in the flight path prior to terrain impact, loss of situational awareness caused the mishap. To the contrary, I believe the mishap aircraft's flight path did change. The mishap pilot did have sufficient time to arrest the descent rate in order to land just past three deep wadis, executing a near-perfect roll-on landing. In summary, nothing in the ASIST report caused me to believe that loss of situational awareness was the cause of the mishap by clear and convincing evidence.

The ASIST and structural engineers from NAVAIR prepared extraordinary reports considering the short time frame and limited information they were given. The accident investigation board had previously requested formal engineering and animation support from the Air Force Safety Center and Naval Air Systems Command. Unfortunately, the resources were always unavailable, or reported to be "non-existent."

The convening authority stated that he was unaware of any testimony indicating an aircraft issue during the last 22 seconds of flight. I respectfully disagree. The mission tail scanner testified that there was an "excited conversation" in the cockpit. He described it as, "something catastrophic" going wrong with the airplane between the one-minute call and ground impact. One of the Army Rangers, and his wife, also testified the mission copilot told them something happened after the one-minute warning. The crew was doing everything they could to try to belly land the airplane to save it.

Finally, I analyzed the mishap aircraft's speed in order to validate the calculated proprotor rpm (Nr). The greater weight of credible evidence shows the mishap aircraft's speed was 80 knots at touchdown. The speed, when used *with the distance between initial blade strike marks to calculate Nr, indicates that the Nr was lower than normal. Therefore, I conclude engine power loss was a substantially contributing factor in the mishap.*

EXECUTIVE SUMMARY

On November 15, 2010, the Air Force Chief of Staff reopened the accident investigation. The accident investigation board President and selected members of the accident board considered information prepared after submission of the original report. The board President also consulted with the imagery analyst who performed the initial video analysis for the accident investigation board. The imagery analyst used an updated resource to assess the video and accurately measure distance and the mishap aircraft's speed. The board President determined the mishap aircraft's speed was 80 knots instead of 75 knots as stated in the original report.

After considering the additional information, the board President was still unable to determine a cause by clear and convincing evidence. He considered the speed at initial impact, the aircraft's deceleration rate on the ground during the mishap sequence, and the spacing of the blade strikes on the ground, as well as testimony of crew discussions and computer-generated voice warnings. He determined that the greater weight of credible evidence supports engine power loss as a substantially contributing factor. The Board President's original conclusion that ten factors substantially contributed to the mishap remain unchanged. [17]

I tapped the edges of the several sheets along both edges and waited for my remarks to register with the board.

"Should I add anything else?" I asked.

"Sir, Kelly and I will study this in detail before we submit it," said Winsett.

"It sounds perfect to me, sir," added O'Leary.

We worked for a few more hours before finishing late Saturday afternoon. I released the board members to return to their home bases a day earlier than planned. Again, we parted with considerable emotion. I tempered my pleasure at seeing everyone again by the fear for the careers of the individuals assigned to the investigation. I'd like to think they wouldn't suffer from the reluctance of the senior leadership of Air Force and AFSOC to accept the accident board's honest evaluation of evidence. I had learned not to underestimate how the power and influence of jilted leaders can cause bad things to happen to highlighted subordinates' military careers.

Winsett delivered the addendum to AFSOC on Monday morning. I had little confidence AFSOC leaders would invest time to read the report. They would cut to the addendum before considering if it would be worthwhile to read the entire report. AFSOC would not be satisfied accepting the report and the unchanged tenth contributing factor of power loss. After three attempts to change the cause of the accident to "pilot error," they would forever deny the evidence and the truth of what caused the accident to occur.

The AFSOC Public Affairs office worked overtime preparing for public release of the accident report. They braced for the onslaught of media who would dissect the findings of the investigation and requests for additional information. I hoped the families would be briefed and provided a full copy of the accident report before Thanksgiving Day. At that point, I had no influence on what did or did not happen. Once again, I settled into my home routine and military retirement.

The evening of December 16th, my wife and I arrived home from the grocery store. As I carried in bags, I noticed we had messages on the telephone answering machine. I listened to the first message.

"This is Bob Cox from the *Fort Worth Star-Telegram*. I am calling for Brigadier General Don Harvel. Could you please return my call at your earliest convenience?"

I wrote down his name and skipped to the next message.

"General Harvel, this is Robert Dorr from the *Air Force Times* magazine. I read the AFSOC news release and your executive summary from the CV-22 accident investigation. I would like to discuss the results of your investigation at your earliest convenience please."

I wrote a one-line note and listened to the next message.

"I'm looking for retired Brigadier General Don Harvel. My name is Bruce Rolfsen. I write for the *Military Times*. I would appreciate a call back as soon as possible."

"General Harvel, this is David Axe. Please call me at your soonest opportunity."

AFSOC must have released the accident report earlier in the day. The calls were from reporters who read the press release or portions of the accident report. I googled "CV-22 AIB Report." Numerous sources popped up, each with links to the accident report. I clicked on the AFSOC news release. The first three paragraphs gave background information about the accident. The fourth paragraph discussed the ten substantially contributing factors from my opinion. The fifth paragraph stated:

CV-22 Accident Investigation Board Results Released

> *The Convening Authority approved the board president's report, with comments. While legally sufficient, the assessed evidence in the accident investigation board report did not support a determination of engine power loss as one of the ten substantially contributing factors. The Convening Authority made this decision based upon evidence in the accident investigation board report, and through additional analysis of the evidence. The primary purpose of the accident investigation board was to provide a publicly releasable report of the facts and circumstances surrounding the accident. Please contact the Air Force Special Operations Command Public Affairs Office for a link to view the entire report.* [18]

AFSOC leaders and public affairs personnel stopped talking to me in August … the day I turned in the accident report. The news release gave me insight as to what the convening authority (Dobrinski) wrote after reading my response to the weak AFSOC addendum. The news media quickly picked up on the fact that there was a difference of opinion regarding the cause of the Osprey accident. It all came down me saying power loss substantially contributed to the accident and the convening authority saying that it didn't. Me stating the Osprey went into a sudden and rapid descent and the crew attempted to go-around, but engine power loss prevented the maneuver versus the convening authority thinking it did not happen that way ... the crew lost situational awareness and hit the ground ... pilot error.

I had nothing to gain from a contentious battle with AFSOC or the media. I prepared to meet their microscopic examination of what I had written and to defend my conclusions.

Design engineers and test pilots plan for a multitude of controllable malfunctions. They provide crews with the tools and knowledge to deal with them safely. Failure outside this regime ... a wing falls off, all engines fail, a fuselage splits apart in mid-air ... these fall into the category of "unacceptable or catastrophic failures." There are no emergency procedures published for dealing with such failures. But, as improbable as they are, they happen ... a DC-10 loses all hydraulic pressure to the flight controls, or birds take out two engines of an Airbus A-320 airplane after takeoff from New York's LaGuardia airport. What stands between ultimate disaster and safety, or a lesser catastrophe, is the crew. Sometimes, all the crew can do is mitigate a tragedy.

I marshalled my resolve and recalled the facts supporting my assessment of the accident and called Mr. Cox of the *Fort Worth Star Telegram*. We spoke for twenty minutes. He focused his questions on facts and spoke in a direct manner. He ended by saying his story would be published the following morning.

Cox, Robert. Findings on Osprey Crash Overturned.

Ft. Worth Star-Telegram. December 17, 2010.

Senior Air Force generals overturned the findings of their own investigation team and ruled the fatal crash of a CV-22 Osprey in Afghanistan last April was largely due to flight crew mistakes and not a mechanical problem. But *the general who led the crash investigation said Thursday that there was strong evidence to indicate the $87 million plus aircraft, which has a history of technical problems, experienced engine trouble in the final seconds leading to the crash. In his report, Harvel wrote that the preponderance of evidence pointed to an engine problem. "It is unlikely that this very experienced and competent [pilot] would have chosen to execute a roll-on landing on rough terrain if he had power available to go-around and set up for another approach."*

But the senior Air Force officer who ordered the investigation disagreed. "I find the preponderance of evidence does not support a determination of engine loss as a substantially contributing factor," said Maj Gen Dobrinski, vice commander of Air Force Special Operations Command, wrote in a response that stands as the official Air Force position.

Release of the public investigation report had been delayed for months due to internal Air Force wrangling.

Brian Alexander, a prominent New York aviation safety lawyer and former Army helicopter pilot, said the official Air Force response to the accident report showed the service leadership is more interested in preserving the controversial V-22 than the safety of its own personnel. [19]

I also participated in an interview with the *Air Force Times* a few weeks later. The following article was published as the headline story.

Rolfsen, Bruce. Generals Clash Over Osprey Crash.

Air Force Times. January 17, 2011:

One says engine problems caused deaths, his boss faults the crew – and no evidence can settle the dispute. In a rare public display of disunity, two generals are at serious odds over the cause of a fatal aircraft accident. Brig Gen Don Harvel, president of the accident investigation board, said he believes engine problems brought down the special operation's Osprey on its landing approach. Maj Gen Kent Dobrinski, to whom Harvel answered during the investigation, argues aircrew errors caused the crash. Despite his strong disagreement with Harvel's conclusion, Dobrinski signed off on the report November 23rd because Air Force accident investigation rules left him little choice. With the investigation finally wrapped up, Air Force Special Operations Command leaders began meeting with families and survivors to explain the conclusions. Usually, the board president handles the duty, but Harvel was not invited. Harvel was not asked to meet with service members and families because he had retired, said AFSOC spokesman Lt Col Randy Rogel. Harvel sees the exclusion as AFSOC's snub of his opinion. "I thought they were very wrong not to let me brief the families," he said. "I had gathered a lot of insight and kept personal notes to share with each family. I even volunteered to brief the families at no expense to the government. My request wasn't acknowledged. [20]

Requests for interviews waned then ceased altogether within a few weeks. I had expected interest in the story to fade over time.

I remained interested and held the aircraft accident investigation process in high regard. I volunteered to attend National Transportation Safety Board (NTSB) accident investigation courses. I had just returned home after attending the first course, when my cell phone rang.

No name appeared on my cell screen and I didn't recognize the number from which the call originated.

"Hello," I said.

"Hi. Is this Brigadier General Harvel?"

"Yes."

"My name is Jill Voas. My husband died in the Osprey accident you investigated."

CHAPTER FORTY EIGHT

WIFE OF MAJOR RANDY VOAS

I had not expected to hear from any family members after I completed the accident investigation and retired. I had been told Jill Voas did not regard AFSOC's explanations with any degree of confidence and trust. She didn't pass on opportunities to press the command for answers to her many questions. I had looked forward to meeting her in an official capacity to debrief our investigation and express my regard for her husband and sympathy for her family.

On a cool and rainy Georgia night in January of 2010, I would finally have the opportunity to hear what the deceased pilot's wife thought about the accident investigation board report and my opinion of the accident.

"General Harvel, excuse me for bothering you, do you have a few minutes to talk?" she asked.

"Hi. I'm surprised, but very pleased, to hear from you. Of course, I have time. How are you and your family doing?"

"We are still struggling. Every day is a challenge for the children, and especially for me."

"Please accept my most heartfelt sympathy for your loss. I'm so sorry," I said.

"Thank you, sir. I don't mean to seem angry and frustrated, but that's what I am. I apologize for intruding on your private life, but if you have a few minutes to answer questions?"

"Of course, what do you want to know?"

"Sir … first, thank you. Thank you for having the courage to write the truth about the accident. Thank you for your integrity to stand up against the people who pressured you to tell their skewed version of the truth. You've given me and my kids hope. My deceased husband is not here to defend his honor and the truth … he was a hero when he made decisions during that early morning flight on April 9th … and saved sixteen lives. I want my children to grow up knowing their father was a hero. It makes my heart sick to read media accounts attributing the accident to pilot error. I know it's not true. Every day, I have to wake up and smile … but inside I just want to die. The pain does not go away … even with time. Now, thanks to your accident report, I know something went wrong with the airplane's engines, forcing my husband to attempt a night roll-on landing."

"I'm at a loss for words," I said. "I regret I was not allowed to brief the families … especially your family. Your husband was a great officer and outstanding pilot. The more I learned about him during the accident investigation, the more I wished I could have met him. I can't imagine the grief you and your family have gone through."

"Sir, to be honest, it's a struggle. I have a giant hole in my heart. I lost the love of my life, my soul mate. Our children will grow up without the influence of a wonderful father. I never knew it was possible to cry so many tears, and I still can't stop. I thought there'd come a time when, but …"

She struggled with her composure but recovered venting her disappointment in the AFSOC leadership who sought to throw her husband and his crew "under the bus" in order to protect the Air Force and the Osprey from more negative scrutiny.

"When the AFSOC general and his support staff came to my home to brief the accident investigation report, they never mentioned anything about loss of engine power. They looked me in the eye and lied. I was getter angrier by the minute. I couldn't stand for them to be in my … Randy's house. Since then, I've read the accident report cover to cover. I highlighted, and tabbed parts of the report that make no sense to me. I helped Randy study for many hours. I feel like I know quite a bit about the mission and the airplane. While reading the report, there was a reference to a video of the accident taken by an A-10 airplane. My copy of the report had a special page for a compact disk (CD), but it had been removed from my report. The morning following the briefing at my house, I drove to AFSOC Headquarters and demanded to see the commander. I was escorted upstairs to the command suite. They told me Lt Gen Becker was out of town. I was told Maj Gen Dobrinski would be meeting with me.

"Before we exchanged the first word, I demanded to see the video. He excused himself and placed a couple of phone calls. Before I knew it, officers were filing into the office. They sat me at a conference table in front of a laptop and without a word of introduction of themselves or the video, I watched the last half minute of my husband's life.

"I asked them to play it a second time and saw what appeared to be faint white smoke streaming off the wings in the seconds before the aircraft touched down. I asked them to enlarge the video and slow it down so I could see it again. After three times, I asked about the white smoke coming off the wings ... what is the white smoke coming from? They looked at one another like little boys caught with their hands in a cookie jar looking for an excuse. I waited for an answer. Dobrinski, like he'd just seen the video for the first time, asked the squadron commander (Compton) about the white puffs trailing the aircraft. 'Hot sand' ... Compton told me ... like I would believe sand could stream off the wings of an airplane in flight and appear white (cold) in an infrared video. Hot sand ... really? That's what they told me. More lies. I demanded a copy of the CD, which AFSOC reluctantly provided a day later. The fact that senior officers could be so callous sickened me. I pitied the junior officers and enlisted who work for them. Who are *their* heroes?"

I'd said little thus far. I was very impressed with her knowledge of infrared and the fact she noticed the white smoke/vapor trail on the wings of the airplane as it descended to the ground. She said nothing that had not been discussed, many times, around the accident investigation board conference table.

"I apologize, sir," she said. "I'm rambling. You should know how much your report means to me. To me, and my kids, this report provides proof their dad was not the cause of the accident. I have a few questions. Would you mind if I emailed them to you?"

"Please, send me your questions. I'll answer them as quickly as I can. Would you mind if I ask you a question?"

"No, sir, go ahead."

"Please tell me about your husband."

"Sir, he was a calm, confident, reserved, and humble man, with a dry wit. A kind, loving, trusting husband and father who at times could be very serious … and very silly. To get him excited, I'd call him 'monotone man.' He was a confident and proud military pilot. He never boasted about his many achievements. He shunned military politics. He just wanted to fly.

"One of the happiest days of his life was when he reported to flight school and started a career that made him a warrant officer flying the Apache helicopter. Whether a student or instructor, he strove for perfection. He was known for sharing experiences and techniques not found in flight manuals. He loved the world of aviation.

"His two children made him proud. He would beam when a stranger commented on their resemblance to him. Both in appearance, mannerisms and interests. Randy loved spending time with his kids. He tended to their every simple need. He read them bedtime stories and proudly doted on them. He hated their sad faces when they got in trouble for misbehaving. He refused to make them feel worse. I was the disciplinarian of the family.

"He loved cycling, swimming, and running. He spent countless hours outdoors with our daughter, who also loved running. In 1992, while stationed in Germany, we attended a stage of the Tour de France bike race. It was a dream trip for him. He loved watching bicycle racing.

"Unlike many of his comrades and peers, and under advice from his grandfather, Randy rarely consumed alcohol. His favorite drink being a cola of any brand.

"Randy seldom showed emotion or raised his voice, though I knew him to be more sensitive than he ever let on. He spoke in a low hushed manner, a monotone that became high pitched when he got excited or angry.

"He appreciated the camaraderie of friends but didn't need or cultivate it. He accepted everything for what it was and didn't attempt to culture events or his family to meet his personal expectations.

"True to the axiom that opposites attract, we fit together like pieces of a jigsaw puzzle, our whole being larger than either of us could expect to be separately. My heart aches for him constantly. No words could describe how much I miss him."

The clock on the mantle told me I had been on the phone for over ninety minutes. Sensing the end of our conversation, Jill asked if she could share a personal story with me.

"Sir, before going to bed the night of April 7th (in Afghanistan), Randy had set his alarm for 5:30 a.m. on April 8th (in Afghanistan). When the alarm woke him, he carried a satellite phone into the dark, cool Kandahar morning looking for a quiet and private location. He wanted to talk without disturbing the other crewmembers who were still sleeping nearby. He dialed our home number and I answered. It was a few minutes after 8:00 p.m. (Florida time) on April 7th. Excited to hear his voice, I called the children to come say hello to their dad. They exchanged small talk for a few moments. Eventually, I shared news about a puppy we saw at a nearby pet shop. The kids reengaged in the conversation now that the puppy was the main topic. I remembered his reaction … 'Oh no, we don't need more pets,' he said laughingly.

"I knew the decision to get a new puppy was totally up to me. Over the years, Randy always trusted me to make financial and other household decisions. Randy would support my decision 100%. The kids told their father they loved him and handed the phone back to me.

"The next afternoon, April 8th, I loaded my sister, Julie, and the kids into the car and headed for the pet shop. We made one stop along the way, finally arriving at the pet shop at about 3:05 p.m. The kids were very excited about the prospect of bringing a new puppy home. They ran into the store and headed directly to the puppy's crate. My daughter opened the door and removed the puppy from the crate. They begged me to let them bring the puppy home. They shared the excitement of the moment by passing the puppy from person to person. As they tried to hand the puppy to me, I felt something was very wrong.

"An intense anxiety washed over me, sending chills cursing down my spine and raising the hairs on the nape of my neck. Overcome with a strange sense of dread, I told my sister and the children we needed to go immediately. I turned and quickly walked to the car. Julie, sensing something very strange was happening, put the puppy back into its crate and ushered the very disappointed kids toward the car. I motioned for everyone to hurry up and get in. The kids did not understand and persisted in asking why they couldn't bring the puppy home? I shushed them and whispered to Julie that I sensed something was wrong with Randy. I wanted him to call. I was overwhelmed with dread. I had an unexplainable need to be home. I had to be by our telephone, just in case Randy called again.

"I seldom concerned myself with Randy's safety when he deployed … until that day and at that time. The rest of the afternoon and evening I remained huddled with the house phone in one hand and my cell phone in my other hand. I'd never experienced such a feeling of anxiety. I asked my sister if she thought something might be wrong with me. She assured me I was fine and told me to get some rest.

"I went to bed but couldn't sleep. I stared incessantly at a framed picture with the word *Dream* printed in large letters, hanging on the wall directly in front of the bed. If Randy would just call, I would be all right. I prayed for him to call. I needed to hear his voice. If he would call and just say 'Hi,' then I would be okay. My anxiety built with each passing minute.

"A few minutes after 11:00 p.m., I heard a faint knock at the front door. My heart raced and pounded in my chest. My mind went crazy with thoughts. Somehow, I got out of bed and walked to the landing at the top of the stairway. I looked down at the front door. The door had frosted glass panels on each side. I could see blurry figures through the glass. I rubbed my eyes. It looked like the people at the front door were wearing blue uniforms. I screamed for Julie as loud as I could. My knees folded underneath me like pieces of warm spaghetti. I struggled to get to my feet but couldn't. I thought if I didn't answer the door the pending nightmare would go away. After many minutes, I marshalled the strength to get to the door with my sister's help. I unlocked the door and slowly turned the knob to open it.

Two uniformed Air Force officers greeted me from the stoop and asked me my name. When I couldn't answer, they pulled me back into reality by saying my name. I only remember the words 'your husband,' then screamed, 'No, not Randy, no,' as my sister wrapped me in her arms and held me tight.

"That night and the following days seemed like a tear-filled blur of hurt and pain. I remembered the pet store and the time, 3:10 p.m. (Florida time), almost the same minute that Randy's airplane impacted the ground in Afghanistan.

"That's when it started, sir. It's not over. My husband doesn't deserve the blame."

CHAPTER FORTY NINE

MORE POWER LOSS ACCIDENTS

The months passed by quickly as I refocused my time on family, work, and safety projects for the Air Line Pilots Association. It had been over a year since anyone had called to ask me questions about the Osprey or the accident investigation.

In March of 2012, I started getting calls from Japanese media, including newspapers and television stations. Apparently, news had leaked out about the U.S. Marine Corps plan to base twenty-four V-22s at the controversial Marine Corps Air Station (MCAS) Futenma. The Ospreys would replace the retiring CH-53s stationed at the base. The Futenma base is in the city of Ginowan, on the island of Okinawa. For years the relocation of the base had been, and still is, a major political issue for the U.S. and Japan. The local Japanese people protested the base for many years, fearing the Marine Corps flying operations endangered the local civilian population. Hearing the aging CH-53s would be replaced by MV-22s added fuel to the fiery protests, not only by Japanese civilians, but also by Japanese politicians.

As a Japanese television crew set up equipment at my home, I asked the interviewer why they wanted my opinion. She responded the Japanese media had read the news stories about my Osprey accident investigation.

"Our research indicates you will tell us the truth. You will be getting more calls from other Japanese media outlets," she said.

She was right. I conducted three telephone and two more television interviews over the next week and a half. Every interviewer asked a few questions about the accident investigation. Most questions were about the danger of the V-22 flying over a large Japanese civilian population. I was told about a CH-53 crash, or controlled emergency landing, depending on whose version (the U.S. Marine Corps or Japanese officials) of the report. The CH-53 damaged a building on a university campus near the military base. No one was hurt on the ground, primarily because the university was closed for a scheduled student break. The accident served as a reminder of the threat to the city's population. During each interview, I expressed I was not an opponent of the Osprey. I told them the V-22 would not pose a higher degree of danger to the local population than the CH-53.

The controversy of basing Ospreys in Japan became more difficult and complicated after a MV-22 crashed in Morocco on April 11, 2012. The copilot was flying. He lifted the airplane off the ground and made a right 180 degree turn when the Osprey was twenty feet off the ground. After turning, he began lowering the angle of the MV-22's nacelles to convert to the airplane mode of flying. Within three seconds, the nacelles moved from 87 degrees to 71 degrees, below the allowable level for the phase of flight. The copilot violated a warning in the MV-22 flight manual stating severe pitch down and altitude loss can occur if nacelles are rotated too far forward too quick of a rate after takeoff. As the copilot felt the Osprey's nose begin to plunge downward, he pulled the cyclic control stick full aft. The nose continued downward until the airplane hit the ground at a 45 to 60-degree angle, just fifteen seconds into the flight. The pilot and copilot survived. The two Marine crew chiefs, sitting behind the cockpit, were killed.

Japanese and U.S. officials agreed the MV-22s would not fly in Japan until the results of the accident investigation were determined and briefed to Japanese officials.

On Wednesday, June 13, 2012, I had just finished an early dinner in Seattle, Washington when my cell phone lit up with numerous text messages. As I started to read the first message, my phone rang. I recognized the number and immediately answered.

"Sir, how are you?" said the familiar voice of MSgt (retired) Bryan Scott. "Check the news when you can. Also, look at some of the links I've texted to you. A CV-22 crashed at Eglin AFB a few hours ago. The news is going crazy here at Fort Walton Beach."

"Were there survivors?" I asked.

"Sir, the news is reporting five crewmembers were taken to the hospital. No word yet on casualties or extent of injuries. But I thought you should know the copilot from the Afghanistan accident, Major Brian Luce, was one of the pilots flying the airplane. I wanted to make sure you knew about the crash; you'll probably be getting media calls very soon. I'll keep sending you information as it is released."

"Thanks. I appreciate your call Scotty. Send me a link if any of the local news stations report on the status of the crew."

The next morning, I found a news story verifying all five crewmembers survived. I was called by two national news channels to provide a sound bite about the Air Force accident investigation process.

A few days later, multiple news stories were published that confirmed Maj Brian Luce was the aircraft commander of the mishap airplane that crashed at Eglin AFB. The stories also linked him to be the copilot of the Osprey that crashed in Afghanistan in April 2010. They went on to say that Maj Luce suffered undisclosed injuries but was released from the hospital two days after the accident. The 1st SOW commander said:

"The results of the Accident Investigation Board will guide our decisions. If there's some misbehavior on the part of the crew or if they performed in a way that was unsatisfactory, it's too early to say whether they will face disciplinary action. Currently, there is no reason to suspect mechanical flaws."

The wing commander confirmed the mishap airplane was the number two airplane in a two-ship formation flying in the Eglin AFB range conducting live-fire training.

The Japanese Ministry of Defense and Ministry of Foreign Affairs reiterated the MV-22s would not fly in Japanese airspace until the Morocco and the Eglin accident investigations were completed and the findings personally briefed to Japanese officials.

Both investigations were completed by the end of July. The Japanese officials were invited to the Pentagon to be briefed in August of 2012. After the briefing, the officials cleared the Marine Corps to start MV-22 operations in Japan at the end of September 2012.

On May 18, 2015, I was contacted by ABC World News reporter, Randee Elaine, to make a brief statement about a deadly V-22 accident in Hawaii.

"I haven't had a chance to gather information about the accident. Is there something about the accident that led you to me?" I asked.

"It's still early, and we know there will be an accident investigation, but videos of the accident make it appear the engine power could be suspect. We would like to get your comments concerning the engine power issue on the accident you investigated in Afghanistan."

The reporter asked a few questions about the Osprey ... nothing about the Hawaii accident. The interview gave me the incentive and piqued my interest to follow the story until the investigation was complete. Speculation was growing about engine power loss being a factor. After a week, the story disappeared from the news and publications. All eyes were turned to the Marine Corps Judge Advocate General Manual (JAGMAN) to complete the investigation and publish a report of the findings. In September 2015, I received an email from Bill Sweetman, a writer for *Aviation Week and Space Technology* magazine. He attached a copy of the completed JAGMAN report and asked if I would please comment on the published findings. I opened the attachment and my jaw fell open in shock as I read the first two sentences of the report:

> *A JAGMAN investigation attributes the accident to repeated, sustained flight time in brownout conditions while attempting to land, causing **compressor surge and abrupt power loss** on the left Rolls-Royce AE1107C turboshaft engine. Sand and dust ingestion from the rotor wash caused significant material buildup on the turbine blades.*[21]

I was shocked to see the words "compressor surge and abrupt power loss" in the report. I immediately emailed two pages of comments to Mr.

Sweetman. His article, with my comments, appeared in the *Aviation Week and Space Technology* magazine on October 19, 2015:

> *Investigation of a fatal accident in May involving a Bell-Boeing MV-22 Osprey tiltrotor transport, points to an undiagnosed failure mode in the Osprey's trouble-prone propulsion system and has resulted in tight restrictions on restricted visibility landing (RVL) operations. The preliminary report findings – disclosed in documents obtained by Aviation Week – also reopen questions about an April 2010 fatal accident involving a U.S. Air Force CV-22 in Afghanistan. In that case, a senior officer dismissed investigators' focus on engine problems and put blame on the pilots.*
>
> *A major modification to fix the Osprey's perennial problem – damage to engines caused by the dense and high-energy dust cloud the aircraft creates when landing on any loose surface – is under development, but testing will not be completed until late 2017 and the cost and time to retrofit the fleet is unknown. The fleet wide engine life remains a fraction of the goal for other helicopter engines. If the problem could be fixed, Bell suggests it would increase engine life by a factor of eight.*
>
> *Two U.S. Marines died, and the two pilots and eighteen other occupants were injured May 17 when an MV-22 crashed while attempting a restricted visibility landing (RVL) at Bellows Air Force Station on Oahu, Hawaii.*
>
> *The MV-22 experienced a compressor surge and abrupt power loss in the left-hand engine at an altitude of less than 150 feet, during the second incursion into a RVL for the mission, according to a Naval Air Systems Command (NAVAIR) status report issued September 9. The V-22's*

cross-shafting system and pilot inputs kept the aircraft in level flight, but the pilots were unable to control the rate of descent. The second Osprey in the formation also lost power and was a "near-miss" for an accident.

The likely cause of the power loss, according to the document, was the engine ingested sand containing reactive materials – classified as calcium, magnesium, aluminum and silicon compounds - which melted in the combustor and solidified on the fixed first-stage turbine vane. This restricted airflow and reduced surge margin, but indications of these conditions to the aircrew "are not sufficient," the report says. Throttle movement can trigger a surge with no other warning.

The NAVAIR report identifies three earlier surge (stall) events related to reactive sand, one of which – on August 26, 2013, at Creech AFB, Nevada – resulted in a Class A mishap (an accident that involves death, or a total and permanent disability, or the aircraft is totally destroyed, or the aircraft suffers more than $2 million of damage) and the loss of the aircraft in a post impact fire. In addition, surveys of flight operations have found six more "rapid power loss events."

The newly discovered risk factors in the Hawaii accident parallel known information about the first Osprey combat loss, an Air Force CV-22 that crashed in Afghanistan in April 2010. An investigation board headed by Brig Gen Donald Harvel concluded – from video of the accident, rotor strike marks on the ground and other evidence – the aircraft had experienced sudden power loss, forcing the crew to attempt a rolling landing that ended in a crash after the nose wheel collapsed and the aircraft struck a ditch. Significantly, in view of the recent findings, the investigators noted that the left-hand engine air particle separator (EAPS) had failed in *dusty conditions shortly before the accident and subsequent to the last performance check.*

But Lt Gen (promoted after departing AFSOC for a follow-on assignment in 2011) Kent Dobrinski, vice commander of Air Force Special Operations Command, the convening authority for the investigation board, ruled that engine power loss could not be considered a major factor in the accident, and issued a statement contrary to the mishap report. "The probability of an engine failure, less than two seconds prior to impact, was assessed as being highly remote," Dobrinski wrote – although this appears to have happened in Hawaii.

Today, Harvel tells Aviation Week that the findings are "definitely a possible explanation" for the Afghanistan accident. "They suddenly went into a 2,000 feet per minute rate of descent while less than 200 feet above the ground. If the pilot had appropriate power, there is no doubt in my mind that he would have applied go-around power to get away from the ground and return back to the nearby forward operating base."

In the course of the investigation, Harvel says, the team studied how the V-22 would respond to a sudden power loss. "Even though the pilot commands maximum power, the good engine can only give so much [FADEC limited] and the power demand does not equate to changing blade pitch," he says. "Instead, the flight control system prioritizes rotor rpm over blade pitch – it will reduce the pitch to keep rpm up. The next bad thing to happen in that sequence is for the good engine to be tasked so much that it also compressor surges/stalls." [22]

The article not only gave credibility to the power loss finding of my accident investigation report, but it also addressed the probability of compressor stalls on both engines. Probability has nothing to do with accident investigations. It all comes down to facts and the story the facts tell.

In January of 2016, another article titled, "Forty-Five Seconds," was published in *War is Boring* magazine by Matthew Gault, Joseph Trevithick, Kevin Knodell, David Axe and Robert Beckhusen:

Forty-five seconds of swirling dust was all it took to kill two U.S. Marines and injure twenty other service members. On May 17, 2015, a Marine Corps V-22 Osprey tiltrotor flew into a cloud of sand kicked up by its rotors while the transport was landing on the island of Oahu as part of a training exercise. The Osprey's engines, which run unusually hot owing to the tiltrotor's ungainly aerodynamics, sucked in the unexpectedly fine sand. The Pentagon had advised V-22 pilots that their finicky aircraft could withstand such dust clouds for sixty seconds before risking a major problem. But, on that May morning, the V-22 suffered a catastrophic engine failure after just forty-five seconds of breathing dust. Two Marines – Lance Corporals Joshua Barron and Matthew Determan – died when the transport tumbled to the ground and burst into flames. In the aftermath of the crash, the military amended its flight rules for the V-22, advising that pilots evacuate a dust cloud after just 35 seconds instead of a full minute. The policy change might seem like a tacit acknowledgment that the Osprey and the Pentagon bureaucracy that set the rules for flying the tiltrotor – rather than the pilots of the crashed aircraft – was to blame for the Oahu fatalities. [23]

The pilots involved in the Hawaii accident didn't violate any aircraft operating regulations or limits. The engine lost power due to sand ingestion. The engine air particle separators were proven to be inadequate. The time for V-22s to be in dust during landings was lowered from sixty seconds to thirty-five seconds, six weeks after the accident. I was shocked and disgusted … how could the pilots be blamed for this accident? Somehow, they were. "Pilot error" was the official cause stated by the investigation board's conclusion. The accident report accused the pilots of not accomplishing an adequate risk assessment of the landing zone. Pilots could be blamed for every accident in the history of aviation using that flawed logic. Pilots always conduct risk assessments. It is the nature of the job. Assess risk, mitigate it properly, and proceed accordingly.

Attached to the magazine article was a PowerPoint™ presentation given by the V-22 Engineering Team on September 9, 2015. The presentation covered "Rapid Power Loss and Surge during Reduced Visibility Landings (RVLs)." It was a detailed presentation explaining the effect of dirt or sand on the Osprey Rolls-Royce engines. I expected the presentation would explain what happened in Hawaii. I was very surprised to see the engineering team admitted the Hawaii V-22 event was not the first-time compressor stall was positively identified as a "contributing factor" for an accident or incident. How many accidents or incidents does it take before an airplane or engine manufacturer decides "enough is enough?"

CHAPTER FIFTY

CONCLUSION -
WHAT REALLY HAPPENED

At the bottom of the first page of the NAVAIR PowerPoint™ presentation was a list of four compressor stall/surge events to date. The May 17, 2015, Hawaii accident was at the top of the list, clearly indicating it was the fourth Osprey accident involving compressor stalls. Disruption of the airflow through the compressor section of the engine, which causes a compressor stall, was the primary cause of accidents on February 24, 2015, December 1, 2013, and August 29, 2013. It was remarkable to see that NAVAIR was publicly admitting a problem with engine power loss due to compressor stalls.

The April 9, 2010, CV-22 Afghanistan accident should have been on the list; however, without the 100% concrete-hard evidence of power loss, it would never be added. The sad part is the Afghanistan accident was not the first time a compressor stall/surge caused an accident or incident. Pilots knew "other pilots" who had a sudden power loss and had to land airplanes in fields and even a parking lot, prior to the Afghanistan accident. A deficiency report published by Detachment 1, 18th Flight Test Squadron (performing an Operational Utility Evaluation (OUE) at Edwards AFB, CA in 2006), published a report titled "Engine Degrades During Austere Environment Hovers." The testing was a prerequisite for certifying the CV-22 training unit at Kirtland AFB, NM. The report details tests of hovering over dirt, resulting in quickly degraded engine power. Despite numerous requests, I was never able to get information about these known events from NAVAIR during our accident investigation. The battle of hiding engine power loss facts about the Afghanistan accident and other incidents involving power loss was won by AFSOC and NAVAIR public affairs until the V-22 accident occurred in Hawaii. But the public relations war is not over. I believe the truth about what really happened at thirty-nine minutes after midnight on April 9, 2010, will eventually prevail.

Many people will wonder why I took the time to write this book. I wanted the truth about the accident and the accident investigation to be shared. I wanted the people affected by the accident - the families, the four heroes who lost their lives, and the others on board the Osprey who were injured to varying degrees to know what really happened. None of the survivors have ever been told why the accident occurred. French philosopher Voltaire once said, "To the living we owe respect, to the dead we owe only the truth."

On May 6, 2016, CBS news correspondent David Martin reported the following story about the V-22 accident that took the lives of nineteen Marines in Arizona on April 8, 2000:

> *After sixteen years, two Marine Corps widows saw their husbands vindicated. The Pentagon now says the two pilots were unfairly blamed for the fatal crash of a V-22 Osprey in April of 2000.*
>
> *A review of the investigation found no fault with the airplane, but says the pilots were not adequately trained and weren't warned about potentially dangerous flight maneuvers.*
>
> *The two Marine widows and their families met with the Deputy Secretary of Defense to hear their late husbands cleared of blame for the deadly crash. Brooke Gruber was eight months old when it happened and has grown up with the shadow hanging over her father.*
>
> *"Did your father cause the crash, since he was the pilot?" Brooke said friends would ask her. Brooke would reply, "Of course not."*
>
> *The two pilots, Lt Col John Brow and Maj Brooks Gruber, were killed instantly along with seventeen other Marines.*
>
> *Announcing the findings of the accident investigation, a Marine Corps press release stated, "the fatal factor," was Brow and Gruber's decision to complete that night's mission*

by attempting a landing that required them to descend too rapidly.

For Connie Gruber, that made the loss of her husband even more painful.

"It felt like he had died once in the Arizona desert and it felt like he died again in the press," Gruber said. She said by using the phrase "the fatal factor," the Marines appeared to basically protect the aircraft over the pilots."

At the time of the crash, the V-22 with its revolutionary tilt-rotor technology was a controversial aircraft in danger of being cancelled.

"I felt betrayed for my husband," Gruber said.

Finally, Deputy Defense Secretary Bob Work – himself a former Marine – reviewed the evidence and issued a letter, which read, "I disagree that the pilots' drive to accomplish the mission was 'the fatal factor' that contributed to the accident."

"I knew right then that that's exactly what we needed to have said publicly," Gruber said.

Work concluded, "I hope this letter will provide the widows… some solace after years in which the blame for the…accident was incorrectly interpreted…to be primarily attributed to their husbands."

When she received the letter, Gruber said, "We went out to the cemetery, my daughter and I, and we placed it on the grave."

We rubbed our hands across his name, and we said, "This is your legacy," Brooke Gruber said. "Now it's honorable and you can finally rest in peace, the way you should have sixteen years ago." [24]

In 2002, Connie Gruber had enlisted the help of her Congressman, Representative Walter Jones (Republican from North Carolina) to push the Pentagon to review the accident and reverse the unfair blame placed on the pilots. Jones made the cause a personal quest. He made over 150 speeches on the floor of the U.S. House of Representatives to bring attention to the family's request. In every speech, he asked for a military review and an elimination of blaming the pilots for the accident. Once he heard the news that the Pentagon would publish a letter of apology to the families of Lt Col John "Boot" Brow and Maj Brooks "Chucky" Gruber, Congressman Jones announced he would make one more speech on the floor of the House, this time in celebration of the pilots' vindication.

The U.S. Air Force and Air Force Special Operations Command (AFSOC) owe the same type of apology to the families of Maj Randell Voas and SMSgt James Lackey. They performed heroically in dealing with the engine power loss issue they suddenly encountered in the final seconds of their mission on April 9th. It would take courage, honor, and integrity for the Air Force and AFSOC to admit they mistakenly blamed the crew for an accident that was engine power related. The future will tell whether the Air Force, and especially AFSOC, has the moral courage to admit the error of their unforgivable actions. The command had concluded "pilot error" within days of the accident. Rather than finding a theory which fit all the facts, they looked for facts to fit a convenient theory. Every decision was based on protecting the CV-22, the platform of the future for the command. It had to be protected from public and political scrutiny for funding to continue to flow. Pilot error was a convenient way to resolve the cause of the accident and quickly move on with procuring more money to maintain and purchase Ospreys.

It has been a decade since the accident. Amazingly, it still strikes a deep emotional tone among the AFSOC CV-22 community. They are still reeling from this tragic event that caught the command by surprise. The fact that AFSOC did not deal with the accident openly and honestly has haunted CV-22 crews to this day. Not only are surviving families still hurting from the way the event was handled, even some of the subsequent events meant to commemorate the accident and the crew are shockingly ill-planned and disrespectful to the families of the wrongfully blamed pilot and flight engineer.

On April 6, 2017, Boeing donated a large CV-22 replica to be permanently displayed in the middle of a roundabout at Hurlburt Field. The model was donated to showcase the capabilities of the CV-22 and to show appreciation of their partnership with the Air Force. Distinguished guests were entertained by speakers and the unveiling of the CV-22 model with the tail number "0031" blazed in white paint on the tail of the airplane. The event marked a generous gesture by Boeing, but it was truly disrespectful to the families of those killed in the accident, as well as those who were injured and not invited to the event. Once again, the wives and children of the affected crewmembers were left angry and heartbroken.

"Neither me, nor Cassie Lackey (wife of deceased flight engineer SMSgt Lackey) knew

anything about the event," said Jill Voas (wife of deceased pilot Maj Voas). "I just shake my head and swallow these inconsiderate oversights. Being told you'll always be part of the 'AFSOC family' seems like such a hollow promise. It hurts to be disregarded by the command our husbands served so faithfully and honorably."

In March of 2018, AFSOC honored Major Voas and Senior Master Sergeant Lackey by naming streets and dedicating busts of the two fallen CV-22 crewmembers. The event was meticulously planned and well attended. This time, the command made sure the families were invited and played a key role in the honorable ceremony as the street names were unveiled and busts of the two crewmembers were revealed and dedicated. The most striking part of the ceremony was not what happened during the ceremony, but rather how it reflected a small change of heart about how the current AFSOC leadership viewed the actions of the two airmen on the night of the accident. For the first time, the ceremony gave credence to the idea that the crewmembers were heroes for their actions on the morning of April 9, 2010 when they attempted to safely land a severely crippled CV-22. Instead of continuing to hide the accident behind the mantra of "pilot error" and continuing to blame the crew, the command opened the door for recognizing the crew for their actions. Eight years earlier, during the fall of 2010, rather than accept the accident investigation board's report of engine power loss being a contributing factor, AFSOC spent a great amount of time, money, and effort ensuring the crew was shamelessly blamed.

The AFSOC CV-22 community has been very slow in dealing with the lessons it may have or could have learned from the accident. To this day, active duty CV-22 squadrons still do not discuss the Afghanistan accident, even within private forums such as flying safety meetings. It is as if those involved in CV-22 leadership positions were sworn to secrecy or signed a special pact of silence in the days following the accident. Sadly, secrecy does little to help the wives, children, parents, and other family members heal. Secrecy also does little to help flawed organizations learn, improve, and move forward to be better.

As incredible as it seems, I have never been asked my opinion of what caused the accident by anyone except a few members of the media. The accident investigation board report contains a detailed description of my official opinion. The opinion was based on official testimony and credible evidence. My opinion of causal factors included events not having 100% proof of happening (dual engine power loss). But, when added together with the facts discovered during the investigation, it makes a perfect, and complete, picture of how the accident occurred.

My Unofficial Opinion of "What Really Happened"

The mishap Osprey lifted off from forward operating base Delta after loading sixteen Army Rangers onto the airplane. The takeoff was described as "very wobbly" and "unstable," by Army Rangers. One Ranger even commented that one of the engines suddenly made a "very unusual noise," as the CV-22 lifted into the air. The copilot, Capt Luce, commented during the takeoff that the Osprey felt "very heavy." The right engine coanda valve failing in the open position would account for the unusual noise and the very wobbly takeoff. The open valve could reduce power available (up to 20%) from the already power limited right engine (95.3% during its last power check on the day prior to the mishap mission).

The crew maintained a higher than normal speed to make up time enroute. They told the Army Rangers the time over target would be forty minutes after midnight local time. Maj Voas had taken over the flying duties from the copilot after the first checkpoint on the low-level route to the landing zone. He flew a non-standard approach to the landing zone as he continued to keep the speed up, in order to make up time. When the flight computer indicated they were finally on time, Voas quickly reduced power to idle and stated, "Descending to 100 feet" (above ground level) over the airplane's intercom. The one-minute warning was passed to the Rangers in the back of the Osprey. As the crew continued configuring the airplane for landing, Voas noticed the left engine had a compressor stall. The "caution" warning illuminated, causing the flight engineer, SMSgt Lackey, to immediately start dumping fuel to reduce the airplane weight. The crewmembers are overwhelmed by the sudden loss of engine power and do not make any distress radio calls. The pilot, Major Voas, advances the thrust control levers to full power to reverse the rapid rate of descent and gain altitude. The left engine compressor stall causes a surge in torque to the right engine. The surge breaks the right proprotor gearbox clutch, rendering the engine to be useless and unable to add power to the proprotors (even though the engine is probably still running). [The right engine was never recovered from the accident site. The only explanation is Afghan citizens recovered the engine from the site and drove it to an unknown location. I find it interesting that no one has ever expressed concern about the disappearance of the right engine]. The crew had no idea of what caused the power loss situation. There were no procedures, and no information in their flight manuals about clutch failure. However, they would get other "cautions" posted on their engine instruments relating to driveshaft and gearbox components attached to the right engine. The confusion would explain the "excited conversation" heard by the tail scanner on the airplane intercom. Major Voas told his crew, "it's all in," indicating he had advanced the thrust control lever to maximum power. Unable to go-around or even maintain altitude, the Osprey continued descending toward the ground at a rapidly increasing rate. In just a few seconds, Maj Voas and SMSgt Lackey had depleted all available options, except one, which was extremely dangerous.

He converts for landing as the engine rpm decays and the rotors move into the conversion mode. Voas is committed to attempting an emergency roll-on landing. Instead of landing like a helicopter, he attempted to keep as much forward speed as possible and land on the sand, like an airplane landing on a runway.

The *roll-on landing* emergency procedure in the CV-22 flight manual instructs the crew to configure the Osprey nacelles at eighty degrees and attain 80 knots airspeed. When the nacelles were at sixty degrees, SMSgt Lackey lowered the landing gear. Voas checked his forward-looking infra-red radar display and noticed the Osprey was descending on a path to impact a deep ditch. At the last second, he slightly raised the nose of the airplane to adjust the glide path to clear the ditch. Using his night vision goggles, he could see what appeared to be a fairly flat area on the other side of the ditch. Lackey stops the fuel dumping as the Osprey approaches the ground. Voas made a perfect roll-on landing with the main wheels gently touching down on the soft sand. As the weight of the Osprey caused the wheels to sink into the sand, the ramp scraped across the ground. Voas lowered the nose wheel onto the ground and rolled across the sand for forty-five feet. As the Osprey traveled across the desert, the nose wheel hit a rock and collapsed, causing the nose of the airplane to plow deeper and deeper into the sand. The airplane slid another fifteen feet before tipping up onto its nose, crushing the cockpit, and flipping tail over nose onto its back.

The Rolls-Royce analysis of the left engine concluded the engine was running when the airplane touched down. I agree. The engine was running, but the proprotor gearbox clutch was broken. In fact, I think both engines were running. They were operating at an abnormally low power, as proven by the proprotor rpm calculation made using the proprotor marks in the sand and the NST proprotor calculation of rpm while the airplane was in flight.

There are still two very interesting and important questions, though, to be answered. The first question - why did AFSOC repeatedly send the report back to the accident investigation board? The report was completed in July. Maj Gen Dobrinski sent the report back citing it was "insufficient due to lack of evidence that engine power loss was a significantly contributing factor" for the accident. Once we had other experts verify the calculations and information, the unchanged report was sent back to AFSOC. Dobrinski could have accepted the report with comments and the process would have moved forward to briefing the families of the deceased and injured personnel in August of 2010. To me, briefing families had always been one of the most important aspects of the investigation. Instead, he sent a few pages of information to NAVAIR engineers and asked them to analyze the data and decide whether engine power loss could have been a "significantly contributing factor." The process took three months to produce reports and information that did nothing except give the convening authority a source to cite as support for the probability of power loss being low. The accident board was reconvened in November of 2010 and told to analyze new information and write an updated addendum. The accident investigation board complied and submitted an addendum as requested.

Only one change was made in our updated addendum. The touchdown speed was confirmed to be eighty knots, instead of seventy-five knots as published in the original report. It took nearly another month for AFSOC to accept the addendum, with comments, and finally send out a team to brief the families the week prior to Christmas. In the end, the report was accepted with comments from AFSOC, exactly what should have happened five months prior when the report was originally submitted in July. The only reason the families ended up being "held hostage," was so the convening authority could pursue every legal option to challenge the credibility of my opinion, and especially "engine power loss" as a substantially contributing factor.

The second question was also important … what was the mysterious "white vapor trail" or "mist," that suddenly appeared coming off the wings of the Osprey as it went into the rapid descent during the last eighteen seconds of flight? The accident board had imagery experts study the video to give us their opinions. Even though they could not positively identify the mist, they all agreed it was a cool substance. Hot sources in the video were black, such as when the airplane flipped over and caught on fire. If the mist was "hot sand," as proclaimed by the squadron commander during a meeting with Jill Voas, it would have been a dark colored mist. It wasn't … it was white. The data transfer module (DTM) recovered from the airplane gave the accident investigation board information about fuel flow to the engines (in pounds per hour) for every ten seconds of the flight. Normal fuel burn for an Osprey in the hover mode would be approximately 4,900 pounds per hour. At the last measured DTM point at 20:09:08 (nine minutes and eight seconds after 2000 hours Zulu time, or thirty nine minutes and eight seconds after midnight local time in Afghanistan) … seven seconds before the airplane hit the ground, showed the airplane's fuel flow at 26,640 pounds per hour. Abnormally high. The most logical explanation for the dramatic increase in fuel flow is the crew dumping fuel to decrease the airplane's weight for an attempt to go-around, or as a last resort, attempt a roll-on emergency landing. The mist, or vapor trail, that was so predominant to nearly everyone who viewed the A-10 video of the accident, was fuel being dumped. It was a "cool" source that showed up white in the video.

I have commented numerous times about the professionalism and superior flying skills of Maj Voas and SMSgt Lackey. Both crewmembers were very experienced on the MH-53 helicopter. All MH-53 crewmembers were taught to immediately dump fuel during a power loss situation. It was second nature to the crews since it was practiced frequently during simulator training. Having the presence of mind to dump fuel while attempting to troubleshoot as the Osprey was uncontrollably falling out of the sky was just one more example of their exemplary airmanship.

The accident investigation and subsequent "arguments" were summed up very well by Mr. Robert Dorr, a writer for the Air Force Times:

> Two generals disagree over the cause of a fatal Osprey crash in southern Afghanistan. Because of a big mistake the Air Force made at the accident site, no evidence exists to settle the argument over what happened to the CV-22. The black box was not recovered. The brigadier general in charge of the accident investigation board wrote: "The greater weight of credible evidence supports engine power loss as

a substantially contributing factor." His two-star boss, in a dissent, attributed the crash to pilot error.

The difference is important because the Osprey is controversial. Marine Corps versions have been in four crashes that claimed 30 lives. A finding of engine failure could point to a mechanical problem in the fleet. A finding of pilot error would acquit the CV-22 of any design flaw.

The Air Force needs to take a hard look at how it trains the airman who swoop down on crash sites. They need to know what to look for and understand just how crucial the flight data recorder is to an investigation ... apparently, they don't. Unfortunately, the mistake made in the Osprey investigation can't be undone.

So, the dispute goes unsettled. The CV-22 aircrew members can't ... and shouldn't be blamed for the accident, but they can't be "officially" exonerated, either. It's a sad day for the families and the Air Force. [25]

There is no doubt the sixteen survivors of the accident should be forever grateful to Major Randell D. Voas and SMSgt James B. Lackey who were in the cockpit making life-saving decisions during the early morning hours of April 9, 2010.

BOOK CHARACTERS

CV-22 Crew Involved in April 9, 2010 Accident:

Major (Maj) Randell "Randy" Voas – Aircraft Commander of Mishap Airplane (accident casualty)

Captain (Capt) Brian Luce – Copilot of Mishap Airplane (accident survivor)

Senior Master Sergeant (SMSgt) James B. "JB" Lackey – Flight Engineer of Mishap Airplane (accident casualty)

Staff Sergeant (SSgt) Chris Curtis – Tail Scanner of Mishap Airplane (accident survivor)

Army Rangers onboard CV-22 During April 9, 2010 Accident:

Major (MAJ) Keith Carter – Army Ranger, Ground Forces Commander for mission (accident survivor)

Captain (CPT) Christopher Grates – Army Ranger, Alpha Company Fire Support Officer (accident survivor)

Captain (CPT) Erick McFerran – Army Ranger, Interpreter Coordinator (accident survivor)

Staff Sergeant (SSG) Robert McGuire – Army Ranger (accident survivor)

Staff Sergeant (SSG) Matthew Tennill – Army Ranger (accident survivor)

Sergeant (SGT) Thomas Blaylock – Army Ranger (accident survivor)

Sergeant (SGT) Charles Claybaker - Army Ranger (accident survivor)

Sergeant (SGT) – Brent Hernandez – Army Ranger (accident survivor)

Sergeant (SGT) – Thomas Nigro – Army Ranger (accident survivor)

Sergeant (SGT) – Christopher Wooten – Army Ranger (accident survivor)

Corporal (CPL) Michael D. Jankiewicz - Army Ranger (accident casualty)

Specialist (SPC) Jim Hansen (alias) – Army Ranger (accident survivor)

Private First Class (PFC) Timothy Davis - Army Ranger (accident survivor)

Private First Class (PFC) Philip Tilley – Army Ranger (accident survivor)

Mr. Mohammed Naheed (alias) – Afghan Civilian Contractor, Interpreter (accident survivor)

Reeta Sandozai – Afghan Civilian Contractor, Interpreter (accident casualty)

Accident Investigation Board:

Brigadier General (Brig Gen) Don Harvel – Accident Investigation Board President

Lieutenant Colonel (Lt Col) Chance "Doc" Harper (alias) – Medical Member of Accident Board

Lieutenant Colonel (Lt Col) Gordon Winsett (alias) – Legal Member of Accident Board

Lieutenant Colonel (Lt Col) Jeff O'Leary (alias) – Pilot Member of Accident Board

Captain (Capt) Christie Kelly (alias) – Assistant Legal Member of Accident Board

Master Sergeant (MSgt) William Dolan (alias) – Maintenance Member of Accident Board

Technical Sergeant (TSgt) Nicole Adams (alias) – Recorder Member of Accident Board

Technical Sergeant (TSgt) Bryan "Scotty" Scott – Communications Specialist Member of Accident Board

Other Book Characters:

Brigadier General (Brig Gen) Guy Walsh – 451st Air Expeditionary Wing Commander, Kandahar Air Base, Afghanistan

Brigadier General (Brig Gen) Michael Kingsley – Safety Investigation Board (SIB) President

Captain (Capt) April Pierce – Communications Officer assigned to Commander's Action Group (CAG) with additional duty as Executive Officer for Brig Gen Don Harvel

Captain (CPT) Jay McKenna – Battalion Surgeon for 3rd Battalion, 75th Ranger Regiment (Doctor)

Captain (Capt) Keith Nystrom (alias) – 8th SOS Maintenance Officer – temporary duty in Afghanistan

Captain (Capt) Luke Porsi – Special Operations Forces Medical Element (SOFME) Flight Surgeon

Colonel (COL) Dan Walrath – Army Ranger/Task Force Commander (Commanded the Joint Operations

Center at Kandahar Air Base, Afghanistan)

Colonel (Col) Stuart Lund (alias) – Medical Group Commander 1st Special Operations Wing

Congressman Walter Jones – Republican Congressman from North Carolina

Deputy Secretary of Defense Robert Work – Wrote letter of apology for blaming pilots (pilot error) as the cause for the Marana MV-22 accident on April 8, 2000.

Doctor Carlos Godinez – Combat Army Support Hospital (CASH) Surgeon (on duty at forward operating base Apache the morning of the accident)

Doctor Anthony Pistilli (alias) – Attending physician for SSgt Curtis at Walter Reed Medical Center

First Sergeant (1SG) Lloyd Drennen (alias) – 3rd Battalion, 75th Ranger Regiment 1st Sergeant

General (Gen) Norty Schwartz – U.S. Air Force Chief of Staff

Lance Corporal (LCpl. – Marine Corps) Joshua Barron – Hawaii V-22 accident May 17, 2015 (accident casualty)

Lance Corporal (LCpl. – Marine Corps) Matthew Determan – Hawaii V-22 accident May 17, 2015 (accident casualty)

Lieutenant Colonel (Lt Col) Chuck Coulter (alias) - Commander's Action Group (CAG) Commander

Lieutenant Colonel (Lt Col) Drew Daugherty (Alias) – 8th SOS Operations Officer

Lieutenant Colonel (Lt Col) Randy Rogel (alias) – AFSOC Public Affairs Officer

Lieutenant Colonel (Lt Col) Schultz (alias) – Chief of Standardization and Evaluation for CV-22

Lieutenant Colonel (Lt Col) Sean Compton (alias) – 8th SOS Squadron Commander

Lieutenant General (Lt Gen) Charles Becker (alias) – AFSOC Commander

Major (Maj) James Young – Human Factors expert, 720th Special Tactics Group (STG), Hurlburt Field, FL

Major (MAJ) Robert Kocher (alias) – Task Force Mission Planner, Joint Operations Center (JOC)

Major (MAJ) Mike McCrossin (alias) – Army Commander of forward operating base Apache

Major (Maj) Warren Bildstein (alias) – AFSOC Commander's Action Group (CAG)

Major (Maj) William Smith (alias) – Officer in Charge (OIC) of Kandahar Legal Office, Afghanistan

Major General (Maj Gen) Clay McCutcheon – Air Force Reserve Advisor to AFSOC Commander

Major General (Maj Gen) Kent Dobrinski (alias) – AFSOC Deputy (Vice) Commander

Mr. Bill Sawtelle (alias) – NAVAIR ASIST engineer

Mr. Bill Sweetman – *Aviation Week* and *Space Technology* writer

Mr. Bob Cox – Writer for the *Ft Worth Star Telegram* newspaper

Mr. Brian Alexander – Prominent Aviation accident lawyer in New York

Mr. Bruce Rolsen – Writer for various military magazines

Mr. David Axe – Writer for *War on The Rocks* magazine and other publications

Mr. Eric Jason (alias) – NAVAIR ASIST engineer

Mr. Gary Wilshire (alias) – NAVAIR ASIST lead engineer

Mr. Henry Brucker (alias) – Civilian CV-22 Flight Simulator Instructor, Hurlburt Field, FL

Mr. Jack Miller (alias) – NAVAIR ASIST engineer

Mr. John Tsaio – Aircraft engine expert from Air Logistics Center, Oklahoma City, Oklahoma

Mr. John Vulgamore – National (Geo-Spatial-Intelligence) Support Team (NST)

Mr. Joseph Trevithick - Writer for military publications

Mr. Kevin Knodell - Writer for military publications

Mr. Matthew Gault – Writer for military publications

Mr. Robert Beckhusen - Writer for military publications

Mr. Robert Dorr – Writer for the *Air Force Times* magazine

Mr. Ronald "Curly" Culp – Civilian Maintenance Pilot (retired Marine V-22 pilot)

MSgt Frank Stookey (alias) – CV-22 Engine Maintenance Specialist, Kirtland Air Force Base, NM

MSgt Coby True – AFSOC Rotary Wing Propulsion Manager, Hurlburt Field, FL

Ms. Nan Morton (alias) – NAVAIR ASIST Rotary Wing Loads and Dynamics Technical Specialist

Ms. Randee Elaine (alias) – ABC World News reporter based in Atlanta, Georgia

Staff Sergeant (SSG) Paul Montoya (alias) – 3rd Battalion, 75th Ranger/ Regiment Medic (flew on chalk two)

Technical Sergeant (TSgt) Pat Dooley (alias) – Flight Line Expeditor, 801st SOAMXS

Technical Sergeant (TSgt) John Brown – Combat Search and Rescue (CSAR)

Technical Sergeant (TSgt) Kim Smith (alias) – Kandahar Legal Office, Afghanistan

Note: "Alias" names were used for personnel not contacted for permission to use their given names. A real name was used if given permission via written communication, or if the person was named in multiple public news articles and associated with the April 9, 2010 Osprey accident. Alias names are fictitious and not intended to represent anyone in a negative manner.

"80 Jump" Takeoff – A technique used by V-22 pilots to get off the ground in a short distance

A-10 Thunderbolt – Air Force fighter airplane used for close air support missions

ACD – Afghanistan Customs Department

AFB - Air Force Base

AFLOA – Air Force Legal Operations Agency

AFSOC - Air Force Special Operations Command (U.S. Air Force Major Command)

AIB - Accident Investigation Board

AMC – Air Mobility Command (a U.S. Air Force Major Command)

AMXS – Aircraft Maintenance Squadron

AOR – Area of Responsibility (the Middle East is an AOR)

Army Rangers – Army personnel that have completed Ranger school training

ASIST – NAVAIR Engineering team – Aeromechanics Safety Investigation Support Team

BDU - Battle Dress Uniform

BG – Brigadier General (1-star / Army abbreviation)

Brig Gen – Brigadier General (1-star / Air Force abbreviation)

CAG - Commander's Action Group

Cannon Air Force Base – Clovis, New Mexico

Capt – Captain (Air Force Abbreviation)

CASEVAC – Casualty Evacuation

CASH – Combat Army Support Hospital

CCP – Casualty Collection Point

CCT – Combat Control Team

CFIT – Controlled Flight into Terrain (airplane flying into the ground – usually "pilot error" accident)

Class "A" Mishap –Total cost of damage to government or other property is $2 million or more, or a DoD aircraft is destroyed, or a fatality or permanent disability occurs

CMSgt – Chief Master Sergeant (Air Force abbreviation)

Col – Colonel (Air Force abbreviation)

COL – Colonel (Army abbreviation)

COMM-SEC – Communication Security

CONUS – Continental United States

CPT – Captain (Army abbreviation)

CSAR – Combat Search and Rescue

CV-22 - Osprey Tilt Rotor airplane assigned to Air Force/AFSOC (See "Osprey")

DFAC – Dining Facility

DOS – Department of State

DTM – Data Transfer Module

EAPS – Engine Air Particle Separator

EPP – Engine Performance Percentage

FAA – Federal Aviation Administration

FAC – Forward Air Controller

FARP – Forward Air Refueling Point

FOB - Forward Operating Base (small base – usually closer to enemy forces than Main Operating Bases)

FOB Apache – Forward Operating Base in Zabul Province, Afghanistan

FOB Delta - Forward Operating Base in Zabul Province, Afghanistan

Gen – General (4-Star / Air Force abbreviation)

GMT - Greenwich Mean Time (also known as "Zulu" time)

HHQ – Higher Headquarters

HMMWV – High Mobility Multi-Purpose Wheeled Vehicle (commonly called "Humvee")

HQ – Headquarters

HR – Human Remains

HUD – Heads-Up Display

Hurlburt Field – Hurlburt Air Force Base, Ft Walton Beach, Florida

HVT – High Value Target

ISB - Interim Safety Board

ISR – Intelligence Surveillance and Reconnaissance

JACC – Judge Advocate Corp Commander

JAG – Judge Advocate General (legal advisor to commanders)

JAGMAN – Judge Advocate General Manual

JOC - Joint Operations Center

JPO – Joint Program Office

JSOAC – Joint Special Operations Air Component

JTAC – Joint Terminal Attack Controller

KIA – Killed in Action

KAB - Kandahar Air Base

Lt Col – Lieutenant Colonel (Air Force abbreviation)

Lt Gen – Lieutenant General (3-star / Air Force abbreviation))

LVA – Low Visibility Approach (standard approach for CV-22 when landing on dirt or sand)

LZ - Landing Zone

Maj – Major (Air Force abbreviation)

MAJ – Major (Army abbreviation)

Maj Gen – Major General (2-star / Air Force abbreviation)

MCAS – Marine Corps Air Station

MFD – Multi-Function Display

MFR – Memorandum for Record

MOB - Main Operating Base

MOTT – Multi-Service Operational Test Team

MPF – Military Personnel Flight

MSgt – Master Sergeant (Air Force abbreviation)

NASA – National Aeronautical Space Administration

NATO – The North Atlantic Treaty Organization

NAVAIR – Naval Air Systems Command

NCO – Non-Commissioned Officer

NGA – National Geospatial-Intelligence Agency

NST – National Support Team

NTSB – National Transportation Safety Board

OGE – Out of Ground Effect

OPEVAL – Operational Evaluation

ORE – Operational Readiness Exercise (training conducted to prepare for unit's "Operational Readiness" Inspection – used to determine a unit's readiness to deploy into combat)

Osprey – CV-22 tilt-rotor airplane nickname

PFC – Private First Class (Army abbreviation)

PMO – Program Management Office

POC - Planning Operations Center

"Q" - Quarters

Qalat – Afghanistan City nearest to CV-22 accident site on April 9, 2010

ROE – Rules of Engagement

RRESO – Rolls Royce Engine Services Oakland (California)

1SG – First Sergeant (Army abbreviation)

SEAL – Sea and Land (Specially trained Navy and Marine personnel)

SGT – Sergeant (Army abbreviation)

SIB - Safety Investigation Board (accident investigation members that investigate an accident within days after an accident occurs. The findings of the SIB are not made public. The findings of the SIB are briefed to the MAJCOM Commander and select personnel only)

SIPRNET – Secret Internet Protocol Router Network

SMSgt – Senior Master Sergeant (Air Force abbreviation)

SOFME – Special Operations Forces Medical Element

SOS - Special Operations Squadron

SOW - Special Operations Wing

Sparkle – An illumination beam emitted from airplane flying over an area that can only be seen with the aid of night vision devices

SPC – Specialist (Army abbreviation)

SSG – Staff Sergeant (Army abbreviation)

SSgt – Staff Sergeant (Air Force abbreviation)

Stand-Up Briefing – High level unit leadership meeting conducted each weekday morning at 8:00 a.m.

Stan Eval – Standardization and Evaluation (aircrew members that train and check aircrew proficiency by periodically flying with crewmembers)

STU III – Secure Terminal Unit (Telephone with encryption capability to prevent eavesdropping)

TXANG – Texas Air National Guard

TCL – Thrust Control Lever

TOLD – Takeoff and Landing Data

TOT - Time Over Target

TSgt – Technical Sergeant (Air Force abbreviation)

USAF – United States Air Force

VOQ -- Visiting Officer's Quarters - "The Q"

VSLED – Vibration/Structural Life and Engine Diagnostics

VVI – Vertical Velocity Indicator

WWLR – World-Wide Language Resources

ZULU time – Based on GMT (Greenwich Mean Time). Greenwich Mean Time is based upon the time at the zero-degree meridian crossing through Greenwich, England.

CONFIRMING SOURCES

1. Robert Wall, *CV-22 Crashes in Afghanistan* (London: Aviation Week, April 9, 2010).

2. Donald D. Harvel, *United States Air Force Aircraft Accident Investigation Board Report* (Hurlburt Field, Florida, 8th Special Operations Squadron, 1st Special Operations Wing, April 9, 2010), Y3-Y4.

3. Donald D. Harvel, *United States Air Force Aircraft Accident Investigation Board Report* (Hurlburt Field, Florida, 8th Special Operations Squadron, 1st Special Operations Wing, April 9, 2010), V1.1-V1.25.

4. Donald D. Harvel, *United States Air Force Aircraft Accident Investigation Board Report* (Hurlburt Field, Florida, 8th Special Operations Squadron, 1st Special Operations Wing, April 9, 2010), EE15-EE21.

5. Donald D. Harvel, *United States Air Force Aircraft Accident Investigation Board Report* (Hurlburt Field, Florida, 8th Special Operations Squadron, 1st Special Operations Wing, April 9, 2010), EE51-EE52.

6. Jamie McIntyre, *Exclusive: First V-22 Combat Crash Likely "Pilot Error"* (War Magazine, May 18, 2010).
Thom Shanker, Helene Cooper, Richard Oppel Jr. and Alissa J. Rubin, *Elite U.S. Units Step Up Effort in Afghan City Before Attack* (New York Times, April 25, 2010).

7. Donald D. Harvel, *United States Air Force Aircraft Accident Investigation Board Report* (Hurlburt Field, Florida, 8th Special Operations Squadron, 1st Special Operations Wing, April 9, 2010), 48-53.

8. Donald D. Harvel, *United States Air Force Aircraft Accident Investigation Board Report* (Hurlburt Field, Florida, 8th Special Operations Squadron, 1st Special Operations Wing, April 9, 2010), II51-II53.

9. Donald D. Harvel, *United States Air Force Aircraft Accident Investigation Board Report* (Hurlburt Field, Florida, 8th Special Operations Squadron, 1st Special Operations Wing, April 9, 2010), 53-54.

10. Donald D. Harvel, *Memorandum for Convening Authority Letter* (Hurlburt Field, Florida, AFSOC HQ, August 25, 2010)

11. Convening Authority, *Action of Convening Authority* (Hurlburt Field, Florida, AFSOC HQ, November 23, 2010).

12. Norton A. Schwartz, *Memorandum for Brig Gen (RET) Donald D. Harvel* (Department of the Air Force, Washington D.C., November 15, 2010).

13. Donald D. Harvel, *Addendum to United States Air Force Aircraft Accident Investigation Board Report* (Hurlburt Field, Florida, 8th Special Operations Squadron, 1st Special Operations Wing, April 9, 2010), B-35.

14. Donald D. Harvel, *Addendum to United States Air Force Aircraft Accident Investigation Board Report* (Hurlburt Field, Florida, 8th Special

15. Operations Squadron, 1st Special Operations Wing, April 9, 2010), B-36.

16. Donald D. Harvel, *Addendum to United States Air Force Aircraft Accident Investigation Board Report* (Hurlburt Field, Florida, 8th Special Operations Squadron, 1st Special Operations Wing, April 9, 2010), D9-D10.

17. Donald D. Harvel, *Addendum to United States Air Force Aircraft Accident Investigation Board Report* (Hurlburt Field, Florida, 8th Special

18. Operations Squadron, 1st Special Operations Wing, April 9, 2010), 1-7. Donald D. Harvel, *Addendum to United States Air Force Aircraft Accident Investigation Board Report* (Hurlburt Field, Florida, 8th Special Operations Squadron, 1st Special Operations Wing, April 9, 2010), C3-C4.

19. Robert Cox, *Findings on Osprey Crash Overturned* (Ft Worth Star-Telegram, December 17, 2010), 18A.

20. Bruce Rolfsen, *General's Clash Over Osprey Crash* (Air Force Times, January 17, 2011).

21. Bill Sweetman, *Hawaii V-22 Accident Investigation Points to New Ingestion Issue* (Aviation Week and Space Technology, October 19, 2015).

22. Bill Sweetman, *Hawaii V-22 Accident Investigation Points to New Ingestion Issue* (Aviation Week and Space Technology, October 19, 2015).

23. Matthew Gault, Joseph Trevithick, Kevin Knodell, David Axe and Robert Beckhusen, *Forty-Five Seconds – Military Unfairly Blames Crews For V-22 Crashes* (War is Boring, January 18, 2016).

24. David Martin, *Marines: Pilots Not to Blame for Deadly 2000 Osprey Crash* (CBS News' National Security Correspondent, March 2, 2016).

25. Robert Dorr, *CV-22 Crash Leaves Only Questions* (Air Force Times, January 31, 2011) 5.

** All Chapters with personnel interviews are summarized and edited for improved readability. The editing did not change the character or meaning of testimony in any way. The reference for all interviews:

Donald D. Harvel, *United States Air Force Aircraft Accident Investigation Board Report* (Hurlburt Field, Florida, 8th Special Operations Squadron, 1st Special Operations Wing, April 9, 2010) Tab V.

All book conversations are based on letters, notes, personal diaries, memory recollection and recorded phone messages. Conversations were edited for clarity only.

Convening Authority. *Action of Convening Authority,* Hurlburt Field, Florida. AFSOC HQ, November 23, 2010

Cox, Robert. *"Findings on Osprey Crash Overturned,"* Ft. Worth Star-Telegram, December 17, 2010

Dorr, Robert F. *"CV-22 Crash Leaves Only Questions,"* Air Force Times, January 31, 2011

Gault, Matthew, Joseph Trevithick, Kevin Knodell, David Axe and Robert Beckhusen. *"Forty-Five Seconds – Military Unfairly Blames Crews for V-22 Crashes,"* War is Boring, January 18, 2016

Harvel, Donald D. *United States Air Force Aircraft Accident Investigation Board Report,* Hurlburt Field, Florida 8th Special Operations Squadron, 1st Special Operations Wing, April 9, 2010

Harvel, Donald D. *Addendum to United States Air Force Aircraft Accident Investigation Board Report,* Hurlburt Field, Florida, 8th Special Operations Squadron, 1st Special Operations Wing, April 9, 2010

Martin, David. *"Marines: Pilots Not to Blame for Deadly 2000 Osprey Crash,"* CBS News, March 2, 2016

McIntyre, Jami. *"Exclusive: First V-22 Combat Crash Likely 'Pilot Error',"* War Magazine, May 18, 2010

Pawlyk, Oriana. *"V-22 Osprey Engines Still at Risk in Sand and Silt, Watchdog Report Finds,"* Military.com, November 13, 2019

Rolfsen, Bruce. *"Generals Clash Over Osprey Crash,"* Ft. Worth Star-Telegram, December 17, 2010

Shanker, Thom. Helene Cooper, Richard Oppel Jr. and Alissa J. Rubin, *"Elite U.S. Units Step Up Effort in Afghan City Before Attack,"* New York Times, April 25, 2010

Sweetman, Bill. *"Hawaii V-22 Accident Investigation Points to New Ingestion Issue,"* Aviation Week and Space Technology, October 19, 2015

Wall, Robert. *"CV-22 Crashes in Afghanistan,"* Aviation Week, April 9, 2010

Whittle, Richard. "*The Dream Machine, The Untold History of the Notorious V-22 Osprey*", New York, New York: Simon & Schuster, 2010

Rotors marks in the sand – after Osprey flipped over on its back Photo published: United States Air Force Aircraft Accident Investigation Board Report (Hurlburt Field, Florida, 8th Special Operations Squadron, 1st Special Operations Wing, April 9, 2010), page Z-9.

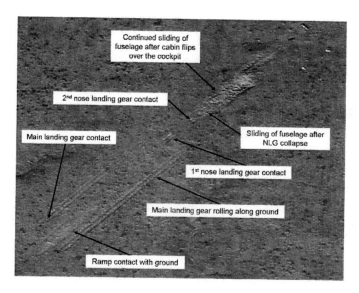

Ground markings of Osprey as it attempted roll-on landing. Direction of landing is from bottom of photo to top of photo. Photo published: Response to Request For Structural Evaluation of CV-22 Mishap (NAVAIRSYSCOM, Patuxent River, Maryland, September 30, 2010), page 8.

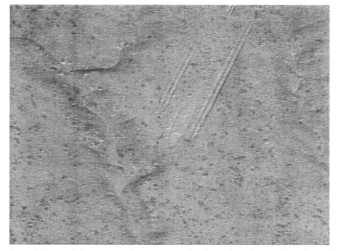

Ground markings of Osprey as it attempted roll-on landing. Direction of landing is from bottom of photo to top of photo. Photo published: United States Air Force Aircraft Accident Investigation Board Report (Hurlburt Field, Florida, 8th Special Operations Squadron, 1st Special Operations Wing, April 9, 2010), page Z-5.

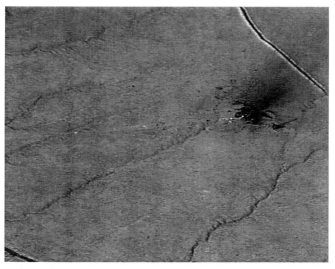

Accident site and ground markings (left to right) of Osprey as it rolled across the sand. Photo published: United States Air Force Aircraft Accident Investigation Board Report (Hurlburt Field, Florida, 8th Special Operations Squadron, 1st Special Operations Wing, April 9, 2010), page Z-15.

View from CV-22 Osprey cockpit.

CV-22 Osprey air refueling from C-130.

Osprey wreckage discovered at forward operating base Apache five weeks after the accident. The accident Investigation Board was told the accident wreckage had been totally destroyed. (Photo published: United States Air Force Aircraft AccidentInvestigation Board Report (Hurlburt Field, Florida, 8th SpecialOperations Squadron, 1st Special Operations Wing, April 9, 2010), page 27.

Tribute patch honoring the crew flying the April 9th, 2010 mission.

Hurlburt	Zulu	Kandahar
0000	0500	0930
0100	0600	1030
0200	0700	1130
0300	0800	1230
0400	0900	1330
0500	1000	1430
0600	1100	1530
0700	1200	1630
0800	1300	1730
0900	1400	1830
1000	1500	1930
1100	1600	2030
1200	1700	2130
1300	1800	2230
1400	1900	2330
1500	2000	0030
1600	2100	0130
1700	2200	0230
1800	2300	0330
1900	0000	0430
2000	0100	0530
2100	0200	0630
2200	0300	0730
2300	0400	0830
0000	0500	0930

*Time Conversion Chart Hurlburt Field, Florida
to Zulu time to Kandahar, Afghanistan local time*

Map of Afghanistan

*THE
END*